TRANSFORMATIONAL
NURSING LEADERSHIP

A Vision for the Future

TRANSFORMATIONAL NURSING LEADERSHIP

A Vision for the Future

Anne M. Barker, EdD, RN

WILLIAMS & WILKINS
Baltimore • Hong Kong • London • Sydney

Editor: Brigitte Pocta, Susan M. Glover
Associate Editor: Marjorie Kidd Keating
Developmental Editor: Rhonda M. Kumm, RN, MSN
Design and Production: Sandy Renovetz
Compositor: Nancy Segal

ISBN 0-683-00324-0

90 91 92 93 94
1 2 3 4 5 6 7 8 9 10

To Vera, Charlie, and Barbara

Foreword

In this book, Dr. Barker has added a new dimension to nursing leadership literature. She addresses that which is being eroded by our current emphasis on learning the *how to's*. She shows us how to understand the basic meanings in our changing societal environments. These are translated into effect on the lives of all people in healthcare systems. The professional nurse is moved beyond the gathering of knowledge of managing change, conflict resolution, and leadership, popular and valuable courses in nursing education. Dr. Barker challenges the provider to dramatically reshape the world in which nursing practice occurs, and she identifies the opportunities for doing this.

Her central theme, the issues of change, provides a new and artistic perspective on nursing management. Dr. Barker takes the reader on a journey through the history of leadership theory development and emerging societal trends. In this process, the need for change becomes vivid and a new approach to leadership becomes imperative. Differences between leadership and management are discarded. She sees all nurse managers as leaders; and leadership as an exciting practice and discipline. She works from the conceptual framework of James MacGregor Burns and uses the application of Warren Bennis and Burt Nanus to map out the route to leadership success. The case study method facilitates the reader's grasp of these theories.

The compelling conclusion is that the emerging healthcare environment is transforming the way we work and utilize available resources. People rather than dollars, technology, equipment, or machines are seen as the most significant asset. People are identified as the source of creativity, diversity and skill; and people issues and influencers surface as the determinants of organizational success. For a professional group that has traditionally emphasized the value of getting the task done, the perceptual shift to the significance of the individual as the quality factor in the practice of nursing requires a dramatic and revolutionary mind shift. Dr. Barker issues this challenge to the reader.

This book is written for several audiences: nurse managers at all levels, in-service educators, collegiate educators, and graduate students.

For nurse managers the pivotal function the leadership component has in the scheme of corporate life is identified. The various interactive skills in management and utilization of resources are played out with the constant of transforming "what is" to "how it can and should be." This is Dr. Barker's theme. She addresses ways and means for promoting leadership succession via new knowledge development, wisdom accrual, talent maximization, skill upgrading and staff participation in decisions that order their work and shape their lives.

In-service educators will find this document challenging them to refocus how they perceive their world and how that compels the reshaping of their role. *Transformational Nursing Leadership* moves the function of in-service educator to career developer and emphasizes the role of the nurse educator in healthcare delivery systems. The people issues stimulate reflection on the pedagogical approaches currently being used in teaching adult learners and the nurse educator responsibility in healthcare delivery systems to prepare nurses for leadership roles in organizations and society.

Collegiate educators can learn much about current and future issues in change, leadership, and the new world presenting itself in healthcare delivery. In addition, Dr. Barker provides content and format that is compatible with sound educational method and teaching strategies. The case studies presented provide the basis for stimulating student discussion and offer an excellent proving ground for professional socialization.

Graduate students pursuing a career in nursing management have in this book the challenge and stimulus for life long learning. *Transformational Nursing Leadership* can be a launching pad for looking at new worlds in nursing. Here they will discover the "Aha!" experience that thrills the spirit and shapes dreams of budding nurse executives.

For all nurses who worry about the dearth of effective leaders, and the profession of nursing in corporate settings, and how nurses can begin to develop strategies for shaping healthcare delivery in the next century, this book provides ways of beginning. Here is an agenda for nurses committed to influence and transform how healthcare is being delivered.

Eleanor Barba, Ed.D., M.B.A., R.N.
Marion A. Buckley School of Nursing
Adelphi University

Preface

Although the struggles to implement one's dream of nursing are real, challenging, complex and, at times seemingly futile, there is help. This book is blatantly optimistic about nursing and the role it can play in the future. This optimism stems from the abundance of workable, contemporary leadership theories and strategies that are available to guide nurse leaders. By thinking about and adopting the advice from these strategies, nurse leaders can begin to design work environments that satisfy the needs of nurses and enhance the quality of care received by patients.

Being a nurse in a leadership position is not easy. The woes of nursing are frequently blamed on "nursing's leaders." (Whoever they are!) The cry for nursing leadership has been heard for decades. It is an echo of the cry for leadership in our society. But this leadership crisis need not be lamented. It can be looked upon as a time to reassess one's values about people, leadership, leaders, nurses, and nursing. In this reassessment, one can find threads of hope. Nurses are more assertive and more educated than in the past. In one way, this means that work environments should undergo major renovations—an awesome task. From another perspective, it means nurses are increasingly capable of contributing to the care of the individual patient and to the healthcare of the society as a whole. Employees and nurses have new values, including a paradoxical need to belong while at the same time achieving as an individual. In nursing, it is relatively easy to create a climate that appeals to these needs because nursing involves helping others. This is not necessarily true for people employed in other types of work. By focusing on our heritage of caring and by designing nursing organizations that both facilitate team work and recognize and allow the individual to achieve, nursing leaders can proactively address the current list of dissatisfactions in the profession.

Traditional management skills, such as finance, budgeting, marketing, and staffing, are important ingredients for successful nursing leadership in today's healthcare environment, but they are not enough. Nursing needs leaders with new skills to transform nursing organizations into spirited, excited, successful work places where nurses can excel. This book attempts to weave together current and classic leadership theories and strategies and apply them to contemporary nursing. The seminal work of James MacGregor Burns, *Leadership*, provides the theoretical framework for the book. His inspirational work focuses on political leaders. Warren Bennis and Burt Nanus, the authors of *Leaders: Strategies for Taking Charge*, apply Burns's theory to business organizations. Specifically, the chapters on vision, social architecture, trust, and deployment of self (self-regard) are the four transformational leadership strategies proposed by them and each are the subjects of chapters in this book.

This book differs from most books on the topics of nursing leadership and nursing management. Many of these books tend to be mere "how to" guides for managing and leading. This book poses the belief that the survival and achievement of nursing *today*, although important, are not the final goals. It suggests that nursing can thrive and be excellent *tomorrow* if nursing leaders learn to focus on their vision, appeal to the values and aspirations of contemporary nurses, discover and support collective purpose, and care for one another, for our patients, and society with excellence.

This book was written for two audiences: nursing students and practicing nurse leader-managers. To help readers apply the theories to actual practice, I have included a case study and discussion questions at the end of each chapter. Explanations of the discussion questions are in Appendix A. These "answers" are to be used to stimulate further discussion. In the real world of nursing management, there is seldom only one correct approach. Similarly, there are many ways to interpret the case study questions. The case studies can be used in the classroom for group discussions or the reader can study them independently to gain insight from applying theory to practice.

In this book, I struggled with semantics, particularly in my attempt to avoid sexist language. Because this goal of unbiased wording (pronouns) often clouded my meaning, I used the words "she" and "her," acknowledging the overwhelming percentage of women in nursing, but ever mindful of the contributions of men to the profession as well. The second struggle was a more difficult one—avoiding the use of terms such as "subordinate," "superior," and "boss." These terms in many ways contradict the philosophy of the book. Some authors and organizations are beginning to use the term "associates" to refer to employees. I opted not to use this or any other unfamiliar term, but limited my use of traditional hierarchical language to those instances when their use clarified the discussion. Lastly, this book evolved out of a conviction that all nurse managers must be leaders; therefore, I have used the term "leader-manager" throughout the book to convey this ideal.

Acknowledgments

Since this work is a compilation of many years of experience, there are many people who have contributed to my thinking, my values, and convictions. To all those people who have touched my life, I am truly grateful.

In my work as a nurse executive, I was most influenced by Jennie Umbal McKoy, the first transformational nurse leader with whom I had the privilege of working. She was, without doubt, my best mentor. I am further appreciative of many nurses who throughout my career have challenged me and helped me to develop my leadership beliefs. In particular, I am indebted to the Veterans Administration (VA) Nursing Services. In my 14 years of professional work with the VA, I was allowed to grow and develop my skills as a nurse leader. While serving in my last position with the VA, as the Chief Nursing Service at the West Haven, Connecticut Medical Center, I was privileged to work with some of the best nurses I have known. These individuals taught me that by providing an exciting, participatory work environment in which people are recognized, people will respond and achieve excellence for nursing and patients. Because of them, I am convinced that the ideas in this book work.

In my life as a doctoral student, I am grateful to my advisor and sponsor, Eleanor Barba. From the beginning of my student experiences at Teachers College, she taught me to have a world view, to be concerned about the future, and to have a dream of nursing. She suggested that I undertake this book as my dissertation project. During the process of writing both a dissertation and a book, she was patient, provocative, and persistent in helping me to frame my thoughts and to commit them to paper.

In my personal life, I am thankful for friends and family who have supported my endeavors for many years. They have understood and accepted my commitment to study. Most especially, I am grateful to Barbara who read, critiqued, and explored many drafts and who saw me through the ups and downs. Her support and encouragement helped me endure! And I appreciate my parents who love me and whom I love. I contribute my success to their support and encouragement throughout my life.

This book also reflects the ideas and work of other people. In preparing Chapter 5, "Organizational Vision," I thank Andrea O'Conner who served as a consultant to me and to the West Haven Nursing Service to assist us in the development of a philosophy statement. The vision statement in the case study in Chapter 5 is a result of her work and the work of Rose Emmett who coordinated the revisions and distribution of the statement. Further, I am grateful to Ken Sittnick and Rose Emmett who assisted me with scenarios to include in the case studies.

In preparing the book, I would like to thank the developmental editor, Rhonda Kumm. She helped me to rework the dissertation into a book that is practical yet theoretical. I would also like to thank National Health Publishing for having faith in me and in this book.

About the Author

Anne Barker, Ed.D., R.N., is currently an Associate Professor of Nursing at Sacred Heart University in Fairfield, Connecticut. She is Program Director of a graduate program in Nursing Service Administration.

Anne was educated at the University of Virginia (B.S.N.), Catholic University of America (M.S.N.), and Teachers College, Columbia University (Ed.D.). Her doctoral dissertation formed the foundation for this book.

Prior to her position at Sacred Heart, Anne worked for the Veterans Administration for 14 years. She was the Chief Nursing Service for four of her last six years at Philadelphia and for two years at West Haven, Connecticut.

Contents

1

Leadership in Crisis: The Need for New Theory

Chapter Objectives

1. Discuss and cite examples of the leadership crisis in nursing and society.

2. Recognize the need for new leadership theory and strategies in nursing.

3. Describe the historical development of leadership theory over the past century.

4. List five major theories and describe their basic premise.

5. List the strengths and weaknesses of five leadership theories.

6. List three components of an effective leadership theory.

7. List five characteristics of a successful nursing leader.

Introduction

There is today a seemingly unending, universal search for leadership in all of society. This exploration is occurring during an era when a combination of societal forces portends a radically different future. With the rapid development of technology, society is being transformed from an industrial to an information society. Compounding the complexity of this major transformation is a general shortage of people entering the work force in Western society. Moreover, the values of this work force are changing. In the industrial era, from which present society is emerging, the importance of human resources was secondary to energy and mass production. In an information society and because of the scarcity of people, the maximization

1

of human potential is the single greatest challenge for managerial leadership today.

These forces are increasing the demands on managerial leadership in organizations. At the same time, there is a decrease in the authority of managers, a questioning of the infallibility of management decisions, and uncertainty regarding management tasks. Moreover, the potential of the rest of the work force to contribute to the organization in meaningful ways has increased. The relationships between managers and their staff are undergoing significant change. This change requires new leadership theory and new strategies that will appeal to the values of the contemporary work force. Organizational employees will no longer be satisfied with hierarchical organizational structures and depersonalized, bureaucratic policies and procedures.

As society searches for leadership during this time of rapid fundamental change, the nursing profession searches as well. For nursing, there are additional forces and issues to consider, both in the healthcare industry and within the profession. The cost-constrained healthcare environment of the 1980s has resulted in the beginning of major transformations in the healthcare industry including changes in the organizational structure of healthcare facilities, new modes of healthcare delivery, alterations in where patients receive their care, and competition in the marketplace. Within the nursing profession, there is pervasive, expressed dissatisfaction of nurses with their professional work and a supply and demand inequity of nursing resources.

These complex, interrelated forces demand new leadership—in society and in nursing. The conceptual framework for this book, transformational leadership (see Chapter 3), can provide a new leadership paradigm. Transformational leadership can provide guidance to leaders in nursing to make the profession successful and to thrive.

The Leadership Crisis

Leadership in society as a whole is plagued by three problems: increased complexity, lack of commitment, and decreased faith in leaders (Bennis and Nanus 1985, 7-12).

First, society and organizations are becoming more and more complex:

This is an era marked with rapid and spastic change. The problems of organizations are increasingly complex. There are too many ironies, polarities, dichotomies, dualities, ambivalences, paradoxes, confusions, contradictions, contraries, and messes for organizations to understand and deal with (Bennis and Nanus 1985, 8).

The changes in our society profoundly affect how leaders lead organizations, and so many traditional management techniques have become obsolete. Managerial leaders will be seeking new ways to communicate, to make decisions, to think, and to act.

Further, there is evidence of a second crisis in leadership. This crisis involves employee commitment to their work which results in decreased productivity in much of our nation's organizations. Yanklevich and Associates (1983, 6-7) surveyed the nonmanagerial work force and found that fewer than 25 percent of the people surveyed said they were currently working at their full potential; 50 percent said they did not put effort into their job more than is necessary to keep it; 75 percent said they were not as effective as they could be; and 60 percent said they did not work as hard as they used to work.

The third leadership problem is lack of leader credibility which affects the relationship between managers and employees. Due to the mass media which publicizes the unethical behaviors of public leaders and more assertive behaviors on the part of followers, leaders are being scrutinized and criticized by followers as never before. People are questioning and challenging authority. This questioning and challenging is not limited to political leaders. For example, within a few weeks in 1980 several popular lay magazines blamed the current failures of American businesses on the managers of organizations (Peters and Waterman 1982, 34). The roots of this problem may be found in our nation's emphasis on the "bottom line" and personal material success.

A similar leadership crisis exists in nursing. Recent studies of nursing, the Institute of Medicine report (1983), the National Commission on Nursing report (1983), and the Magnet Hospital Study (American Academy of Nursing 1983) revealed an alarmingly long list of dissatisfactions that nurses have with their practice. These include:

- the attitude and behaviors of nurse managers;
- limited professional growth, advancement, and achievement;
- inadequate salaries, insufficient staffing, and unacceptable work schedules;

- relationships with other nurses and physicians;
- oppressive organizational hierarchies which hinder autonomy of practice; and
- lack of job status and power.

These same issues and problems remain unresolved for nurses today. This is evidenced by the current labor shortage and the highly publicized concerns of the nursing profession reported in both the lay press and professional journals. Because nurses in leadership positions have failed to solve these ongoing concerns on any wide scale, there has been a resultant lack of credibility of nursing leadership and a lack of commitment on the part of nurses. These two factors, combined with the rapid changes facing nursing as part of a changing society, call for proactive leadership in nursing.

Historical Development of Leadership Theory

As early as the times of Plato and Confucius, scholars and philosophers have attempted to understand and describe leadership. But the real impetus to study leadership in a systematic, scientific manner occurred during and following World War I. The leadership theories of the last century have their base in industrial organizations and society. They have provided significant knowledge which has facilitated current and future theory development. However, no schools of leadership have emerged out of the immense reservoir of data and analysis about leadership. This is true partly because scholars have worked in separate disciplines and subdisciplines in pursuit of different questions and problems. However, society is on the brink of an intellectual breakthrough in leadership theory (Burns 1978, 3).

The following review of leadership theories is important to the understanding of transformational leadership. However, the theories reviewed are incomplete because they are limited to basically two dimensions: the tasks of managers and their relationship with others. The theories do not consider the values of people, nor do they help explain why some organizations are successful and excellent and why others are not. In Chapter 3, a theory which is relevant to an information society and responds to the future will be presented. Books on nursing leadership and management and management books in general abound with similar summaries of the historical development of leadership theories. Appendix B, "Additional

Readings," contains an extensive reference list for further study of leadership theories. For a greater appreciation of transformational leadership, the following concise summary identifies important themes and elements of seminal works of literature on leadership.

One of the predominant themes of the works that follow is that a democratic, participatory style is generally the most effective one. The situational theorists suggested the use of different leadership styles in different situations. This is a concept with much common sense and some research to support it. However, the participatory style of management, overall, has the most support. This style includes having a positive, supportive relationship with followers. Additionally, the theories also suggest that managerial leaders need to attend to the tasks and goals of the organization, as well as to interpersonal relationships with followers. Another important concept that can be gleaned from this review is that the behaviors and attitudes of leaders directly affect follower's satisfaction and productivity. All three of these themes provide a foundation for transformational leadership theory.

Great Man Theories and Trait Theories

The earliest leadership theories centered on the study of the traits and characteristics of the leader, such as personality, social traits, and physical characteristics. By studying "great men" such as Caesar, Alexander the Great, and Jefferson, the theorist searched for and listed attributes that differentiated the leader from the led. Because these studies described the characteristics of important historical figures, they were called "Great Man" theories. These attempts later evolved into trait theories which were developed by observing leaders in groups or by asking people to describe characteristics of preferred leaders.

Both of these early efforts to study leadership, although helpful, failed to identify any sufficiently universal traits of leaders. Characteristics that distinguished the leader from the follower or attributes that could help predict who would or would not be a successful leader were lacking (Stogdill 1974, 35-65).

Nonetheless, the failure to find these traits is important to the understanding and practical application of leadership theory. A person does not have to possess a certain, rigidly defined set of attributes to be a leader. Nursing managers who are responsible for choosing lower level managers are cautioned against making a list of desirable traits and searching for a leader by measuring people against these traits. A better approach is to look at past behaviors and accomplishments of candidates and gain an understanding of the person's values and beliefs about leadership and nursing. However, traits such as initiative and intelligence, which are generally accepted characteristics of leaders, can be nurtured and developed in others.

Environmental Theories

Several early theorists advanced the view that leaders arise as a result of certain circumstances and events. Thus, they proposed that the situation itself plays a large part in determining both the qualities of the leader and who the leader will be. For example, George Washington was a successful leader because the events of the American revolution brought out his skills and abilities.

However, as with trait theories, these environmental theories were inadequate. They provided no assistance in predicting a leader's abilities or in helping to develop future leaders (Stogdill 1974, 17).

An underlying belief of both environmental and trait theories is that leaders are born, not made. This concept is not in tune with the basic values of people in today's society, nor is it accurate. Leaders are and can be developed, it is not an easy task, but it does happen every day.

General Approaches to Leadership Theory

In this category, the major focus is the behaviors, activities, and styles of leaders. It is important to note that little attention is paid to followers and situations in these theories.

Styles of Leadership. One of the earliest and most famous studies looked at specific leader behaviors, primarily that of decision making and control. The researchers described three styles of leadership behavior: *autocratic, democratic,* and *laissez-faire.* These styles were placed on a continuum. At one end is the autocratic leader, described as directive, exerting a high degree of control, and allowing no participation in decision making. On the other end of the continuum is the laissez-faire leader who gives complete freedom to the followership group and provides no direction, resulting in a passive approach. In the middle is the democratic leader who exerts a low degree of control, but who is active in stimulating the group. The democratic leader allows participation in decision making and at the same time provides guidance and direction (White and Lippitt 1960).

The most important finding arising from this work is that leadership behavior directly influences the climate and productivity of the group. Further research and transformational leadership theory strongly embrace this belief. A second, important theme is that, overall, the democratic leadership style is the most successful. This style allows participation in decision making while at the same time supports, guides, and counsels the followership. Although later situational theories suggested that a leader's style should change to fit the situation and the characteristics of the followership group, a participatory, supportive style remains a common premise in many theories and is a basic premise in this book as well.

Leader Behaviors. Over the course of many years, studies of leadership were conducted at Ohio State University. From these studies, two leader behaviors, called *consideration* and *initiating structure*, consistently surfaced. Consideration refers to a wide range of activities that describes leader-follower interactions. Consideration behaviors cause leaders to display regard for the followers, satisfy their needs, and provide a supportive work environment. Initiating structure refers to the role of the leader to provide structure to accomplish the tasks of the organization and to direct the work group toward attainment of organizational goals. It includes such activities as assigning and organizing work, providing feedback for work performance, clarifying roles, and defining policies and procedures. These activities are similar to the classic management principles of planning, organizing, directing, and controlling (Rue and Byars 1986, 385).

Much of the research conducted to verify this theory of leader behaviors has resulted in conflicting findings about the relationship between initiating structure and employee satisfaction. However, leaders that scored high on both initiating structure and consideration questionnaires appear to have more cohesive, harmonious, and productive groups of followers (House 1971, 321). This research further supports and expands the belief that a democratic, participatory, supportive style is effective if combined with attention to tasks and goal accomplishment.

Likert's Four Systems of Leadership. Likert's (1967) four patterns or styles of leadership evolved out of the work of studies conducted at the University of Michigan. These studies revealed that supervisors of highly productive work groups gave general supervision, delegated authority and responsibility, and were employee- rather than production-oriented (Rue and Byars 1986, 387).

Likert's four systems of leadership are described below:

1. The *exploitative authoritative* style of leadership is one in which the leader exploits subordinates.

2. The *benevolent authoritative* style is paternalistic in nature, yet decision making and control is authoritarian, using direct hierarchical pressure for results.

3. The *consultative* style is one in which the leader maintains the decision-making prerogative but seeks input from and consults with employees.

4. In the *participative* leadership style, decisions are reached by group consensus with the leader serving to give direction.

As with previous theories, Likert claimed that the participative leadership style, called the System 4 manager, is the most effective. Effectiveness was measured by the productivity of the work group, the level of cost containment, positive employee attitudes, and good labor-management relationships.

The Managerial Grid. Closely related to the initiating structure and consideration perspective is the *task* versus *relationship* orientation of Blake and Mouton (1985). However, rather than seeing these orientations on a single continuum, they developed a managerial grid which placed the two elements together bipolarly. They described four combinations and styles of leadership.

A leader with a high task orientation and a low relationship orientation is labeled as having the *authority/obedience* style of management. In this style, the leader's efforts are directed at efficiency of task completion with minimal consideration for people. A manager using the opposite style, *country club* management, places emphasis on the concern for people (a high relationship orientation), resulting in a relaxed atmosphere and work place. The *impoverished* manager, who scores low on both relationship and task orientations, exerts little effort to accomplish the tasks or to relate with people. The *team* manager combines a high degree of concern for people with a high degree of concern for the task.

The purpose of the grid and of the work of these two researchers is to help managers identify their style by use of a questionnaire. They claimed that the team management style of leadership is the most desirable.

From this work, empirical research has demonstrated both people- and task-related behaviors of leaders are important. The transformational nurse leader cannot ignore either the people in the organization or the tasks of the organization. Both tasks and people will be explored in this book, however, they will be discussed as integrated rather than as separate entities.

Situational Leadership Theories

The basic premise of situational leadership theories is that different leadership styles are needed in different situations. For example, some research showed that a democratic, participatory, permissive style is not necessarily the most effective in every situation (Morse and Reimer 1956). Vroom (1960) found that the most effective style was, in part, determined by the characteristics of employees. Thus, he suggested that leaders need to adapt their style to the situation at hand. The situational theories contributed two new elements to the development of leadership theory: the situation and the follower. These theories are prescriptive—attempting to tell leaders how to act in a given situation.

Path-Goal Theory. The central underlying concept of the Path-Goal Theory is consideration of what motivates individuals. In this theory, motivation to behave in a particular manner is seen as the result of two related functions. First is the expectation that a particular behavior will result in a particular goal. Second, how strongly a person desires the goal will influence the behavior. The role of a leader is to clearly define desirable goals and to remove obstacles that could stand in the way of goal accomplishment (House 1971).

The Path-Goal Theory also suggests that there are four leadership styles that the leader can choose to employ in a particular situation: 1) *directive*—the authoritarian style previously discussed; 2) *supportive*—the leader is friendly, approachable, and shows concern for others; 3) *participative*—the leader asks for and uses suggestions to make decisions; and 4) *achievement-oriented*—the leader sets goals for subordinates which cause subordinates to strive for higher standards and shows confidence in them to attain these goals.

Depending on the situation, House suggested, the same leader could use varying styles. There are two situational factors: the personal characteristics of subordinates and the environmental demands with which the subordinates must cope to accomplish goals and satisfy their needs. Thus far, research has shown that for ambiguous tasks the leader should use a directive style. For stressful, frustrating, dissatisfying work a supportive style is appropriate. Finally, for nonrepetitive, unclear tasks an achievement style is warranted. A participatory leadership style was prescribed when subordinates were highly ego-involved in a decision or task and when the decision or task was ambiguous (Rue and Byars 1986, 388).

An example of applying varying management styles would be the same nurse manager using each of the four styles in different situations. In an emergency situation where the tasks are ambiguous and seldom faced, a directive style should be used. For handling the daily stressful, sometimes frustrating work, the nurse manager should choose a supportive style. In a situation when the work group is facing a major change, such as the implementation of a new system of care delivery, the leader should use an achievement style by setting high standards and showing confidence in the group. Lastly, to accomplish goals in which people have expressed a variety of opinions and beliefs, a participatory style would be most appropriate.

Fiedler's Contingency Theory. The Contingency Model of leadership effectiveness sought to integrate person, process, and situation (Fiedler 1967; Fiedler and Chemers 1974). The basic premise of the theory is that the effectiveness of the leader is contingent upon two factors: the motivational system of the leader and the degree to which the leader has control and influence in a particular situation. This theory consisted of two parts: ranking the leader's style and analyzing the situation.

To rank the leader's style, Fiedler and Chemers developed and administered a questionnaire called the Least Preferred Co-Worker. The questionnaire ranked the leader as either *task-motivated* or *relationship-motivated*. These two elements are similar to the initiating structure and consideration perspective of previous theories.

Next, Fiedler and Chemers analyzed the situation based on three elements and characterized the situation as either favorable or unfavorable. The first element, the *leader-follower* relationship, is the degree of friendliness of the leader and the extent to which others trust and respect her. *Task structure*, the second element, is the degree of structure entailed in a particular job. The third element is the *position power* of the leader. This refers to the formal power and influence of the leader, particularly her authority to reward and punish. Using these dimensions, the researchers developed eight classification schemes which are prescriptive suggestions for matching a leadership style with a situation.

Fiedler and Chemers viewed leadership situations on a continuum. In the most favorable situation for the leader, the relationship between the leader and followers is good—characterized by mutual trust, respect, and friendliness. The task is structured, i.e., the goals of the task are known, the elements are defined, and goal completion is probable. The leader is powerful, having formal influence over others. In this situation, a task-oriented leadership style is recommended. Likewise, in unfavorable situations where the relationship is poor, the task is unstructured, and the power of the leader is weak, a task-oriented style is prescribed. However, a relationship leadership style is recommended when the elements in the situation are moderate.

Life Cycle Theory. Hershey and Blanchard's (1977) Life Cycle Theory grew out of the Ohio State study of leader behaviors. This theory placed an emphasis on the behavior of the leader as it relates to the characteristics of the follower. First, they looked at follower maturity as it related to a specific task. The elements of follower maturity are 1) the capacity to set high but realistic goals for self; 2) the willingness and ability of the follower; and 3) the education, experience, job maturity, and psychological maturity of the follower. The researchers proposed that as the maturity level of the follower increases in relation to a specific task, the leader should reduce task behaviors and increase relationship behaviors. Hershey and Blanchard had a slightly different definition of task and relationship behaviors than that of previous theories. They considered task behaviors to be the extent to which a leader engages in one-way communication by explaining how to accomplish tasks. They defined relationship behaviors as the extent to which a leader engages in two-way communication by providing socio-emotional support and facilitating behaviors. They viewed these behaviors as bipolar (Table 1-1):

Motivational Theories

These theories focus on the needs and motivation of followers and examine factors that satisfy followers or decrease their dissatisfaction. According to these theories, a satisfied employee is more productive than a dissatisfied one. Further, these theories claim that the performance of the organization as a whole is a function of individual employee satisfaction and morale. There is conflicting evidence in the research regarding these basic premises; some scholars believe that the issues are more complex than

Table 1-1 Hershey and Blanchard's leader behaviors and resultant leadership styles.

Leader Behaviors		Leadership Style
Task	**Relationship**	
High	Low	*Telling*—defines the task; explains responsibilities; gives time frames for task completion; one-way communication.
High	High	*Selling*—balances concern for goal accomplishment with values, needs, and attitudes of followers; leader is in control but seeks input.
Low	High	*Participating*—concern is for how to get the group to work together to accomplish the task.
Low	Low	*Delegating*—leader takes a low profile; is available for consultation.

this simple cause-and-effect relationship. However, few managers would deny that employee satisfaction is a desired end, if not for its ability to enhance productivity, at least for its ability to provide a positive work environment.

Theory X and Theory Y. At the hub of McGregor's work (1960) is the belief that a leader's attitude about human nature influences her leadership behavior. Consequently, he proposed that there are two types of leaders, *Theory X* and *Theory Y*. Theory X leaders consider people as lazy, unmotivated, irresponsible, and unintelligent, and believe that workers will work only as much as is necessary to keep their jobs. These leaders feel they must direct and control people, supervising them closely and motivating them through a system of rewards and punishments. In contrast, Theory Y leaders believe that work itself can be motivating and rewarding and that workers can be trusted to work hard without constant supervision. The major function of Theory Y leaders, therefore, is to provide support for workers. This support includes providing a satisfying work environment by removing obstacles, providing guidance, and encouraging growth.

Herzberg's Dual Factor Theory. The concept that job satisfaction and job dissatisfaction are not direct opposites but are, in fact, separate but related entities is important to understanding Herzberg's theory. Herzberg (1966, 72-74; 1968) labeled factors which affect worker satisfaction and worker dissatisfaction as *hygiene* and *motivation* factors, respectively. Hygiene factors are those elements of the job environment that when present avoid unpleasantness in the work environment. They include company policy, administration, salary, supervision, interpersonal relationships, and working conditions. If any of these factors do not meet worker expectations, the worker will be dissatisfied. Alternatively, motivation factors, concerned with job content rather than job environment, if present result in employee satisfaction. Motivation factors include those elements that people need to grow and develop psychologically such as achievement, recognition for achievement, the work itself, advancement, and responsibility.

In applying this theory, the nurse manager should consider that those factors which cause dissatisfaction, such as salary, do not reversely cause job satisfaction. In other words, if an employee considers her salary appropriate, this does not mean she is necessarily satisfied with her job. Similarly, factors which result in satisfaction, such as achievement, do not cause dissatisfaction, rather they cause a lack of satisfaction.

In his research, Herzberg found that the last three motivation factors— the work itself, opportunity for advancement, and responsibility—were the most important for long-lasting, positive attitudes about work. He believed that the only way to motivate people is to give them challenging work in which people assume responsibility and achieve success. Although his work is over 20 years old and there are valid criticisms of his theory, his premises point leaders in an appropriate direction. His theory suggests to leaders how they may determine what may or may not enhance employee motivation and satisfaction.

Theory Z. Intentionally alluding to McGregor's Theory X and Theory Y, Ouchi (1981, 71-94) described an alternative leadership approach, Theory Z. His basic premise is similar to other motivational theories. An increase in job satisfaction, brought about by attention to humanistic management, results in improved employee satisfaction and productivity. His work is rooted in a comparison of Japanese and American management. He began his work by listing the characteristics of "Type Z" companies. These include long-term employment, slow evaluation and promotion, nonspecialized career paths, collective decision making and responsibility, and a holistic concern for people. Ouchi purported that the theoretical basis for why Z companies are successful is that they have achieved a high state of consistency in their organizational cultures. He likens Z companies to clans in which the associations among people are intimate. In a clan, people's individuality is less important than team work and agreement on working toward a common goal. Yet people in a clan are socialized so that their personal needs and values are naturally consistent with the common good. Thus, people in Z organizations report a higher degree of autonomy and freedom than employees of other organizations.

Implications for Nursing

Almost every article or book written in this decade which discusses leadership begins by arguing the need for new leadership theory and strategies. Berlew (1986, 99), Peters and Waterman (1982), and Bennis and Nanus (1985) are just a few examples. The theories presented in this chapter are not wrong, they are simply unfinished. They do not consider the new values of people who are no longer fulfilled solely by their work and by being treated with respect. These theories do not explain why some organizations are enthusiastic and successful while others are not. The answers to these questions can, at least in part, be found in the theory of transformational leadership.

As the reader proceeds throughout the book, the behaviors of an "ideal" leader will be discussed. These behaviors include some of those already discussed in this chapter, but include many new ones. The effective leader needs to be able to balance the tasks of the organization (organizational goals) with her skills in dealing with people. To best work with others, the key element is to understand the values, motives, and aspirations of others. The motivational theories reviewed in this chapter direct the nurse leader toward providing an environment in which people can achieve and be successful, have a sense of belonging to the team while maintaining a sense of self, and seek self-actualization in their professional work.

Application to Nursing Practice: Case Study

The Setting

A chief nurse executive (CNE) in a 700-bed hospital recently submitted her resignation in order to pursue a new nursing goal. During her four-year tenure, the CNE successfully implemented a clinical ladder, set up joint practice committees, and decreased employee turnover.

Current Situation

The CNE received the following letter from the chief executive officer upon her departure:

Dear Susan:

My reaction to your official announcement that you are leaving the Medical Center is that it is an unmitigated disaster for the institution. Very few departures in recent years will have had a comparable adverse impact on the functioning of this hospital.

You are a rare commodity: a savvy, highly intelligent, highly skilled, professionally adept, wise, insightful visionary. You are an understanding, flexible, firm thinker as well as a doer who works extremely well with colleagues, superiors, and those reporting to you. You can compromise without capitulating, say no without being negative, take chances without being reckless, be innovative without being destructive, and have warmth and charm without being weak. When you lead, others want to follow. When you collaborate, your colleagues are enriched. Your very presence in a meeting is assurance of at least one source of reason, considered judgment, and an attempt to accommodate.

You will be sorely missed. You have made a difference; let there be no doubt about it. I wish you the best in your new endeavors.

Sincerely,
A.M. Bellows

Case Study Discussion

1. What traits does this nurse leader have? Do these traits ensure leadership success?

2. Does this letter indicate the leader's ability to attend to both the tasks of the nursing department and the people with whom she works (i.e., consideration and initiating structure)?

3. How would you classify her leadership style using Blake and Mouton's managerial grid? Using Theory X and Theory Y?

4. What characteristics does this nurse leader exemplify that are *not* included in the theories discussed thus far?

5. How do you think this nurse leader might motivate staff?

6. Does this letter reflect the nurse leader's skills in dealing with the list of dissatisfactions of nurses with their practice? Why or why not?

7. Does this letter reflect the leader's ability to use different leadership styles in different situations?

References

American Academy of Nursing. 1983. *Magnet hospitals: Attraction and retention of professional nurses.* Kansas City: American Nurses Association.

Bennis, W., and B. Nanus. 1985. *Leaders: The strategies for taking charge.* New York: John Wiley and Sons.

Berlew, D.E. 1986. Leadership and organizational excitement. In *The leader-manager,* ed. J.N. Williamson, 99-104. New York: John Wiley and Sons.

Blake, R.R., and J.S. Mouton. 1985. *The managerial grid III.* Houston: Gulf Publishing.

Burns, J.M. 1978. *Leadership.* New York: Harper and Row.

Fiedler, F.E. 1967. *A theory of leadership effectiveness.* New York: McGraw-Hill.

Fiedler, F.E., and M.M. Chemers. 1974. *Leadership and effective management.* Glenview, IL: Scott Foresman.

Hershey, P., and K.H. Blanchard. 1977. *Management of organizational behavior: Utilizing human resources.* 3d ed. Englewood Cliffs, NJ: Prentice-Hall.

Herzberg, F.H. 1966. *Work and the nature of man.* Cleveland: The World Publishing Company.

Herzberg, F.H. 1968. One more time: How do you motivate employees? *Harvard Business Review* 46(1): 53-62.

House, R.J. 1971. A path goal theory of leadership effectiveness. *Administrative Science Quarterly* 16: 321-338.

Institute of Medicine. 1983. *Nursing and nursing education: Public policies and private actions.* Washington, DC: National Academy Press.

Likert, R. 1967. *The human organization: Its management and values.* New York: McGraw Hill.

McGregor, D. 1960. *The human side of enterprise.* New York: McGraw-Hill.

Morse, N.C., and E. Reimer. 1956. The experimental change of a major organizational variable. *Journal of Abnormal and Social Psychology* 52:120-129.

National Commission on Nursing. 1983. *Summary report and recommendations.* Chicago: American Hospital Association.

Ouchi, W. 1981. *Theory Z: How the American business can meet the Japanese challenge.* Reading, MA: Addison-Wesley.

Peters, T.J., and R.H. Waterman. 1982. *In search of excellence: Lessons from America's best-run companies.* New York: Warner Communications.

Rue, L.W., and L.L. Byars. 1986. *Management: Theory and application.* Homewood, IL: Irwin.

Stogdill, R.M. 1974. *Handbook of leadership: A survey of theory and research.* New York: The Free Press.

Vroom, V.H. 1960. *Some personality determinants of the effects of participation.* Englewood Cliffs, NJ: Prentice-Hall.

White, R.K., and R. Lippit. 1960. *Autocracy and democracy: An experimental inquiry.* New York: Harper and Brothers.

Yanklevich, D. 1983. *Work and human values.* New York: Public Agenda Foundation.

2

Societal and Healthcare Transformations

Chapter Objectives

1. Explain how projected future possibilities will impact nursing and healthcare.

2. Compare and contrast industrial and information societies.

3. Define structural change.

4. Discuss how changes in information processing and communications will impact healthcare and nursing.

5. List three major social trends.

6. Discuss how concerns for cost and quality will change healthcare in the future.

7. Define semi-autonomous work units.

8. Describe the required characteristics of future leaders.

Introduction

This chapter is about the predicted future of society, organizations, and healthcare and the implications for nursing and leadership. There is nothing incontrovertible about the information presented here. No one can predict with absolute certainty what the future holds. However, by analyzing current trends and examining them through computerized models, futurists, such as Martel (1986), Naisbitt (1982), and Toffler (1970), have theorized about possible future scenarios.

It may seem difficult, as nurse leaders struggle everyday for the survival of nursing, to think about the future. However, the nurse leader's understanding of projected possibilities for society and healthcare will help her to prepare for and gain a better foothold for nursing in an uncertain future.

Few periods in history can be labeled as transforming. Today we are living in one of those periods. The transformation is unusual as compared to others (the most recent being the Industrial Revolution). Unlike in the past, today's society is aware that the transformation is occurring. It is being studied and hypotheses about the future are abundant. Kuhn (1962) labeled transforming periods in history as paradigm shifts when the working values and assumptions upon which people structure their daily living become inappropriate. These assumptions then break apart to be replaced by more appropriate ones.

Further, the healthcare system in this country faces two major, conflicting challenges in the next decade: control of healthcare costs and provision of quality care to all clients. These two factors, in combination with societal trends and changes in the role of healthcare providers, are fundamentally altering the healthcare delivery system in this nation.

Structural and Cyclical Change

There are two types of societal change: structural and cyclical. Structural changes are fundamental transformations of an activity or institution which are not reversible and require permanent adjustment on the part of society. Cyclical changes, however, do not involve a change in the structure of society, are temporary, and do not require permanent adjustment. Examples of cyclical changes are business, economic, and demand-supply cycles (Martel 1986, 19-34). The structural changes of both society and healthcare are the subjects of this chapter.

There is a variety of ways to classify the structural changes facing society. Simplistically they can be categorized as either technological or social trends. However, as with most attempts to categorize complex ideas, the classification is not exact. The two categories overlap; technological changes bring about social ones and vice versa. In the following discussion, the impact of structural societal trends on healthcare will be discussed.

Technological Trends

The technological changes facing society and healthcare are occurring because of electronic breakthroughs during the past half century. Recently, the miniaturization of electronics with the concomitant decrease in their cost have laid the foundation for fundamental structural changes of both society and healthcare.

The Emerging Information Society

The most pervasive, pivotal, and profound structural trend is the transformation from an industrial to an information economy. This transformation is occurring because of society's increased and growing capability to handle information using the electronic technology of computers. In the last three decades, the development of equipment to store, process, and distribute information has resulted in information replacing energy as the new transforming societal resource. In contrast to fossil fuel, the primary resource of the industrial age, information is a growing resource which cannot be depleted. This fact, combined with advances in electronic, genetic, and other technologies, means that information will be society's most important resource and the demand for it will continue to increase.

Industrial Society. To fully appreciate the changes that are occurring and will most likely continue to occur, it is helpful to first discern the elements of an industrial society. For most of history, human labor was society's principle resource until energy was harnessed in the 1800s, creating the large-scale production of goods and the means to transport and distribute them rapidly.

The primary resources of industrialization are fossil fuel, the energy of steam, and electricity. The industrial society maximized and "massified" the world through mass production and mass distribution of goods, mass communication, and mass education. The values of education were punctuality, obedience, and rote and repetitious work. This resulted in standardization of goods, services, currencies, and even time. The Industrial Revolution was characterized by big cities, centralized governments with concentrated political power, and big corporations. Socially, the family structure changed from large, extended families of the agricultural era to the nuclear family. These smaller family units were more mobile and thus could move to the big cities (Toffler 1986).

The attributes and working assumptions of the industrial society are breaking apart and are no longer working. This is a reflection of the current paradigm shift. There are major problems facing society today, such as:

- The economic strength of our nation is faltering.
- Corporations are breaking up or downsizing.
- Workers are dissatisfied with their work environment and productivity is down.
- The welfare system does not produce recipients which contribute to the productivity of the nation.
- The healthcare system is too expensive and too dehumanized.
- Families are in crisis.
- The environment is polluted.
- Traditional energy sources are becoming depleted.

Centralized, big governments, that in the past were able to respond to crises, are not able to deal with the current problems facing society.

Information Society. Today the new era is called by some the *postindustrial age* and by others the *information society*. The distinction between the two terms is not clear. In this book, the latter term will be used. An economy is labeled an information economy when the percentage of products and employment in the service industries exceeds that in manufacturing and other industrial activities. In an information economy, the major business is information or a major part of the business is processing and distributing information.

The information society began in 1956-1957. Ironically, this was during the height of the industrial economy in this country. In 1956, white collar workers outnumbered blue collar ones for the first time in this nation's history. In 1957, with the space exploration of the Russian's *Sputnik*, global communications became a reality (Naisbitt 1982, 12). Today, in the late 1980s, the information age has a firm footing—over 70 percent of the American workforce is employed in service industries (Martel 1986, 93).

Society's increased and growing capability to handle information means changes in all activities in society, including work. Economically, there are three productive activities: 1) *extractive*—primarily agriculture but also includes mining and other activities to harness the products of the earth; 2) *industrial*—primarily manufacturing of goods; and 3) *services* for individuals, organizations, and society. All three of these activities are undergoing and will undergo significant changes.

As an example, for the agricultural industry, the information derived from the discovery of the double-helix structure of DNA will result in heartier, more disease-resistant crops and more productive animals. In manufacturing, the efficiency of human labor will continue to be enhanced with the application of automation and robotics, resulting in further improvement of processes and more sophisticated equipment. Goods will be produced more cheaply, with improved quality and less standardization. The service sector, including services to producers, services directly to consumers, and services to society as a whole, is and will continue to be the fastest growing component of society. The "high-tech" industries, including computers, software, and related businesses, will grow. However, their growth will not be as rapid as the "low-tech/no-tech service jobs," such as nursing and other healthcare workers (Martel 1986, 91-107).

Further, Toffler (1986, 15) claimed that the major difference in today's and tomorrow's society is diversity. Naisbitt (1982, 231) calls this a move from "either/or" to multiple options. Evidence of this trend is ubiquitous. Scientist are looking at a variety of energy sources besides fossil fuel such as sun, water, and wind. There is no longer a "typical" family structure. A trip to the grocery store and the selection of foods such as salad dressings, ice cream, and ethnic foods clearly demonstrate the trend of diversity.

Healthcare has experienced this diversity as well, primarily due to recent cost-cutting efforts. Hospitals are diversifying into related ventures such as ambulatory care centers, satellite clinics, and home healthcare. Some have begun to sell medical/surgical products. Others have entered ventures not connected with healthcare, such as catering. Alternatives to the traditional system of healthcare delivery have burgeoned, particularly health maintenance organizations (HMOs) and preferred provider organizations (PPOs). As other healthcare providers such as nurses, social workers, and psychologists successfully challenge the physicians' monopoly on healthcare, consumers and payors of healthcare will have more choices about who will provide care at what costs.

Robotics. Although the state of the art of this form of technology is in its infancy, it deserves special attention since the use of robots in healthcare and nursing is not unforeseeable. It has the potential to drastically alter nursing care.

In the 1950s, there were dreams that robots would be able to perform those chores which human's found to be laborious, such as housekeeping and cooking. This dream has not been realized. The sophisticated circuitry and programming to manufacture such robots has thus far proven to be too expensive. Robots are currently used for tasks such as assembling delicate electronic parts, handling nuclear waste, and exploring space. Robots are defined by the Robot Institute of America as:

> a reprogrammable, multifunctional manipulator designed to move material, parts, tools, or special devices through various programmable motions for the performance of a variety of tasks (Cardoza and Vek 1985, 2).

For healthcare, the development of robots is also in its infancy. Most of the uses for robots have not even been conceived. Yet there are a few attempts now emerging to use robots for routine nursing tasks. Although the use of robots in healthcare will be slow to be implemented because of their costliness, their proposed use indicates an important trend in nursing. That is, the importance of psychomotor skills for nurses is slowly diminishing while the need for decision making, creativity, and innovation are expanding.

Technology and Healthcare

The two most important technological advances for healthcare are the miniaturization of electronics and the new biology. In healthcare there will be more and more computer-assisted diagnostic techniques, the development of supple prosthetics, improved therapeutics, and improved management information systems. The biological revolution is likely to be even more pervasive and more important to the future of healthcare than electronics. Genetic engineering offers great potential, such as the elimination of some diseases and new, effective drug therapies including artificial red blood cells, improved chemotherapies, and anti-rejection drugs. Along with improved drug therapy will come the ability to administer them through implantable devices which reduce the side effects of many medications.

The rapid development of sophisticated medical technology over the past 25 years has caused a dilemma for society. In one way, it has contributed to noninvasive diagnosis, improved drugs, improved life expectancy, and less complicated invasive procedures that benefit society.

But technology is also thought to be the second major cause of increased healthcare costs after inflation (Somers 1985, 2-3). Also, the use of technology to unnecessarily prolong death does not significantly contribute to the quality of life of some individuals. Thus, it has become necessary to protect the public from ineffective, unnecessary technology, while at the same time ensuring that the life-enhancing possibilities of biomedical technology can flourish.

Communications

The most important asset of business and healthcare in an information society (besides people) is the rapid communication of dependable information. In order for businesses to successfully compete, decisions have to be based on accurate and timely information; and, parallel to the growth of information, structural changes are altering communications.

The two major structural changes that are occurring in communications involve the print media and the electronic media. These new technologies enable communications to be directed to distinct, small segments of the population, and at the same time, information can be sent to an entire nation, several nations, or even the world. This contributes to the functioning of the world as a "global village," where values and attitudes can be widely shared and adopted.

Print Media. The print media are growing, but slowly. At some time in the future, they may decline. Newspapers have been the most affected thus far. Where once there were two or more major newspapers in most big cities, now there is only one. The next print media to be affected are periodicals. The large, general-purpose magazines have already experienced a decline in readership. Their formats have been revised to appeal to smaller audiences. This change is reflected on the newsstands where there are periodicals and journals (over 20,000) written only for diverse, segmented audiences.

The book publishing industry has the best prognosis of all print media, but it will also undergo changes. For example, book stores may be able to print books in the stores on demand rather than have multiple copies of a book available. Libraries can store books on computer disks. Thus, many people can read the same book at the same time (Martel 1986, 63-79).

In nursing, the technology is already available to replace traditional print sources of information. Administrative and other reference documents, such as procedure manuals, policy manuals, and the *Physician's Desk Reference* can be stored electronically. Communications are then faster, easier to keep updated, and less bulky to store.

Electronic Communications. The second structural change will be in the growth of electronic communications and in interactive electronics. Because of new and emerging technologies, electronic communications have gotten progressively less expensive and the quality has improved. For example, wired cable television provides the hardware technology for interactive communications in the future. Patients may use this technology to communicate with healthcare providers.

Radio, like the print media, is also switching from "broad casting" to "narrow casting" by marketing to smaller segments of the audience. But radio signals can also be used to communicate with people for such purposes as paging, reminding people to take a medication, and warning families or healthcare providers of an emergency. Thus, both interactive electronics and radio signals will alter where people receive healthcare and the frequency of interactions between patients and healthcare providers.

Structural changes in communications are creating new ways of doing business and rearranging relationships between senders and receivers of information. People no longer have to meet face-to-face to exchange ideas, make decisions, receive training, or buy or sell a product. Telephones have already altered communications. With the use of computers, physical contact can be entirely eliminated and the nature of human interactions transformed.

Preliminary studies of people communicating solely through computers show that this interaction is not necessarily positive. In these studies, people frequently resorted to emotional language, took a longer time to reach agreement, and made more extreme final decisions than when they communicated face-to-face (Martel 1986). These findings have implications for nursing leaders who may, in the future, find themselves increasingly using computers to communicate with others.

Social Trends

Along with these technological changes, social transformations are occurring that have implications for nursing and healthcare. In some instances, technological advances beget social changes. For instance, improved technology has increased life expectancy. At other times, the relationship is not quite as clear. Yet the technological and social changes discussed here are best viewed as interrelated and interconnected.

Demographics

The population growth of the world is slowing. In some countries the growth may begin to decline in the next decade. At the same time, the life expectancy of people is increasing. These two structural changes in the population have led to new altered family relationships and changes in the workforce composition. Further, dependency ratios will change with more older adults dependent on a smaller, younger workforce to contribute to Social Security, Medicare, etc. The single most important change in the composition of the workforce is the entrance of women. This lowers the overall fertility rate and is partly responsible for the predicted lowering of population growth. Further, women's participation in the workforce alters social needs such as child care and health needs (Martel 1986, 107-127).

Demographic changes in the next 30 years will have a dramatic effect on healthcare. In fact, in a nationwide survey of 1,600 healthcare experts, the aging of America was identified as the most critical issue facing the future of the healthcare delivery system. This issue was considered more important than even costs and quality of care (Wesbury 1988, 59). Further, the shrinking American family, a disproportionate increase of elderly women who are poorer than elderly men, and an increase in minorities means fewer personal resources for healthcare and an increased need for long-term care programs.

Education

Educational advancement of the entire world population is another of the structural changes occurring today. In 1980, school enrollment of people age 6 through 23 exceeded 50 percent for the first time in the history of the world. In this country, the overall increase in college-prepared workers has increased from 5 percent to 25 percent in the past 20 years. Similarly, in nursing, the number of college-prepared nurses has increased from 10.4 percent in 1966 to 24.7 percent in 1983 (Vestal 1987, 354).

Education changes how people act and think and what they need and want. With education people attain the knowledge and skills to work in higher paying jobs. This improves their purchasing power and standard of living which add wealth to society. Further, education increases people's awareness and facilitates their participation in decision making. Thus, people become less apathetic and submissive.

The improved educational level of society affects healthcare as well. As people become more educated, they are able to better understand and to take responsibility for their own health. Since nursing has traditionally assumed responsibility for teaching healthcare and for valuing preventative healthcare, this societal trend can provide exciting opportunities for nurses as healthcare educators. In the future, the demand for nurses in acute care may decline while the demand for their teaching and preventive care skills may increase.

Work and Values

The values of people in society are changing. With reduced work hours, wages above subsistence level, and higher levels of educational achievement, work is no longer the central feature of people's lives. Workers have acquired property, new skills, and other interests. Like other aspects of society, workers are diverse. They come from a variety of ethnic backgrounds, life styles, family structures, and value systems. Further, workers no longer have a respect for and awe of authority.

These changed attitudes and values indicate that people have new expectations of organizations and managerial leaders. For themselves, people want respect, recognition, dignity, and an opportunity to be successful and advance. They want work that will increase their self-esteem and self-actualization. From the job itself, people want work that is challenging, rewarding, meaningful, and not boring. Employees want a work environment that is conducive to health, safety, and comfort. From the organization, especially managers, employees want organizational structures that allow participation in decision making; having their opinions, attitudes, and beliefs listened to and respected are further needs of contemporary workers.

Specific Healthcare Trends

As has been discussed, trends in healthcare reflect societal trends. There are some other healthcare trends, however, that are specific to the industry. These include cost containment, assurance of quality, access to care, ethical issues, and changing roles of physicians. Each of these trends has implications for nursing.

Costs

The concern over rising healthcare costs became evident in the late 1970s. In 1983, the crisis in the Medicare fund and its projected failure combined with a concern for the overall national deficit resulted in new legislation. The law implemented prospective reimbursement in the form of Diagnosis-Related Groups (DRGs). Hospitals became motivated by the bottom line which forced them to function as cost-effective businesses rather than as altruistic organizations.

These federal efforts to control healthcare have not been effective. In fact, statistics yield some puzzling data. Whereas costs continue to increase despite a decrease in demand for care over the past five years, the demand has leveled off and may be increasing.

Another structural change is also evident in where people receive their care. For example, the decreased length of stays in hospitals has greatly affected other sectors of the healthcare industry. Ambulatory care and home healthcare has burgeoned. The acuity of patients being cared for in their homes has increased, causing opportunities as well as problems for this sector of the healthcare delivery system. Likewise, the acuity of patients in long-term care facilities has also increased. Further, current technology has facilitated this structural change by eliminating the need for hospitalization for some diagnostic tests and surgeries such as cataract extraction and laser technology.

All of these events have caused competition to increase among all sectors of the healthcare industry because every sector is scrambling for the diminishing healthcare dollar. To secure more dollars under a prospective reimbursement system, each healthcare facility has to compete for a greater market share. Theoretically, the winners of the competition will be those who can provide the highest quality of care at the lowest cost.

What does the future hold? The changes already witnessed in the healthcare system are expected to continue. Experts predict that there will be more consolidations, downsizing, mergers, acquisitions, competition and marketing, managed care, HMOs and PPOs, and more bankruptcies in the years ahead. Most, if not all, hospitals will be part of a corporate structure. Several scenarios have been predicted: 1) hospitals will consist of only emergency rooms, operating rooms, and ICUs; 2) hospitals will specialize (e.g., some will be surgical centers, others maternal-child centers, etc.; and 3) short stays of one to two days will occur in areas remote from the major hospital, perhaps by expanding an already existing satellite ambulatory care center.

Quality

With less dollars to finance healthcare, many people are concerned that the quality of care will decrease. At the same time, the consumer movement, which is affecting the provision of goods and services throughout the nation, is demanding the assurance of quality from the healthcare industry.

Quality of care is a nebulous term which must be more clearly defined in the future. More objective, quantitative data that are "agreed upon" indicators of quality will need to be available to consumers. The release of data by the Health Care Financing Administration (HCFA) comparing the mortality rates among hospitals has been the first, although controversial, attempt to provide these data. Data from quality audits of Peer Review Organizations (e.g., the number of readmissions within 30 days and complications from surgery) will most likely be the next sources of this information. The demands of the People's Medical Society, an activist consumers group, further illustrate the need for qualitative data. They feel that each hospital should make the following data public: mortality rates of different procedures; cesarean section rates; nosocomial infection rates; drug error rates; iatrogenic incident rates; number of specific procedures performed; and qualifications of key personnel (Inlander 1988).

Further, quality of care is receiving increased attention from the Joint Commission on Accreditation of Healthcare Organizations (JCAHO) and HCFA. This means that healthcare facilities will need to measure quality and make the necessary improvements or face accreditation and reimbursement penalties.

To process and have this type of data readily available, hospitals will need to purchase and design computerized management information systems. These data will assist hospitals in their efforts to ensure quality to consumers and other interested parties. The information will also help hospitals to demonstrate their competitive edge when marketing their services to the community.

Access to Care

Not only have the costs of healthcare not been controlled, there is less equity in the provision of health services than there was two decades ago.

The current system functions in a piecemeal fashion—funding from both public and private sources is increasingly incapable of meeting the healthcare needs of society. Further, the number of uninsured Americans is reaching a crisis proportion.

National health insurance, one possible solution for this problem, does not appear to be on the horizon. This is due primarily to the concern for the federal deficit. In lieu of national health insurance, it is likely that long-term care insurance will be implemented by private insurance groups in the upcoming decade.

Ethical Concerns

All of these forces challenging the healthcare delivery system have created major ethical dilemmas for the nation and for healthcare providers. Cost containment and quality, combined with new technology and the increasing aging population, warrant and stir debate on many issues. Should there be limitations on who receives what kind of care? For instance, should total hip replacements be limited to people under 70 years of age if it will be paid for with Medicare funds? Can those people over 70 who can pay for it with out-of-pocket funds be allowed to have this procedure? Will the 72-year-old denied a total hip replacement become wheelchair bound and drain even more resources from the system than the procedure?

Physicians

The multiple forces altering the role, status, and finances of physicians portend new opportunities for all healthcare providers. Physicians have dominated the healthcare system, and this dominance has had much impact on the overall system and its functioning. But there is evidence that this is changing. The dominance of the physician is giving way to a more pluralistic system. Physician relationships with healthcare facilities, consumers, other providers, and the government are undergoing fundamental, irreversible changes.

For instance, in this era of competition and cost containment, hospitals are purchasing physician practices and entering joint ventures or mergers with physicians. Fewer physicians are in private practice. These trends alter the nature of the relationship between physicians and healthcare administrators to one of either employee/employer or business partners. In some cases, physicians are buying healthcare facilities and so changing their role to employer. There is also a trend to hire salaried medical directors in hospitals to oversee both the cost and quality issues of physician practices. More and more physicians are becoming employees of healthcare facilities rather than being users of healthcare facilities—a trend which is expected to continue well into the next century. Physicians are now beginning to feel professional/bureaucratic conflicts which they did not feel in the past.

Physician-consumer relations are also changing. With more information about healthcare available to the public, consumers are more aware and more assertive regarding their own healthcare. Physicians are no longer revered and given as high a status in this society as they once were. In fact, often the opposite is true. People are questioning physician salaries as excessive and not warranted given the quality of medical care provided.

Another trend affecting physicians is that they are also being challenged by other healthcare providers such as nurses, psychologists, social workers, and others, who believe they can deliver quality healthcare in a more cost-effective manner than physicians. Many nonphysician providers, including nurses, have successfully challenged the once legally-sanctioned monopoly given to physicians through licensure. Certainly, this trend will continue, with much resistance from physicians, as other providers demonstrate to the payors that they can provide similar services at less cost.

Physicians are facing major changes in how they are reimbursed for their services. Medicare (Part B) is showing the largest increase in expenditures and 75 percent of this money is fee-for-service for physicians. This issue has been discussed in Congress for several years, but as yet no action has been taken. However, it appears evident that the fee-for-service system will be replaced by another funding mechanism. Exactly what other approaches for reimbursement will be chosen are unknown.

The projected physician glut portends more bad news for physicians. Congress is looking dubiously at the financial support given to medical education. The federal sentiment seems to be that with an oversupply of physicians, it would be poor public policy to fund physician education and to continue to increase their supply (Mitchell 1988, 9).

The Future Organization

Two major changes are occurring in organizations. The first is the development of small, semi-autonomous work units. The second is the cry for a new type of leader to guide these work groups.

Semi-Autonomous Work Units

The current and emerging electronic technology of communications and the importance of information as the primary resource will continue to profoundly affect the workplace. The new organization will be composed of small work units. These units will be interconnected with other small work groups and integrated with larger corporations via electronic networks. Different authors have various names for these work groups such as the "electronic cottage" (Naisbitt 1982, 35; Toffler 1986, 18); "atomized organizations" (Deal and Kennedy 1982, 177); and "semi-autonomous federal units" (Kinsman 1986, 20). Kinsman described this change as a move from hierarchy to heterarchies, with each unit supported by a central matrix, the corporation. He likened this central organization to a sponge. Each unit is supported by the central matrix and can absorb the needed support from it. At the same time, the semi-autonomous work groups nourish the central organization by their profitable activity in the marketplace.

Where people work will also change. More and more people will work in their homes or at small local sites rather than in big cities. Toffler (1986, 19), in an informal interview with factory managers, found that from 25 percent to 35 percent of people presently employed could work at home and could communicate with the factory by computer. Although it seems impossible to envision staff nurses working exclusively in their homes to care for patients, some nursing duties can and increasingly more could be done through electronic communications and monitoring. This would probably reduce the number of face-to-face interactions between nurses and their clients.

Why are so many business scholars predicting this change from big corporations to semi-autonomous work groups? One reason is that small work groups are more able to respond locally, quickly, and creatively than larger systems. This is a vital ability in a complex, rapidly changing, highly competitive environment. Further, smaller work units are integral parts of the overall trend from centralization to decentralization.

Appealing to the new workers' need for a sense of belonging, small work units will help foster in workers a sense of the organization belonging to them, rather than they belonging to the organization. At the same time, the individual's innovative abilities and creativity will be highly prized. This appeals to another value of the new worker: meaningful, challenging work. Since the computer will perform "left brain" activities, the role of intuition and creativity in workers will be the most needed and valued asset. Thus, each person will be expected to be an in-house entrepreneur. The relatively intimate, simple work environment will best support this individual entrepreneurship. Kanter (1983, 354-355) explained the importance of what she called "corporate entrepreneurs." She believed top mangers may set priorities, demand quality, and look for ways to cut costs, but it is the middle managers and below who put form to these strategies.

Decisions in semi-autonomous work units will be reached democratically. By reaching a consensus when making decisions, everyone's opinions, ideas, and beliefs will be sincerely listened to and considered by the group. Since it is highly unlikely that everyone will always support the same strategy, there will be an understanding that once a strategy is undertaken, everyone will give it time and support to be tried.

The units will use ad hoc groups to make decisions, to plan, and to forecast trends. Ad hoc groups, committees, or task forces are ones which form, take action, dissolve, and reform again when necessary. They have been used extensively in organizations for some years. The major difference in the new ad hoc groups is that the leadership of the groups will be more flexible than today. The best person for the task at hand will be the best person to lead the group. The leader does not have to be a manager. More and more, staff nurses will be seen as leading those task forces which affect their work.

Each work group will be responsible for its own success. However, there will be some financial arrangements with the larger corporation. The best current example of this is seen in franchises which are tied to the larger corporation and pay a fee for group advertising, purchase of supplies, and so forth.

These small, autonomous units and the parent corporations will need to respond to a number of stakeholders. Bottom-line financial success will not be the only monitor of performance. The new work units will need to show a concern for the environment, customers, employees, communities, society, and shareholders.

Handy (1984) described a slightly different scenario for the organization of the future. He believes that there will be three types of employees:

1. A small, professional/managerial support core.

2. A fringe of self-employed "out workers" who function individually or in cooperation with others on a jobbing basis.

3. An outer ring of part-time, temporary employees which will be a flexible workforce.

Whether or not this design will become a widespread reality is not known. However, elements of the design are already evident. For instance, in nursing, the use of staffing agencies to provide "outworkers" to nursing service and the use of small in-house float pools or occasional work forces are common practices.

The Future Leader

The leader-employee relationship will change in the future. The now sharp distinction between managers and workers will blur. The leader will work alongside followers. She may best be viewed as the first among equals rather than as a person having autocratic or paternalistic power (Kinsman 1986, 20). The new leader will need to exhibit a fundamental belief in human beings by acknowledging their expertise, trusting them, and sharing power with them.

The role of the new leader will be vastly different than today. The primary role will be to empower others to be their own leader. The leader's own creative and intuitive skills will be important, but the new leader will design systems which enhance these skills in others as well. Because decision making will be participatory, the leader will have to develop skills of persuasion, rather than merely ordering people to do tasks.

Deal and Kennedy (1982, 189) suggested that the role of the future leader of semi-autonomous work units will be to structure and negotiate appropriate economic and financial arrangements with the central core organization. In doing this, the leader will need to be able to balance the legitimate concerns and interests of both parties. The leader will also build a culture of pride in being part of the central organization.

Implications for Nursing

In the future, organizations, healthcare, and nursing will be radically different from today. For nursing, the predicted changes can be positive ones. Nursing leaders need to begin to incorporate the ideas and elements of this future into practice today.

All nursing staff have the potential to become in-house entrepreneurs. There are two major benefits of this possibility. If nurses are empowered to be innovative and creative, they will be more satisfied in their need for achievement. Secondly, by empowering nursing staff, the organization will profit. More than any other group in a hospital or healthcare facility, nursing staff have an intimate understanding of how the organization works, its strengths, and its weaknesses. For the most part, however, nurses have not been given the resources to contribute meaningfully to the overall organization. In the future, this can change by giving staff the necessary time, money, space, information, and knowledge to become in-house entrepreneurs.

Society will continue to become even more dependent on information as a resource. Computers, and even robots, will perform psychomotor tasks and monitoring. Therefore, a nurse's skills in assessment, planning, evaluation, teaching, and decision making will be more valued and more important to society. Nursing organizations should be revising the nursing practice environment so that these skills are nurtured and enhanced. Also, the task orientation of professional practice needs to be de-emphasized and the intellectual orientation needs to be enhanced. This change in orientation will not be easy. Nurses, as well as society in general and healthcare providers in particular, often describe the profession by the tasks that nurses perform. Thus, the transition from a task orientation to an intellectual orientation will take time, patience, and much work with the public. Yet, it is an inevitable change for which nursing should prepare proactively.

The workplace itself will undergo significant changes as well. A diminishing number of nurses will be employed in smaller, more acute hospitals. The role of the nurse in this setting will also change. The decreased emphasis on tasks and an increase in intellectual activities will be evident in this setting. The need to somehow balance the increased acuity of patients in hospitals with fewer nurses and more "nurse extenders" is a challenge that nurse leaders will be addressing over the next several years.

All of these changes and challenges call for new leadership strategies. Nursing needs creative, innovative leaders as well as followers. These leaders will be faced with a combination of societal, healthcare, and professional issues that are currently transforming today into an uncertain future. Nursing leaders will need not only a vision of the future, but also a definite strategy for realizing this vision. Transformational leadership theory and strategies are the beginnings of such a blueprint for success.

Application to Nursing Practice

Because of the forward-looking nature of the information presented in this chapter, no case study is given. However, by discussing the following questions readers can review the main concepts presented in the chapter.

1. Describe one positive and one negative outcome of computerization on nursing.

2. What are possible benefits of improved global communications for the nursing profession?

3. What opportunities do cost containment and the growing elderly population open to nursing?

4. Are semi-autonomous work units in healthcare a credible, future reality?

5. What will be the characteristics of future nurse leaders?

References

Cardoza, A., and S. Vek. 1985. *Robotics.* Blue Ridge Summit, PA: TAB Books.

Deal, T.E., and A.A. Kennedy. 1982. *Corporate cultures: The rites and rituals of corporate life.* Reading, MA: Addison-Wesley.

Handy, C. 1984. *The future of work.* London: Pan Books.

Inlander, C.B. 1988. Full disclosure. *Nursing Economics* 6(1):40.

Kanter, R.M. 1983. *The change masters: Innovation for productivity in the American corporation.* New York: Simon and Schuster.

Kinsman, F. 1986. Leadership from alongside. In *Transforming leadership: From vision to results*, ed. J.D. Adams, 19-28. Alexandria, VA: Miles River Press.

Kuhn, T.S. 1962. *The structure of scientific revolutions.* Chicago: University of Chicago Press.

Martel, L. 1986. *Mastering Change.* New York: Simon and Schuster.

Mitchell, K. 1988. The long term focus of DHSS's Otis Bowen. *Nursing Economics* 6(1):7-9, 47.

Naisbitt, J. 1982. *Megatrends: Ten new directions transforming our lives.* New York: Warner Books.

Somers, A. 1985. Demographic, technological, and economic imperatives must be faced if the health care system is to survive. *Medical Director* (Nov./Dec.):2-4.

Toffler, A. 1970. *Future shock.* New York: Bantam Books.

Toffler, A. 1986. Beyond the break-up of industrial society: Political and economic strategies in the context of upheaval. In *The leader-manager*, ed. J.N. Williamson, 9-28. New York: John Wiley and Sons.

Vestal, K.W. 1987. *Management concepts for the new nurse*. Philadelphia: J.B. Lippincott.

Wesbury, S.A. 1988. The future of health care: Changes and choices. *Nursing Economics* 6(2):59-62.

3

Toward a Theory of Leadership

Chapter Objectives

1. Develop a personal belief about transformational leadership.

2. Define leadership, transactional leadership, and transformational leadership.

3. Apply Maslow's theory of hierarchy of needs to nursing practice.

4. List five possible ways to manage conflict in followers' values.

5. Distinguish between power and leadership.

6. Discuss contemporary personal and organizational values.

7. Discuss 10 roles of managers.

Introduction

Transformational leadership is about change, innovation, empowerment of others, and power *with* others not *to* others. In the daily work of nursing, the need to make changes in nursing departments is evident. This need exists not only to solve current problems and dissatisfactions, but also to successfully thrive in the future. To do this, nurse leaders will need to use a variety of strategies:

- Create new visions which give a sense of meaning and purpose to the work of nursing.

- Develop new, trusting relationships between nurse managers and staff.

- Design working environments which support a commitment to organizational and professional visions and goals and which empower employees.

- Use one major resource, herself, to achieve organizational success.

Unfortunately, there are no prescriptions for transformational leadership. There are no questionnaires to rank a person's transformational leadership skills and abilities to help a person in a concrete way to become a transformational leader. Nor is there any empirical research that has identified the traits of or specific methods of shaping this type of leader.

However, there is much descriptive work starting with James McGregor Burns's (1978) Pulitzer Prize winning book entitled, *Leadership*. His work is limited to extensive descriptions of famous political leaders such as Mahatma Gandhi, Franklin D. Roosevelt, Woodrow Wilson, and John F. Kennedy. However, he claimed that his concepts apply not only to this elite group of men. In fact, he argued that transformational leadership can be seen in the daily routines of life. Parents, teachers, preachers, and corporate managers are and can be transformational leaders.

Since Burns's seminal work, other authors have bridged the concept of transformational leadership from the purely political arena to that of corporations (Adams 1986; Bennis and Nanus 1985; Paul 1982; Roberts 1985; Tichy and Devanna 1986; and Vardaman, Wimer, and Dugat 1986). These authors used the concepts from Burns's theory as a foundation for their writings and observations of transformational or transforming leaders.

Further, a number of management books written in this decade have described corporations and corporate leaders that have successfully adapted to a changing environment. The authors of these works described characteristics and practices of leadership which do not explicitly have transformational leadership as their theoretical foundation. These works also are not based on the traditional leadership theories reviewed in Chapter 1 (Kanter 1983; Naisbitt and Aburdene 1985; Peters and Austin 1985; and Peters and Waterman 1982). Other authors have used terms such as "organizational excitement" (Berlew 1986) or "charismatic leadership" (House 1976) to describe new theories of progressive management. In nursing, one work which describes successful, excellent nursing departments is the *Magnet Hospital Study* (American Academy of Nursing 1983).

All these scholars, whether or not they refer to the specific tenets of transformational leadership, have been concerned with common themes: 1) past leadership theories are not enough to help organizations move toward the uncertain, rapidly changing future; 2) people in organizations want to have a sense of purpose and self-worth; and 3) new leaders and new leadership strategies are imperative. However, the most significant finding of all these studies is that all successful organizations have one thing in common: innovative leadership.

A leader's effectiveness can be significantly influenced by her insight into personal behaviors, attitudes, and beliefs. In other words, a leader's ability to be introspective enhances her ability to lead. In the works of the motivational and the behavioral theorists reviewed in Chapter 1, it was seen that a leader's behavior and view of human nature directly affect her ability to be effective and successful. Stated another way, what the leader believes about followers, about leadership, and about the relationship between leaders and followers becomes a self-fulfilling prophecy. This chapter presents a new, philosophical approach to nursing leadership which hopefully will enable nurse leaders to view the leader-follower relationship in a more contemporary way.

Transactional and Transformational Leadership

A general definition of leadership and definitions of two types of leadership, transactional and transformational, are important to the understanding of Burns's (1978) theory. His theory of transformational leadership and his general definition of leadership comprise the conceptual framework for this book. The following is his general definition of leadership:

> Leadership over human beings is exercised when persons with certain motives and purposes mobilize, in competition or conflict with others, institutional, political, psychological, and other resources so as to arouse, engage, and satisfy the motives of followers (Burns 1978, 18).

Several important features of this definition will be considered in further sections of this chapter: 1) the relationship of leaders and followers;

2) the values, motives, and needs of both the leader and followers; 3) the dynamics of competition or conflict with others; and 4) power.

Transactional Leadership

Transactional leadership occurs "when one person takes the initiative in making contact with others for the purpose of exchange of valued things" which may be economic, psychological, or political (Burns 1978, 19). It is thought to be more common than transformational leadership. Transactional leadership is an exchange to satisfy the needs of both the leader and follower. The leader and follower have separate but related purposes; they are not bound together in pursuit of common goals. For example, a nurse manager exchanges a salary for the services of employees to provide care to patients. Both the nurse and the nurse manager have separate purposes. The nurse receives from this transaction a salary that "buys" a standard of living and, perhaps, fulfillment of some personal and professional need. At the same time, the nurse manager receives the benefit of staffing the hospital. Since this is one of the responsibilities of the nurse manager, her purpose is also fulfilled. In this example, the "exchange of the valued thing" is money for the service of a licensed nurse for some agreed upon amount of time.

Transformational Leadership

In contrast, transformational leadership "occurs when one or more persons engage with others in such a way that leaders and followers raise one another to higher levels of motivation and morality" (Burns 1978, 20).

Transformational leadership implies a relationship in which the purposes of the leader and followers become fused, creating unity, wholeness, and a collective purpose. Collective purpose is crucial to the concept of transformational leadership. There is only one measure of success of the transformational leader: the realization of the intended social change (or purpose) which satisfies the needs and motives of both the leader and the followers. The change must impact positively on the well-being of both the leader and followers, consistent with their values.

Transformational leadership changes followers. Followers are able to grow and develop because their needs are met and new needs, aspirations, and values emerge. Thus, followers may become leaders as they grow and develop.

Transformational leadership in nursing is not as rare as one might initially think. It is easier to observe such leadership by looking at results than at the process. A work environment in nursing functioning under transformational leadership would have the following characteristics:

- low turnover of staff
- readily apparent, high morale of staff
- enthusiastic approach to patient care
- staff working together with team spirit
- an understanding on the part of each staff member of the goals and purpose of their unit
- people expressing a sense of achievement and belonging
- satisfied patients and families

To better understand the elements of transformational leadership, a further look at several key components of Burns's general definition of leadership is necessary. As stated before, these include 1) the leader-follower relationship; 2) values, motives, and needs; 3) conflict and competition; and 4) power.

The Leader-Follower Relationship. Burns's choice of the word "engaged" to describe the leader-follower relationship is significant. It denotes binding, interlocking, meshing, and involvement. It is a fully sharing relationship based on trust. The leader has a sense of belonging to the group, yet at the same time has a sense of self.

The engagement of the leader and followers occurs when the leader recognizes, appeals to, and acts on both her own and the followers' values and motivations. The result of the relationship is the arousal and satisfaction of the motives, values, and aspirations of both. It brings out the best in followers.

Values, Motives, and Needs. Central to Burns's theory are the values and needs of both the leader and the followers. *Values* are enduring beliefs that a specific mode of conduct (*modal* or *instrumental* values) or end states of existence (*end* or *terminal* values) are personally and socially preferable to alternative modes and ends. Modal values may be such things as honesty, courage, and fair play. End values may be such things as equality, salvation, and world peace (Rokeach 1968, 159-161).

Values are organized into a hierarchical structure and substructures. In other words, values are a learned organization of rules for making choices and resolving conflicts. Situations often occur where there is a conflict in the values that a person holds. For example, nurse middle managers are often faced with the choice between two conflicting values. The nurse manager may wish to satisfy a value to support her superior and to follow strategies which advance the overall goals of the facility, but this could conflict with another value to support the nursing staff and to enhance their practice. This conflict occurs in many arenas such as policy making and strategic planning.

Values have internalized cognitive and affective components, as well as behavioral components. Specifically, values function to 1) set standards for behavior by defining specific criteria for action; 2) develop and maintain a person's attitude about a particular thing or situation; 3) justify one's own actions and attitudes as well as to judge others; 4) assist in decision making by defining specific criteria by which to make choices among alternatives; and 5) motivate people by internalizing the values so deeply that they help define personality and behavior (Burns 1978, 74-75).

Burns based much of his work on Maslow's (1970, 35-88) hierarchy of *needs* which serve to motivate people. These needs are intrinsic rather than from external sources.

The hierarchy of needs, according to Maslow, includes physiological, safety, belongingness and love, esteem, self-actualization, and aesthetic needs. (Figure 3-1). The needs are organized into a hierarchy of relative prepotency. Once a lower level need is gratified then a higher level need emerges and dominates the person. Satisfied needs no longer serve to motivate the individual.

The *physiological* needs (not an inclusive list) include food, water, rest, sleep, elimination, breathing, and activity. The next level of needs, the *safety* needs, include security; stability; dependency; protection; freedom from fear, anxiety, and chaos; and the need for structure, order, law, and limits. The *belongingness* and *love* needs include such things as affection; friendship; having a spouse; and enjoying affectionate relationships with people in general. The *esteem* needs include self-esteem and the esteem of others. The self-esteem needs include a desire for strength, for achievement, for adequacy, for mastery and competence, for confidence in the face of the

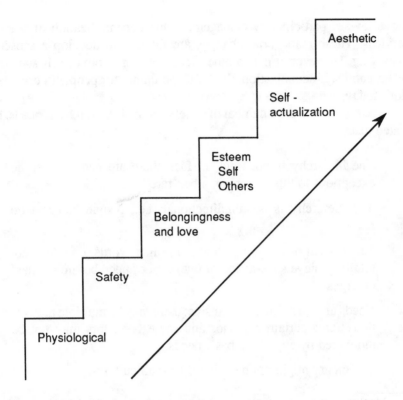

Figure 3-1 Maslow's hierarchy of needs.

world, and for independence and freedom. Secondly, humans desire the esteem of others in the form of prestige, status, fame, recognition, attention, importance, dignity, and appreciation. The need for *self-actualization* is an idiosyncratic need—to be fulfilling one's purpose in life. This is the highest of individual aspirations and involves growth, striving for excellence, and a quest for identity and autonomy. According to Maslow, a sixth level of needs exists in some people. This is the *aesthetic* need which he described as the need to experience and enjoy beauty.

In nursing organizations today, most attention has been paid to the first three levels of need. There has been an emphasis on salaries and on the safety and security of working conditions. More recently, there has been a move toward participatory management and decentralization of nursing services. These managerial changes are thought to develop a sense of belonging. However, it is two other needs, esteem (both of self and from others) and self-actualization, that often go unmet for people in organizations today.

Maslow postulated a number of beliefs about his hierarchy of needs. He stated that:

- The hierarchy is not rigid. In fact, there are people who are exceptions to this hierarchy, albeit rare.

- The hierarchy is not unidirectional; i.e., people can and do regress.

- Satisfaction of needs is relative. In other words, one does not totally achieve satisfaction of one level of need before the next emerges.

- Needs are not mutually exclusive: there may be multiple motivations for a certain behavior and some behaviors may not be motivated by any of the basic needs.

- The theory might not be universal for all cultures.

Maslow's theory has come under a great deal of criticism and scrutiny (Brockett 1975; Fox 1982; Wahba and Bridwell 1976). It is certainly beyond the scope of this work to present the arguments supporting Maslow's theory and those not supporting it. However, the theory should be read and used with some hesitancy and with an awareness of its possible shortcomings. For the purpose of this book, Maslow's theory does not have to be accepted literally. It may be imprecise and does lack conclusive, empirical evidence. However, a hierarchy of needs as such does seem to exist. The needs identified by Maslow are valid and are well documented by both descriptive and historical works.

According to Burns, leaders operate at a level of need and value higher than that of followers, but not so high as to lose contact with followers. Leaders exploit conflicts in the need and value systems of their followers, see contradictions, and arouse a sense of dissatisfaction to force followers to resolve these conflicts. Leaders help followers gratify lower levels of needs so that higher ones emerge and elevate consciousness. The fundamental act of leadership is, thus, to induce people to be aware of and clarify their needs, to be conscious of what they feel, to define values meaningfully, and to induce them to relevant, purposeful action (Burns 1978, 75-76).

Conflict and Competition. Conflict permeates and characterizes the relationships of human beings. No group of people is totally harmonious, a fact that is observed daily in people's work and personal lives. Conflict is not necessarily bad; however, if the level of conflict is either too high or too low, it will not promote growth and change. For instance, a totally compatible group would be void of process and structure. Thus, conflict can be a source of growth, development, learning, interdependence, and pressure for change. Or it can be harmful and only divide people.

Organizational conflict arises because of rapid and unpredictable rates of change, new technological advances, competition for scarce resources, differences in cultures and belief systems, and the variety of human personalities. The organizational conflict with which the leader must be concerned has two forms: 1) conflict within the followership group itself and 2) conflict with others, both inside and outside the organization. For example, the nurse executive finds organizational conflict within the nursing department, from other departments within the healthcare facility, and from outside the organization itself.

To deal with conflict within the followership group, the leader first acts as a catalyst. She arouses followers' consciousness, sees and articulates the contradictions in values and needs, arouses dissatisfaction, and ultimately forces choices that result in the intended change. The leader makes followers dissatisfied with something in order for the followers to mobilize and to act. She constantly assesses the character and intensity of the follower's willingness and ability to act.

For smaller, homogeneous followership groups, the leader will have to primarily deal with the leaders of the other groups with opposing needs and values. For example, the nurse manager of a single nursing unit could find herself in competition with other nurse managers for budget, staff, and recognition of her staff. For larger, more heterogeneous followership groups, the leader will have to face competing interests and goals within her constituency. Nurse executives, for example, manage the conflict existing in the nursing service, as well as conflict with other departments in the medical center.

The role of the leader is to express, shape, and curb conflict. She capitalizes on and embraces conflict in the followership group and with others instead of avoiding it. Her role does, however, differ depending on the source of the conflict. There are a variety of skills the leader brings to handling or managing organizational conflict and each situation calls for a different set of skills.

The skills used depend on whether the conflict is within or outside the followership group and on what resources are available to the leader. She may 1) define the grievances and wants of followers; 2) act for followers in their dealings with other clusters of followers and with others inside and outside the organization; 3) influence the intensity of the conflict; 4) deviate and innovate to mediate between the claims of their groups and those of others; 5) modify leadership in recognition of preferences of followers; 6) act directly on behalf of the followers; 7) bargain with others; 8) override certain motives of followers; and 9) within limits, soften or sharpen the claims and demands of followers (Burns 1978, 36-41).

In nursing and healthcare facilities, many forms of conflict exist: for power and prestige; between managers and employees; between line and staff personnel; between members with different professional affiliations or kinds of expertise; among the various departments, each with different goals that contribute to the overall mission of the organization; and other personal and idiosyncratic conflicts. It is the wise nursing leader who acknowledges the existence of conflict, assesses it sources, and determines how to express and shape conflict for the growth and development of the organization and its people.

Power. Over the past two decades in nursing, there has been an emphasis on power: what it is, how to get it, how to use it, and how not to lose it. This concern for power is a result of nurses, as a group, feeling "powerless." Power has been defined in terms of the personal attributes of people with power; positional resources of power holders; social relationships of power holders and power recipients; control over scarce resources; and in terms of the psychodynamics of power relationships (Gabarro 1978, 298).

Burns (1978, 9-28) has a different perspective on the topic which is valuable to an understanding of transformational leadership. He views both power and leadership as relationships. Leadership is a form of power. "Raw" power has the capacity to be negative; leadership is positive.

He defined power as the process by which a person, possessing certain motives and goals, has the capacity to secure changes in the behavior of others and in the environment. This is done by utilizing resources in one's power base which may include economic, political, institutional, or personal skills. This definition implies that power is a relationship among people. It involves the intention or purpose of both the person with power and the recipients of the power. Hence, power is collective. Thus, power in transformational leadership is best viewed as a means to get things done rather than as an end in itself.

Power has three elements: 1) the motives and resources of the power holder; 2) the motives and resources of the power recipient; and 3) the relationships among all of these. A simple equation is:

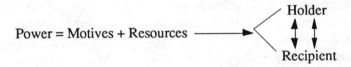

In this equation, the motives of a nurse manager may be to give all nursing staff a salary of over $75,000. However, the resources to achieve this goal are not present in the healthcare system today or in the near future. Thus, there is no power to achieve this goal. In contract, all nurses have the resources to harm patients. Except in rare, pathological instances, there is no motivation to do so. Again, there is no power. When there is no motive to achieve a particular end, resources diminish; likewise, when there are no resources, motives are inactive; and without either motive or resources there is no power. Because resources are limited and motives may be in short supply, power is seen as elusive and limited.

As stated previously, leadership is a form of power having a collective purpose. With power, the purpose may serve only the power wielder. The motives of the power wielder may or may not coincide with the respondents' wants, but may only meet the goals and aspirations of the power wielder. Power may be coercion or control. Leadership is not. Crucial to the power of a transformational leader is purpose which is always in the best interests of both leader and follower.

Transformational leadership is about power and empowerment. Empowerment is the creation of an environment that ensures that people in the organization get the power they need to innovate and be creative. It is power circulation and power access (Kanter 1983, 156-160). Empowering nurses is the way to solve the pervasive feelings of powerlessness in the profession. Both nursing managers and employees need appropriate amounts of power in order to innovate, be creative, and succeed.

Sources of Leadership

Burns (1978, 49-137) departed from previous theories of leadership by considering how people become leaders. He believed there are both social and psychological sources of leadership. The social sources are the family, schools, political system, self-esteem, social role-taking, and sense of purpose. The family rewards the child for compliance and punishes for deviance using standards established by the parents. Later, formal schooling sharpens attitudes and behaviors. In adolescence, the need for self-esteem, the perception of esteem by others, and the need for and capacity for social role-taking work to bring out the potential for leadership.

No definitive work has been accomplished in the study of the psychological sources of leadership. However, some significant information has been gathered. Studies of animals revealed that they do indulge in various forms of leadership, which indicates some evidence of biological sources. Psychoanalysis, a Western invention, has not yielded any helpful results in the study of leadership. Psychobiography, in which the biographies of famous leaders are studied psychoanalytically, has produced a paucity of data. This retrospective approach attempts to look at the formative influences of early life. It has been criticized because it overemphasizes childhood influences and ignores learning from experiences, people, successes, and failures.

Burns stated that Maslow's hierarchy of needs probably furnishes the best information regarding leadership development. Sources of leadership lie in the transformation of biological wants into needs and social aspirations. The lifelong process of needs fulfillment culminates in the skills and motivation for leadership. Although genetic inheritance has a direct impact on the evolving personality, strong cultural, environmental, and political influences work in concert with genetics. Maslow's need for affection may well be the primary source of leadership, combined with social influences and political forces.

Burns's propositions about the origins of leadership in each person are not fully developed nor empirically tested. What is significant in Burns's thesis is that leaders are not born. Although many factors may play a role in one's inclination for leadership, leadership can be developed. The major abilities and competencies of leadership can be learned, enhanced, and nurtured. Most of the learning takes place in the experiences of leadership, in the successes and failures that the leader has each day.

Contemporary Personal and Organizational Values

It is important to understand the values that people in general and nurses in particular are bringing to their work. New values are also emerging within organizations. These values provide the underpinnings of leadership in contemporary organizations.

Personal Values

Complex, interrelated factors are responsible for the fundamental changes in the values of individuals in today's organizations. These factors include higher levels of educational achievement, more leisure time, increased dependence on each other, rapid rates of change, and greater levels of affluence. Work, although important, is no longer the central feature of one's life. Many people now feel that work should contribute to their self-meaning, as well as to the well-being of the organization and society as a whole. Because of this, people are voicing new social values, including the need to 1) have a higher quality of work life; 2) balance their time between work and play for a well-rounded life style; 3) be treated with dignity as human beings; 4) play a role in organizational decision making by having their opinions, attitudes, and beliefs respected; 5) do work that is satisfying, rewarding, and meaningful; and 6) be empowered to be creative and utilize their skills and talents (Martel 1986, 156-174).

Organizational Values

The values of organizations are also changing. Tannenbaum and Davis (1969, 67-86) argued that we are in the midst of value transitions within organizations. Their work, although over 20 years old, is still pertinent to today's organizations and leaders. Their summary of organizational values (Table 3-1) is used as the framework for this discussion.

Views of Human Nature. The old organizational beliefs about human nature were negative. Organizations thus adopted designs which controlled people's behavior such as hierarchical structures with fixed job descriptions; evaluation systems that focused on the negative aspects of performance or avoided evaluation all together; and rigid methods of rewards and punishments.

Table 3-1 Organizational values and behaviors.

Old	New
Man is lazy, incapable of change and untrustworthy.	Man is good, capable of change, and can be trusted.
Resisting and fearing differences; reward loyalty and uniformity	Acceptance of differences and utilization of them for creativity
Ignoring feelings	Use of feelings
Rational, logical decision making using hard data	Use of intuition as well as rational decision making
Maskmanship and gameplaying	Authentic behaviors
Power for personal use and prestige	Power for organization and empowerment of all
Avoidance of conflict	
Avoidance of risk taking	Use of conflict
Competition	Taking risks
	Collaboration

Source: Tannenbaum, R., and S.A. Davis. 1969. Values, man, and organizations. *Industrial Management Review* 10(2): 67-86.

New organizational values see humans as basically good. Organizations are beginning to be redesigned in concert with this belief. Thus, in some progressive organizations, the evaluations of people are focused on their growth and development as human beings. Rather than being confined to fixed job descriptions, people in these organizations are able to use all their talents and skills.

Organizational Behaviors. Old organizational values are reflected in behaviors which are not authentic and carry a negative connotation (see Table 3-1). In contrast, the new organizational values create positive behaviors. In today's organization, there is a move from behaviors such as game playing and avoiding risks and conflict toward risk taking, managing conflict constructively, and collaboration with others. Further, the use of one's intuition and acknowledging one's feeling are slowly becoming acceptable behaviors.

Contemporary Organizational Designs

Values and organizational designs change slowly. The new values held by people and by organizations and current organizational designs are asynchronous. Some organizations more fully embrace the new values than do others. The old, hierarchical structures of organizations are still prevalent today despite new, emerging organizational values. Organizations are just beginning to restructure their designs, management systems, and philosophies not only in response to the new attitudes about human nature, but also because of the productivity crisis in corporate America. One reason the semi-autonomous work unit (see Chapter 2) is predicted to become prevalent is because it responds to the new societal values.

Nurses, too, are bringing new values to their practice and searching for meaning in their professional lives. These values are evidenced in the many new behaviors seen in the nursing profession: the feminist perspective that is now part of the profession; attempts to develop collegial relationships with physicians; the pursuit to raise the educational level of all nurses; the implementation of participatory management in nursing departments; and renewed focus on the tradition of caring in nursing combined with autonomy.

Managerial leaders are faced with a paradox: people want to stand out, to fulfill their own purpose, to be unique, and worthy (independent); at the same time, people have the need to not be isolated and to belong (interdependent). Transformational nursing leaders must appeal to both of these needs in order to achieve organizational and professional success.

Leadership versus Management

There has been much written and talked about regarding the differences between managers and leaders. Missing from Burns's theory is the integration of leadership and management in organizations in a practical sense. Mintzberg (1973, 1975) has provided a useful definition of managers and a model for the managerial role.

A manager is a person in charge of a formal organization or one of its subunits. The manager has two basic goals: 1) to ensure that the organization produces its goods or services efficiently and 2) to ensure that the organization serves the needs of those persons who control it (Mintzberg 1973, 166).

Figure 3-2 Mintzberg's (1975) ten managerial roles.

Managerial Roles	Descriptions
Interpersonal	
Figurehead	Represents the organization in matters of formality which are ceremonial in nature.
Liaison	Interacts with peers in the organization, other colleagues, and people outside the vertical chain of command to gain favors and gather information
Leader	Motivates and guides staff
Informational	
Monitor	Scans the environment for information, asks for information from subordinates and peers, and receives unsolicited information
Disseminator	Transmits information into the organization
Spokesman	Sends information into the external environment
Decisional	
Entrepreneur	Initiates change to improve the unit and to adapt to a changing environment
Disturbance handler	Takes charge when the organization is threatened and when there is conflict and pressure beyond the manager's control
Resource allocator	Decides where the organization will expend its efforts
Negotiator	Deals with situations in which the manager feels compelled to enter negotiations on behalf of the organization

Mintzberg's work unifies the elements of leadership with the managerial role. He found ten roles to be common to the work of all managers. (Roles are a set of observable behaviors belonging to an identifiable position.) Everything a manager does can be categorized into one of these ten roles, however, each role is not isolated. He studied the content and purposes of managers' work and divided these managerial roles into three groups: interpersonal roles, informational roles, and decisional roles (Figure 3-2).

Interpersonal roles are a part of the formal authority of the manager within the organization and involve interpersonal relationships with others. Because of these interpersonal interactions, the manager is a central person in the communications that occur in the organizational unit and so performs

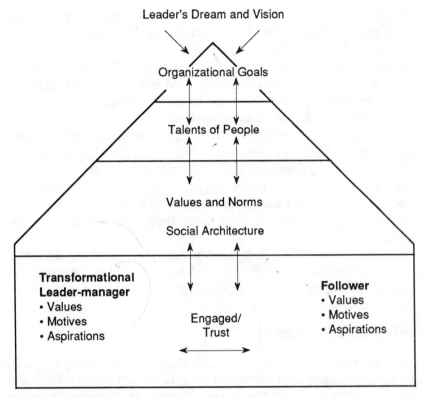

Figure 3-3 A quest for excellence: A model for organizational success.

informational roles. Using the information gathered from these interpersonal and informational roles, the manager plays an important part in making decisions for the organizational unit. This is the *decisional role.*

Model of Organizational Success

Figure 3-3 depicts a model for excellence and success of nursing organizations. Excellence and success can be defined in nursing as the balance of organizational, professional, and personal values. The result of the balance is the provision of quality nursing care to clients (which fulfills organizational and professional goals) and the satisfaction of the staff with their work environment (which fulfills personal needs and aspirations).

At the base of the organizational model, supporting the whole, is the leader-follower relationship. This relationship is characterized by mutual trust and engagement. All members of the organization bring values, purposes, aspirations, needs, and motives to their work. These values reflect those of people in contemporary society. Also, values which are distinctly those of the nursing profession must be incorporated. The leader uses herself to appeal to the values and aspirations of the followers.

The organization as well has a distinct set of values and norms which forms its social architecture. In the successful organization, the talents of the people match the organizational tasks and goals. In other words, the needs of the followers and those of the organization must be in balance and harmony. Therefore, for most nurse leader-managers there is a need to reorganize nursing departments by making changes that will empower the nursing staff.

The essence of leadership is purpose. Practically speaking, the leader must have goals for the organization and for herself. It is the vision and dreams of the leader that provide inspiration and direction to the organization.

Implications for Nursing

In this chapter, a different perspective of leadership theory has been presented. The theory, as applied to nursing, is just a beginning. The nurse leader-manager now should consider how to apply the concepts to practice. But more importantly, she should consider how consistent the theory and her behaviors are.

For example, the leader-manager can consider the definition of transformational leadership and apply it to her practice. Questions to consider during this introspection are:

- How would I describe my relationship with followers?

- Do I trust them?

- What is my view of power? Do I give others the necessary resources to be powerful as well?

- What do I value? What are my goals? What do followers value? What are their goals? Are my values and goals and those of the followers consistent?

- Do I use conflict constructively?

- How does my organizational unit compare to the characteristics of a transformational leadership situation discussed on page 42?

Although many scholars attempt to distinguish between management and leadership, separating the two concepts may not be practical. It has been helpful to the study of both concepts over the past century to study them separately. However, it is not important in the application of theory for organizational success. In every situation a nurse leader or manager doesn't ask, "Is this my leadership role or is this my managerial role?" The basic underlying element of nurse managerial success is the integration of both management and leadership into the role. This person is titled the "leader-manager." The nurse leader-manager is an individual in the nursing organization who holds a formal line position of authority and who engages followers through appealing to their motives, values, and aspirations to achieve the goals of the organization and the nursing profession.

Application to Nursing Practice: Case Study

The Setting

The hospital is a community hospital in an affluent area. The nursing department is decentralized.

Current Situation

Based on the unrelenting complaints of RNs, LPNs, and nursing assistants, a nurse executive has decided that floating staff from unit to unit would be eliminated. She has met with the top nursing management staff and has presented her idea. This group, who is responsible for daily staffing, is pessimistic that this goal can be reached. They are attempting to delay this elimination of the floating staff until there is a full complement of permanent staff. Since there are 40 vacancies and a nursing shortage, reaching a full level of staffing is doubtful in the foreseeable future. The nurse executive believes that until floating is eliminated, the turnover rate of staff will not decrease.

In staff meetings with the nurse executive, some staff express the desire not to float. However, when asked if each staff person will agree to cover their respective units without outside resources, most are reluctant to agree.

The nurse executive is convinced that eliminating floating will improve morale, reduce turnover, attract nurses to work at this hospital, and ultimately improve patient care. She is not sure how to proceed at this point.

Case Study Discussion

1. What is the value conflict in this situation?

2. Would you describe this nurse executive as a transformational leader? Why or why not?

3. What should the nurse executive do?

References

Adams, J., ed. 1986. *Transforming leadership: From vision to results.* Alexandria, VA: Miles River Press.

American Academy of Nursing. 1983. *Magnet hospitals: Attraction and retention of professional nurses.* Kansas City: American Nurses Association.

Bennis, W., and B. Nanus. 1985. *Leaders: The strategies for taking charge.* New York: John Wiley and Sons.

Berlew, D.E. 1986. Leadership and organizational excitement. In *The leader-manager,* ed. J.N. Williamson, 99-104. New York: John Wiley and Sons.

Brockett, C. 1975. Toward a clarification of the need hierarchy theory: Some extensions of Maslow's conceptualization. *Interpersonal Development* 6(2): 77-90.

Burns, J.M. 1978. *Leadership.* New York: Harper and Row.

Fox, W.M. 1982. Why we should abandon Maslow's need hierarchy theory. *The Journal of Humanistic Education and Development* 21(1): 29-32.

Gabarro, J.S. 1978. The development of trust, influence, and expectations. In *Interpersonal behavior: Communications and understanding in relationships,* ed. A.G. Athos and J.S. Gabarro. Englewood Cliffs, NJ: Prentice-Hall.

House, R.J. 1976. A theory of charismatic leadership. In *Leadership: The cutting edge,* ed. J.G. Hunt and L.L. Larson, Carbondale: Southern Illinois University Press.

Kanter, R.M. 1983. *The change masters.* New York: Simon and Schuster.

Martel, L. 1986. *Mastering change.* New York: New American Library.

Maslow, A.H. 1970. *Motivation and personality.* 2d ed. New York: Harper and Row.

Mintzberg, H. 1973. *The nature of managerial work.* New York: Harper and Row.

Mintzberg, H. 1975. The manager's job: Folklore and fact. *Harvard Business Review* 53(4): 49-61.

Naisbitt, J., and P. Aburdene. 1985. *Reinventing the corporation: Transforming your job and your company for the new information society.* New York: Warner Communications.

Paul, M.F. 1982. Power, leadership and trust: Implications for counselors in terms of organizational change. *Personnel and Guidance Journal* 60: 538-541.

Peters, T.J., and N. Austin. 1985. *A passion for excellence: The leadership difference.* New York: Warner Communications.

Peters, T.J., and R.H. Waterman. 1982. *In search of excellence: Lessons from America's best run companies.* New York: Warner Communications.

Roberts, N.C. 1985. Transforming leadership: A process of collective action. *Human Relations* 38: 1023-1046.

Rokeach, M. 1968. *Beliefs, attitudes, and values.* San Francisco: Jossey-Bass.

Tannenbaum, R., and S.A. Davis. 1969. Values, man, and organizations. *Industrial Management Review* 10(2): 67-86.

Tichy, N.M., and M.A. Devanna. 1986. *The transformational leader.* New York: John Wiley and Sons.

Vardaman, B., J. Wimer, and S. Dugat. 1986. Transforming leadership. *Baylor Business Review* 4(1): 5-8.

Wahba, M.A., and L.G. Bridwell. 1976. Maslow reconsidered: A review of research on the need hierarchy theory. *Organizational Behavior and Human Performance* 15: 212-240.

4

Organizational Change

Chapter Objectives

1. Describe three conditions necessary for change.

2. List five characteristics of a transformed future.

3. Discuss four techniques to create a sense of urgent dissatisfaction.

4. List five indications that people are resisting change.

5. Explain why it is difficult to understand the change process.

6. Describe three change tools that the leader-manger can use on a daily basis.

7. Compare and contrast responding to change with solidity versus resilience.

Introduction

Change involves the crystallization of new action possibilities (new policies, new behaviors, new patterns, new methodologies, new products, or new market ideas) based on reconceptualized patterns in the organization. The architecture of change involves the design and construction of new patterns, or the reconceptualization of old ones, to make new, and hopefully more productive, actions possible (Kanter 1983, 279).

This definition implies that change can take on many forms and can occur in a variety of ways. Seldom is change a dramatic, one-time breakthrough. Rather it is a step-by-step accumulation of accomplishments which have been implemented deliberately and slowly. Thus, change is elusive and hard to measure. Seldom can a person pinpoint an exact time when a change began or ended. Change may mean a complete overhaul of the mission, goals, and people of the organization. More often, change may be the act of rethinking and repackaging already existing organizational elements.

Transformational Change in Organizations

The purpose of transformational leadership, as its name denotes, is change—change that appeals to the values and needs of both the leader and followers. In organizations, change is revitalization through the development of and commitment to a realistic, successful future. But commitment to a vision is not enough. For nursing, organizational transformation also includes the redesigning of the organizational structure of nursing departments.

Three conditions are necessary to transform a nursing department: 1) dissatisfaction with the present, 2) a vision of a preferred future, and 3) a social architecture which commits people to the vision.

This chapter and the following three discuss change from the perspective of transforming nursing services slowly over time to create departments characterized by success and excellence.

Planned Change

Most books that discuss organizational change propose models of *planned* change. These proposed models focus on changes *within* the existing structure of the nursing department. They provide valuable guidance to the leader-manager for instituting new programs such as a new medication administration system, or for solving well-defined problems such as a high IV infection rate. However, these planned change techniques do not give complete guidance for transforming organizations.

Transforming Change

In contrast to changes within the existing structure, *transforming* changes are those made to the structure itself. Nursing departments are structurally transformed by leaders who appeal to the values and goals of the people in the organization, manage dissatisfaction, provide vision, and structure the organization for professional nursing practice. Transforming change, like planned change, is well thought out and deliberate.

Recognizing the Need for Change

The traditional approach to change is that the leader recognizes and desires a particular change. She then orchestrates a complex process to bring about the desired outcome. The elements of this process differ among theorists, but generally include 1) assessing the people and the environment, 2) determining change strategies, 3) implementing the strategies, and 4) evaluating the effect for intended results. There is one common concept of change theories: others will resist the change. Thus, in order to be successful, the leader persuades and coaxes others. However, it is generally agreed that change is much too complex and people are much too diverse for any one theoretical prescription to guarantee success. Further, in the confusion and muddle of day-to-day activities, the leader-manager seldom has the opportunity to apply the concepts of planned change models. Change is not accomplished by manipulation of people by applying some arbitrary change formula, but rather by appealing to the values and motivation of people in order to realize excellence for all.

At times, the leader-manager may not see the need for change where it exists. Thus, the first thing that happens before the transformation of a nursing department can occur is for the nurse executive to become dissatisfied with current reality. If a nurse executive is not sensitive to the need for or is not willing to change, she will be less likely to allow others in the nursing department to be innovative and creative. In other words, she will not be able to empower others to enact change.

Ironically, healthcare organizations and the people who run them are not always sensitive to the need for change to occur. This phenomenon happens because organizational thresholds of awareness for change are set too high; often, they do not recognize the need for change until there are disastrous consequences (Tichy and Devanna 1986, 44). For example, in the 1970s, the concern for rising health care costs became a national issue, yet nothing was done by the healthcare industry to curb costs; they kept rising. In 1983, prospective payment became a reality, taking most healthcare institutions by surprise and having devastating effects on many.

Nursing is facing a similar scenario of change coming "too little, too late." The current nursing shortage, which is following closely on the heels of the previous one in the late 1970s, is signaling the need for major changes in the profession. The delivery of nursing services to clients and the role of nursing in healthcare must be reevaluated. Instead, short-term solutions are being implemented primarily in the form of more money to recruit people into a particular facility. More people then become aware of the favorable starting salaries and thus more people enter the profession. This money is important, but it distracts administrators and nursing leaders from tackling other central issues. For example, nothing significant has been done to address the salaries of nurses who have many years of experience. Further, the role and utilization of registered nurses and their dissatisfaction with their practice are not being aggressively addressed. Until these problems and others are solved, such as participation in decision making, empowerment of staff, and an improved image of nurses, the nursing shortage will recur cyclically. Further, financial resources are limited; society cannot continue to pay increasing rates for nursing care without receiving higher quality of care in return. To compound the problem, other professions are stepping in to suggest alternative healthcare providers such as registered care technicians. What has happened, as mentioned previously, is that the threshold of awareness of the need for fundamental change has been set too high. Exactly what is going to trigger the recognition of the need for these changes in nursing is still not evident.

A Model of Organizational Change

The model for understanding the managing transformation in nursing departments is illustrated in Figure 4-1. After the leader recognizes the need for change, she helps followers to also recognize this need by raising their level of dissatisfaction. Dissatisfaction is a result of followers recognizing that the present situation does not meet their needs or conflicts with their values. Next the leader-manager depicts a future that does appeal to the values, needs, and aspirations of the followers. This is called defining a vision. Thirdly, the social architecture is redefined and revised. This is when behaviors are changed to reach intended outcomes.

Managing Dissatisfaction

The experience of most big corporations that have undergone major transformations is that it was the external environment which caused the leader to become dissatisfied, to arouse dissatisfaction in others, and to mobilize commitment to a new vision (Beer 1987, 51). Similarly, external environmental factors are providing the climate for transformational changes

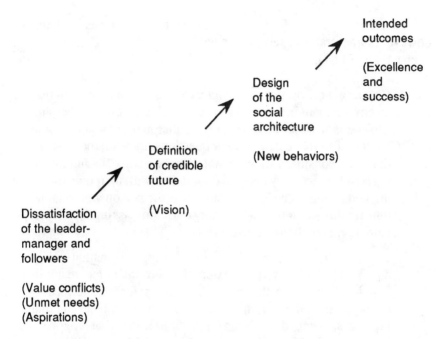

Intended
outcomes

(Excellence
and
success)

Design
of the
social
architecture

(New behaviors)

Definition
of credible
future

(Vision)

Dissatisfaction
of the leader-
manager and
followers

(Value conflicts)
(Unmet needs)
(Aspirations)

Figure 4-1 Barker's model of organizational change.

to occur in nursing departments. These factors include the transformation to an information society, the need to control healthcare costs, and the dissatisfactions of nurses with their practice. Now is the time for nurse leader-managers to respond to the external environment positively and use these factors to transform nursing organizations.

The effort a transformational leader needs to spend in convincing the organization of the need for change is inversely proportional to the urgency for the need to change (Tichy and Devanna 1986, 47). For example, in the early 1980s, many nurse executives found that salary increases and other benefits for nurses were difficult to achieve. This was because the supply and demand for nurses was in balance, i.e., at that time, there was no urgency. However, in 1987, when some hospitals had to close beds because of the unfulfilled demand for nursing services, a sense of urgent dissatisfaction became apparent. Thus, there was a significant increase in the salaries of nurses.

To create a sense of *urgent* dissatisfaction is not easy. There are, however, some practical techniques available to do this (Tichy and Devanna 1986, 53-57).

1. *Creating an Environment Conducive to Interchange.* Creating an environment in which people can challenge one another and explore issues can foster a sense of dissonance. When people feel comfortable enough to ask questions, they are then able to think and consider various sides of issues. People, including the leader-manager, may become dissatisfied with their own thinking and actions. The leader-manager is the person who sets the tone for this environment by asking questions, asking for advice, listening, and allowing discussion.

2. *Broadcasting Pertinent Information.* Sharing information widely about both the internal and external environment can result in people appreciating the challenges facing them. The leader-manager should share specific information such as internal problems, intended strategies for the future, and what is happening in other healthcare facilities that are considered the "competition." Publicizing quantitative data such as budgets and quality assurance audits is important and helpful if used to help increase dissatisfaction and a sense of dissonance.

3. *Discussing Future Goals.* Discussing the future can arouse excitement in an organization, increase the motivation of people, and stimulate the development of team work. For example, some nursing services are considering the implementation of case management. The leader-manager should discuss what case management is and how it can positively affect nursing practice in the future. This can result in people working together toward a desirable future goal.

4. *Interacting With Similar Organizations.* By using external networks and interacting with people outside the organization, key staff can become aware of problems that could also be present in other organizations. Thus, people can become aware that the dissatisfaction they are feeling is not limited to their organization only. The issue takes on a wider significance—"This is not

a unique problem at hospital X, but is a problem faced by all nursing." Additionally, people may become increasingly dissatisfied by seeing what is happening in other settings, i.e., seeing that a particular professional practice can be better or seeing similar problems and concerns in other organizations.

5. *Altering Management Processes.* By intentionally altering management processes, the leader-manager can increase the level of staff dissatisfaction. For instance, the performance appraisal system can be used to create dissatisfaction. If a new expectation is created, people may become dissatisfied with the ability of environmental support to fulfill the expectation. If the evaluation system is changed to evaluate staff on their use of the nursing process rather than on punctuality, the staff may become dissatisfied with some organizational elements hindering their ability to do the nursing process. Thus a sense of dissatisfaction is created and change becomes possible.

Managing Dissatisfaction—The Individual

During this phase of engendering dissatisfaction with the past, the individuals in the organization are undergoing psychological changes. Lewin (1958) calls this stage "unfreezing" and Bridges (1980) calls it "endings." The individual is letting go of past beliefs and behaviors. This process must happen first in order for people to adapt new beliefs and behaviors. At this time, the role of the nurse leader-manger is to make the future appear brighter and better than the "good old days." At the same time, she acknowledges the past, both its successes and failures.

Complexities of the Change Process

As stated previously, prescriptions for planned change are fraught with difficulties and uncertainties. Understanding the change process is complex for a variety of reasons. It is almost impossible to have a clear understanding of change because of three interacting forces which make change elusive: paradoxes, resistance, and distortion.

The Paradoxes of Change

Tichy and Devanna (1986, 27-28) present four paradoxes of change that shed light on the complexities of organizational change.

Paradox 1. There is a conflict between the forces of stability and the forces of change. It is human to want adventure, variety, and change, and at the same time to yearn for safety and security. Organizational leaders have to balance holding on too tightly to the old ways of doing things with moving too quickly, going out of control, and thus failing.

Paradox 2. The tension between denial and acceptance of reality portends failure if the tendency toward denial is stronger.

Paradox 3. A conflict between fear and hope exists in the hearts of people. In nursing, this paradox is evident every day. Generally, the nursing profession views the future optimistically. The changing health care environment provides opportunities for new roles for nurses and nursing, both in the workplace and in the policy-making arena of the nation. However, the fear for the actual survival of the profession is expressed daily.

Paradox 4. The leader-manager has to grapple with being both a manager and a leader. The managerial side of the leader-manager wants to organize and keep the organization from experiencing the turmoil of change whereas the leader yearns for changes and progresses toward goals.

To illustrate these paradoxes in nursing services, consider the head nurse who wishes to move from team nursing to a modified primary nursing system of delivery of nursing services. First, she and the staff will struggle with the desire for the stability of team nursing. In this system, everyone is familiar with their roles and expectations. However, the staff is also aware of the disadvantages of team nursing, and may desire a different patient care approach that improves their satisfaction with their work. The leader-manager in this instance will also need to balance implementing the change too quickly with not moving fast enough.

Also at this time of change, both the leader-manager and the staff may deny the need for change. This is similar to the previously discussed phenomenon of having a threshold for change that is set too high. Yet each day the staff may be confronted with evidence that change is necessary.

The third paradox may also be operating in this example, i.e., there may be fear of letting go of the past and fear that the new system will not work. At the same time, there may be a sense of hope that the new system will improve the quality of work and the satisfaction of staff. Lastly, as the head nurse works with others to implement primary nursing, she may struggle with the tasks of implementing a new system in an organized, controlling manner. Yet she also may find that in being too organized and managerial, she will be stifling the creativity of the staff.

Resistance to Change

Resistance to change is a well recognized phenomenon in organizations. In fact, resistance to change and techniques to overcome it are the subjects of most of the management literature about change. An understanding of resistance to change helps the leader-manager cope with the complexities of the change process. There are many forms of resistance: 1) rejection of the leadership in the organization; 2) low performance levels and productivity; 3) clinging to old ways of doing things; and 4) passivity and avoidance of responsibility.

Resistance is harmful. One of the basic laws of physics is that energy will travel along the path of least resistance. Thus, when faced with organizational resistance, the energies of most people will not be directed toward change to actualize the vision. Resistance to change comes from several sources including people in the organization, the lead-manager herself, and organizational norms and values. Tichy and Ulrich (1984, 61) describe nine causes of resistance.

1. *Habit and Inertia.* At times, resistance occurs because people are comfortable with the routines related to the tasks that are performed. In nursing, an example of this type of resistance is seen when implementing a computer system for medication administration and documentation. Such a system can radically alter the task of medication administration. Staff may raise many barriers to the process of implementing a computerized system, although in reality the system will be a great benefit to the staff.

2. *Fear of the Unknown.* Not knowing the future and not being able to predict organizational behavior can cause anxiety among the staff. This may result in resistance.

3. *Sunk Costs.* Organizations are sometimes unable to implement a change because of costs already spent in doing things in a particular way. Thus, there are no available resources to try new approaches.

4. *Threats to Powerful Coalitions.* Often with the onset of change, power relationships shift as do the status of some people. Or there may be a conflict between the "old" guard and the "new" one. One of the difficulties in implementing an environment that empowers everyone is that power and status become dispersed. Ironically, the people the nurse executive needs to rely on the most, a critical mass of middle managers, have the most to lose.

5. *Limited Resources.* In today's healthcare environment, change almost always involves how to do more with less. It means that there are less resources to distribute and someone or everyone is going to lose. This is not easy to sell to people, and thus they resist the change.

6. *Indictment of Leadership.* When managerial leaders lament problems facing their organizations, they are also recognizing that they are part of the problem. Thus, recognizing the need for change is an indictment of their past behaviors and decisions.

7. *Selective Perceptions.* Organizations have certain values and norms of behavior. Thus, people in the organization may only see issues from this perspective. They see limited possibilities for making changes. This is why outsiders and consultants can more readily see opportunities and need for change.

8. *Security Based on the Past.* The past frequently seems more secure than the future. There are people who resist change hoping for the return of the "good old days."

9. *Limited Climate for Change.* Organizations vary in their conduciveness to change. Some require a great deal of conformity and do not support its members in implementing changes.

Distortions: The Elusiveness of Change

Change, as has been stated previously, is elusive, and so the processes of change are not easy to understand. Kanter (1983, 282-284) provides an interesting approach to the study of the change process in organizations. She suggests that in the attempts to tell about or write about how organizational change transpires, distortions occur. It is through the distortions that one can learn some of the "truths" about change and gain a fuller appreciation of its complexities.

The major distortion is time. When relating the process of change to others, the "changer" will label some event as the beginning of the change process. This may be the time she became consciously aware of a problem, decided to establish a new goal, or began to seek alternate courses of action. However, there is a "prehistory" for change which lays the groundwork for the events to come. Something occurred *before* the changer became aware of the need for change. Because these events are generally unknown to the changer, any conclusions that are made about the change process are suspect and any attempts to replicate a change are impossible. In other words, the recognition of a need for change is not the beginning, but rather some midpoint of the process.

It can be seen then that the history of the organization and the nursing department, which can either assist or block changes, is important. If the leader-manager is aware of the past, she will be able to capitalize on it for the future. This helps to provide security and stability within the department.

The histories of most nursing departments have their strengths and weaknesses. The leader-manager needs to be aware of both. For example, in some nursing departments, the past is characterized by a high degree of respect for the nursing department throughout the organization. Thus, an awareness of the past can support future efforts in ensuring that nursing plays a significant role in decision making in the organization. In contrast, some elements of the past could negatively affect plans for the future. In the same organization, there may be a history of lack of trust permeating the nursing department. The leader-manager would then need to first build trusting relationships with the staff before proceeding with other programs.

Other distortions besides those of time can occur. Kanter (1983, 284-289) explains them below.

1. *One person initiates change, not the group.* Generally, one person may be the "shaker and mover" who initiated the change. However, for change to be truly change, it involves the entire organization. In fact, part of the success of the initiator is getting the team to buy into the innovation and to become part of the process. Thus, the initiator often keeps her role invisible, with the cooperation and the power of the team in the forefront.

2. *Early events and people are just as significant as later ones in producing change.* When relating a change that is occurring or has just happened, the people and events that are currently in the forefront are the ones credited with the change. In reality, many past events and past people have contributed to the state of the organization.

3. *After a consensus is reached, conflict is forgotten.* During the process of transformation, conflict may be intense. However, once a decision is made and a course is charted, those who were on the "winning" side generally forget the conflict, disagreements, and negotiations and avoid holding grudges. They do this in the interest of organizational harmony. Those opposed to the change may, likewise, choose to forget the conflict and may even benefit from the new events.

4. *There were many workable courses of action available.* Once a course of action is chosen, in order to sell it to others, it is presented as the best, most obvious choice. Although equally good and plausible choices existed, they are now forgotten.

5. *Periods of uncertainty, confusion, and experimentation often precede a clear-sighted strategy.* When selling a strategy, the uncertainty that often precedes the consensus is discounted. Once a decision is made, people want to take pride in its rationality, thus its elements of confusion are minimized.

6. *Only significant events are remembered.* A large number of happenings that are important to the change process become reduced into one or two significant events. These events are then thought to be the most important and are the only ones that are used to explain change to others. This occurs, not purposefully, but because people often naturally forget events.

All of these distortions make change a difficult phenomenon to understand. The "stories" about change frequently omit important data about the timing of events. The actions and ideas of one or two people become credited to the entire group. Confusions, conflicts, diversity, and uncertainty fade when one course of action is chosen and implemented. Thus, when the leader-manager is confronted with muddling events, the supposedly clear-sighted prescriptions for change seldom appeal to her or seem useful.

Strategies of Change

Peters (1978, 8) suggested tools for change which he divided into four categories (see Figure 4-2) using speed of effect and control of outcomes as his two variables. These include low control, low speed (cell 1); low control, high speed (cell 2); high control, high speed (cell 3); and high control, low speed (cell 4).

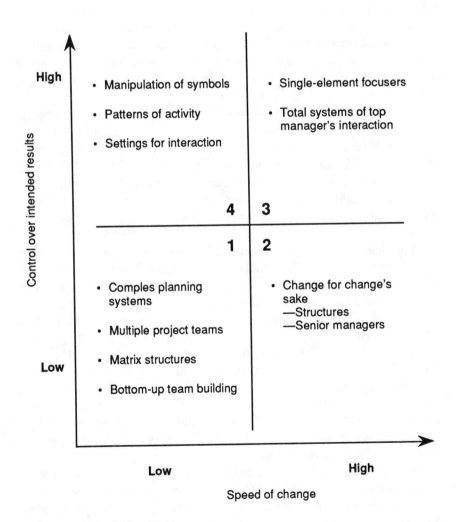

Figure 4-2 Tools for change.

The first category, cell 1, includes complex planning schemes, project management teams, structural considerations such as matrix organizational designs, and bottom-up team building. Although intended originally to be high-control, low-speed change techniques, they have not realized their intended effect despite years of use in a variety of organizations. They are now labeled as low-control, low-speed techniques. These tools have failed for three reasons. First, they take too long to be implemented and to see the effects of their use. There is a significant time lag between when a matrix design, for example, is implemented and when behavioral changes are obvious in the organization. Also, once these tools are used, their use cannot be easily reversed. Thus, they often outlive their usefulness. Thirdly, some tools tend to over-organize and produce a rigidity while others, such as bottom-up team building, are too loosely structured.

A low-control, high-speed tool is used to implement change for change's sake (cell 2). The form may involve a wide range of alternatives such as a "shake-up" of managers or a new structure such as decentralization. The change can occur rapidly, but it seldom has the intended effects. Its use is limited and rarely recommended for situations characterized by confusing, muddling problems. The main outcome of the use of this tool is a sense of novelty which may provide an opportunity to see things in a new, fresh way.

For change that is needed *now*, high-control, high-speed changes are recommended (cell 3). These include using temporary systems to redirect the organization's attention and energies. Examples of these approaches are *single-element focusers* and *systems of interaction*. Single-element focusers are limited, temporary organizational designs such as pilot projects. Pilot projects are successfully used in nursing to implement new care delivery systems such as primary nursing and case management. The entire nursing organization watches the pilot project and focuses attention on it. A second approach is to use new systems of interaction. These systems can range from formal mechanisms such as retreats and forums to informal mechanisms such as social activities. By designing situations in which people interact differently than in the past, organizations can help shift people's attention to new directions.

For high-impact, low-speed change (cell 4), Peters recommended the use of what he called "mundane" tools. These are appropriate tools for slow, deliberate transformation of nursing departments. They are called mundane because as described below, they are simple occurrences that managers are involved in each day. Yet the leader-manager seldom thinks about these as tools of change. It is these occurrences and events that can be managed daily to effect change by sending out and receiving messages that direct the energy in the organization.

Change occurs slowly as a result of the use of many of these tools (cell 4), not just one. Also, in view of the fact that the organizational focus of today is temporary, will change, and may be greatly different in four to five years, these tools are not rigid or over-organized and are sensitive to the vision and purpose of the organization. They are grouped in three categories: manipulation of symbols, patterns of activity, and settings for interaction.

Manipulation of symbols includes calendar behavior, reports, agendas, public statements, physical settings, and staff organization. These tools have the power to reshape beliefs and expectations over time. The way a manager spends her time is the single most important statement about what is important to her. Review of reports, the use of agendas, minutes of meetings, and public statements shape expectations and focus attention. They place importance on or ignore particular themes and issues. Physical settings, such as operating out of one's office versus operating in the work sight, provide further evidence of concerns and focus. The use of personal staff also sends messages about not only the manager's style, but also the direction of her concerns. Such things as the size of this staff, their perquisites, and the scope of their authority and responsibilities send important, unspoken messages.

Patterns of activity include positive reinforcements and the frequency and consistency of the leader-manager's own behavior. Frequent, consistent, positive reinforcement shapes expectations and induces change better than any other technique. People need to know directly from the leader-manager that their behaviors and accomplishments contribute to organizational success. By acting consistently and in concert with her vision, the leader-manager can reinforce this vision every day and in every situation.

The third category of mundane tools is *settings for interaction*. The presence or absence of the manager at particular functions and the manager's minor activities can shape points of view. Where meetings take place, how the agenda is controlled, who attends and participates at meetings, the format for presentations, and what questions are asked can be used to focus attention and signal new directions.

Responding to Change

> Thus, a branch floats peacefully down a river whose waters are high with the spring run-off. Although the branch is floating rapidly and occasionally bumps gently into a rock, it is almost effortlessly motionless in relation to the water it floats in. A similar branch has become wedged between some rocks, and is thus resisting the swift flow of water around it. This branch is buffeted, whipped, and battered by the water and debris floating past it, and will soon be broken by the pressure against it. If branches could experience, the one wedged into the rocks would be experiencing change with intense pain and distress; the floating one would experience ease and, paradoxically, comfortable stability even in the midst of rapid motion (Enright 1986, 60).

The leader-manager has one of two choices when responding to the rapidly occurring changes of today's world. She can be the wedged branch, forcefully and painfully resisting changes which have been thrust upon her, or she can be the floating branch, comfortably adjusting to the turbulence of these times.

Change can be distressing for people because it affects their level of need gratification and deprivation. As has been discussed, people have needs for belonging, self-esteem, and self-actualization. As people have different life experiences, these needs are met through the attachment to specific people, specific jobs, and so forth (Enright 1986, 60-61). For example, a nurse may meet her need for belonging and self-esteem through her work on a particular nursing unit, with a particular group of people, and through mastery of particular tasks.

When something happens that threatens the way a person gratifies her needs, she can react in one of two ways: with *solidity* or with *resilience*. Solidity means holding onto the current situation and those things which satisfy needs. Resilience, however, is the ability to step back and see possibilities (Enright 1986, 61-62). To do this, one keeps in mind the purpose and vision of nursing and the organization. For example, staff nurses in some settings are assuming responsibility for quality assurance on their nursing units. To do this, they had to break from the past when these activities were performed by a centralized committee. Staff did not have to worry about quality assurance except for occasionally responding to negative feedback. When staff nurses were asked to assume quality assurance responsibilities, they had two choices: to respond with resilience or with solidity. By responding with resilience, the staff would concentrate on deeper purposes, in this case, quality patient care. Thus, a sense of achievement can now be obtained not only from care delivery, but also from performing quality assurance activities.

By reacting to events with resilience, a person maintains an attitude of and believes that "things turn out for the best." This is not easy to do when threatened by change and adversity. By remembering past difficult situations that were resolved positively, the leader-manager can see hope in times of uncertain change.

When a person reacts to change with solidity, she relies on procedures and policies of the past, or attempts to plan and control the situation. For example, to respond to a nursing shortage with solidity, a leader-manager might develop a comprehensive, written plan to increase salaries and benefits. A leader-manager who responds with resilience would see the opportunity to redefine the roles of nursing staff in order to provide a long-lasting change that would satisfy people's needs for belonging, esteem, and self-actualization.

Implications for Nursing

Change is elusive, difficult to manage, and rarely fully understood. Knowing this gives the leader-manager better control over change and transformation of the nursing department. It also makes change less threatening and the challenges less frustrating.

What exactly are the changes necessary in nursing? The answer to this question can be found by reflecting on the dissatisfactions facing nurses and the profession (Chapter 1) and understanding societal and healthcare trends. Table 4-1 suggests the necessary organizational changes which nursing departments must undergo. Nursing needs to move from traditional centralized/decentralized organizational hierarchies to semi-autonomous work units. Power should be vested in all. Trust, versatility, innovation, and creativity are desirable characteristics of nursing organizations. Paradoxically, both the individual and the team should be promoted. These ingredients form the conceptual framework of the remaining chapters of the book.

Table 4-1 Necessary transformations for nursing departments.

Past	Transformed Future
1. Decentralized/centralized organizational hierarchies	1. Semi-autonomous work units
2. Power vested in management positions	2. Empowerment of all which brings out the best in each person
3. Distrust	3. Trust
4. Solidity/rigidity	4. Versatility/resilience
5. Equity in pay	5. Pay for performance
6. Quantitative productivity management	6. Development of human resource potential
7. Reliance on rational decision making	7. Intuition and creativity
8. Team	8. Importance of the individual as a member of the team
9. Formal communications	9. Informal communications
10. Depersonalization	10. Respect and caring for the individual
11. Striving for survival	11. Striving for excellence

Application to Nursing Practice: Case Study

The Setting

The medical center is a 400-bed, not-for-profit facility in an urban area. It offers a wide range of services and is a tertiary care center. A new ambulatory care center has recently opened. The nursing service was centralized with head nurses reporting to one of three supervisors. The current nurse executive has been in her position for slightly over two years. When she assumed the position, the management systems, policies, procedures, budget, etc., were well organized. The nursing department enjoyed a good reputation within the hospital community.

However, as with any large nursing organization, a variety of problems existed including 1) a large turnover of staff nurses (38 percent) and 2) a low level of trust which was explicitly talked about by nursing staff, peers, and the chief executive officer (CEO).

The nurse executive determined the following goals for her first year in the position. Her overall objective was to enhance the retention of registered nurses. Her goals were to 1) build trust; 2) decentralize the nursing service; 3) stabilize staffing by eliminating the practice of floating staff from one unit to another; 4) attain a tuition reimbursement benefit for nursing personnel to assist in recruitment and retention of staff; and 5) develop a resource-driven model of nursing care delivery starting with a philosophy statement.

Within the first year, the nurse executive achieved several of her goals. Although still tentative, there was evidence of more trust. Floating had not been totally eliminated, but it had decreased significantly. This was achieved by having each unit responsible for its own coverage and by the establishment of a small float pool. The turnover of staff had decreased from 38 percent to 21 percent. One goal was not realized: negotiations with the CEO for tuition reimbursement proceeded slowly and were eventually not approved.

Current Situation

The nursing department is now experiencing a shortage of registered nurses and an alarming increase in turnover. Bed closures have occurred in three of the four ICUs and on two medical units. Staff are expressing concern over staffing and workload.

Recently, the nurse executive led a retreat of 25 nursing personnel to discuss recruitment and retention issues and to develop a plan for enhancing both. This strategy resulted from the concern of the CEO about the need to close two more ICU beds. He asked the nurse executive, "What can we do about getting more staff and keeping those we have?" The nurse executive proposed that the answer should come from the staff itself because she felt that the final recommendations would be considered more seriously if direct input from the staff was attained. All levels of staff attended the retreat, however, staff nurses had the largest representation.

At this retreat, many recommendations were prepared for the CEO. Priorities were determined and later presented to him by the nurse executive. After salary increases, tuition reimbursement was the second major concern. The nurse executive and nurse recruiter presented a number of options to the CEO for funding the tuition reimbursement package. Their primary concern was that the eventual system be competitive with area hospitals. The program was approved and served to decrease turnover for about six months at a time when other facilities were suffering major losses of staff.

The recommendation and plans derived from the retreat were shared with all nursing personnel through a written summary distributed shortly after the retreat and through discussion at all meetings. Several follow-up reports were written as recommendations were accepted and implemented.

Follow-up meetings with the staff attending the retreat occurred monthly for six months.

Case Study Discussion

1. Did the nurse executive recognize the need for change? What measure did she use?

2. Why was the nurse executive not successful the first time in negotiating for a tuition reimbursement benefit? Why was she later able to achieve this goal?

3. What high-control, high-speed tool of change did the nurse executive employ?

4. What "mundane" tools of change did the nurse executive use?

5. How would you classify the nurse executive's response to the external problem of the nursing shortage? Why?

References

Beer, M. 1987. Revitalizing organizations: Change process and emergent models. *Academy of Management Executives* 1 (1): 51-55.

Bridges, W. 1980. *Transitions: Making sense of life's changes.* Reading, MA: Addison-Wesley.

Enright, J. 1986. Change and resilience. In *The leader-manager*, ed. J.N. Williamson, 59-73. New York: John Wiley and Sons.

Kanter, R.M. 1983. *The change masters.* New York: Simon and Schuster.

Lewin, K. 1958. Group decision and social change. In *Readings in social psychology*, ed. E.E. Maccoby, 197-211. New York: Holt, Rinehart and Winston.

Peters, T.J. 1978. Symbols, patterns, and settings: An optimistic case for getting things done. *Organizational Dynamics* 7 (8): 3-23.

Tichy, N.M., and M.A. Devanna. 1986. *The transformational leader.* New York: John Wiley and Sons.

Tichy, N.M. and D.O. Ulrich. 1984. The leadership challenge: A call for the transformational leader. *Sloan Management Review* 25 (3): 59-68.

5

Organizational Vision

Chapter Objectives

1. Define organizational vision.
2. Discuss the positive impact that a vision has on organizational functioning.
3. Describe the envisioning process.
4. List the elements of a vision statement.
5. Discuss practical ways to engender commitment to a vision statement.

Introduction

Providing a vision for a nursing department is the first strategy of transformational leadership. A vision makes visible the invisible element of collective purpose. In doing this, it can stimulate the nursing organization toward desired goals. Authors have used such terms as "shared values" (Deal and Kennedy 1982, Peters and Waterman 1982); "superordinate goals" (Bradford and Cohen 1984); or "central belief systems" (Britton and Stallings 1986, 21) to describe organizational vision. For this book, the term *vision* is used because it best denotes a futuristic approach to values and beliefs.

Definition and Characteristics of Vision

Vision is an image of a possible and desirable future state for an organization. It is an articulation of a realistic, attainable, credible, and attractive future (Bennis and Nanus 1985, 89). Visions that have proven to be successful in transforming organizations have several common characteristics. They reflect the core purposes of the organization; are feasible, yet challenging; and have a significance that transcends the organization and impacts society as a whole. Further, these visions appeal to the values, emotions, and imagination of the people in the organization. Since the goal of leadership is to have people invest their talents and skills toward organizational success, having vision is vital. In a nursing organization, the vision should have at least two dimensions: the services provided to patients and the management and organization of these services.

Much of the work written about vision has been focused on overall organizational vision versus vision for sections and subsections of the organization. However, the nurse leader-manager, at the executive level and at the nursing unit level, can have an articulated vision for their area of responsibility. This vision cannot conflict with the explicit or implicit organizational mission and vision. Yet it is more than a restatement of organizational purpose. A vision statement for nursing entails distinct, unique statements and goals. These statements are suited to the organization, the profession of nursing, and the individuals working in the department. For instance, the mission of a healthcare facility may or may not be explicitly described. Often, a mission statement may vaguely describe a primary mission of patient care and a secondary one of medical education. The vision of the nursing department in such a medical center, therefore, would include a statement about nursing's contributions to patient care and to medical and nursing education.

To understand why vision is important it is necessary to look at why organizations exist. People join organizations for rewards—both economic and psychosocial. The financial rewards include profits, prestige, power, and status. The changing values of people and of organizations can serve as guidelines to determine exactly what psychosocial rewards people are seeking in their organizations. For example, a successful vision statement would appeal to the need to belong to a group that does challenging, creative, and meaningful work.

People also seek psychosocial rewards through their position in the external environment. When the organization has a widely-shared, clear sense of its purpose, direction, and desired future state, people in the organization are able to define their own roles both in the organization and in society (Bennis and Nanus 1985, 90-91).

If vision is such an important element in effective, successful organizations, why isn't it more widely used? The answer lies in the inherent complexity of organizations. Organizations have a diversity of people who have varying and conflicting purposes and values (Bennis and Nanus 1985, 94). For example, in a hospital, the social workers, nursing staff, physicians, administrators, etc., view the mission and goals of the organization from different yet equally important perspectives. Within a nursing department, a similar disparity may exist between staff and managers, educators and administrators, and clinicians and managers. Developing and maintaining an organizational vision is difficult because of this diversity. Another reason that vision is not more readily seen in today's organizations is that its importance is just being recognized. Thus, the skills of leaders to develop and maintain visions have not yet been developed.

The Functions of Organizational Vision

A simple model elucidates the importance of vision:

Vision $\longrightarrow$ Energized action for change $\longrightarrow$ Success and excellence

In this model, vision is necessary to generate energy in organizations. This energy results in action, and action can lead to organizational success. By having an optimistic, credible vision, the organization functions more smoothly and in a unified direction.

Organizational Alignment

The major function of the vision is to catalyze alignment. When the members of the team are committed to a shared vision, the relationship among the team and even one's self-concept may change. *Organizational alignment* is a situation:

in which the members operate as a whole, knowing that the actions taken will allow each of them to be true to themselves as well as to the organization. They see that the purpose and vision of the organization is worthy of the commitment of their life-spirit. And they, in effect, expand their definition of self, to enjoy a sense of unity with every other person in the organization (Kiefer 1986, 191).

Alignment pulls together a disparate, heterogeneous work force. Yet at the same time, each person can feel that their contributions are important. A nursing unit which is noted for its superb patient care, teamwork, and low staff turnover is most likely composed of an aligned staff.

Empowering people, i.e., giving them the resources and power to be creative and innovative, works best when people in the organization are aligned. When there is no alignment, empowerment may be difficult to manage. Everyone may wish to "do their own thing" without regard to others and organizational goals. This creates organizational disharmony and dysfunctional conflict.

Performance

Studies have shown that organizations with a strong vision and a strong sense of values and beliefs outperform those that do not (Bennis and Nanus 1985; Peters and Waterman 1982). Further, companies with widely shared values are more successful than either those without any stated values or those whose visions were expressed in financial terms only. The explanation of the latter phenomenon is that financial values alone may motivate the top administrative group, but do not filter down and motivate the entire work force (Peters and Waterman 1982, 281).

Vision can provide a stimulus towards excellence by setting goals that exceed current performance levels and by challenging staff to stretch and reach. It can alter the nature of the leader-follower relationship with the impetus for performance being attainment of goals rather than a system of rewards and punishments.

Change and Adaptability

Employees are more likely to adapt to and respond to change with versatility and resilience if there is a commonly held belief system. This may seem contradictory. People with firmly held beliefs are sometimes thought to be rigid and inflexible. But in reality, with a firm vision, employees are more willing to adapt to small, short-term changes that are consistent with their vision and belief system (Britton and Stallings 1986, 22-23). Further, the vision serves to describe what can be and serves as a guide to making changes.

Decision Making

Providing a vision facilitates decision making at lower levels in the organization. People do not have to appeal to higher levels of authority when the vision provides a frame of reference for decision making (Bennis and Nanus 1985, 92). Further, the vision provides a framework for making decisions about the future because of its focus on long-term versus short-term gains.

Commitment and Meaning

By explicitly articulating the organizational purpose, the organization creates an environment where commitment is the norm not the exception. Commitment is a way to empower people in the organization because committed individuals have the emotional resources to be creative and to innovate.

Conflict Resolution

By focusing on a clear vision, the members of the organization can resolve conflicts more easily. The vision provides the framework for conflict resolution rather than by using power plays, game playing, and personal idiosyncrasies.

Envisioning: The Role of the Leader-Manager

Developing a vision for an organization or a department is a dynamic process. It involves the art of discovery and requires a profound knowledge of both oneself and the organization. The vision that is ultimately articulated should be realistic and feasible. This means that the skills and resources of the organization must be considered. In a bureaucratic organization, (which characterizes the majority of healthcare facilities and nursing departments) the act of envisioning is necessarily limited by organizational constraints. Rules, procedures, historical decisions, and contracts among the parties may limit the leader's freedom to act. Thus, the vision that emerges is organizationally feasible, not merely an expression of the leader-manager's dreams (Mintzberg and Waters 1983, 70).

To envision, the leader-manager uses the skills of foresight, world view, hindsight, depth perception, peripheral vision, and revision (Bennis and Nanus 1985, 102). Each of these skills are described below with sample questions a nurse leader-manager might ask herself while developing a vision for her organization.

Foresight

Foresight involves exploring how the vision will fit into the way the organization may develop. In other words, the leader must have a sense of a possible future for the organization and society. In order to do this, the nurse leader-manager needs to be aware of trends in healthcare and nursing. Predicting the future is, of course, not possible. However, the leader-manager's awareness of what is likely to happen is important:

- What are the long-range opportunities and risks for the department?
- What are the issues and trends in healthcare?
- What are the likely outcomes of prospective reimbursement for the organization?
- What are the characteristics, both qualitative and quantitative, of nurses in the community?
- What will be the role of nurses in the future?

World View

Similarly, a world view involves awareness of the impact of new trends, not only in healthcare, but also in society as a whole. This perspective will enhance the leader-manager's envisioning:

- What societal trends will impact healthcare and nursing?
- How will the information age impact healthcare in general and nursing in particular?
- What values will people be bringing to their work?

Hindsight

Likewise, to envision, the leader uses hindsight: an appreciation of the traditions and cultures of the organization and its mission in the community. To develop an appreciation for the organizational history, the leader-manager might ask:

- What is the current mission of the organization?
- Has it changed recently or does it have a long historical presence in the community?
- What is the history of the nursing department? Is it stable or in constant states of change?
- What are the past and current strengths of the staff?

Depth Perception

Depth perception means that the leader must survey the entire picture—both the internal and external environment. This should be done in appropriate detail and perspective:

- What does the nursing department contribute to the organization, the profession, patients, and society?
- What are my own interests, skills, and dreams?
- What are the internal resources of the department?
- What is the match between the internal strengths and external needs?

Peripheral Vision

Peripheral vision refers to the leader's awareness of competitors and stakeholders and their futures. The leader-manager might ask:

- What is happening to other professions such as social work and psychology which may affect nursing or place the disciplines in competition?
- How will the predicted physician glut affect nursing practice and the role of nurses?

- What is happening in nursing at other institutions and what are the community standards of practice?

- What are patients demanding of healthcare and nurses?

Revision

Further, the leader reviews and reassesses the vision as the environment changes. This is necessary because one risk of a shared value system is that the external environment can change and then the vision becomes no longer helpful to organizational success (Deal and Kennedy 1982, 34). Periodically, the leader-manager should assess the vision by asking, Where were we?, Where are we now?, How well have we done?, Where do we go and by when?

Developing a Vision Statement

Philosophy Statements

Unlike in many other departments in healthcare institutions and other organizations, written philosophies of nursing have existed for decades. However, with rare exception, the development and review of the philosophies have been a paperwork exercise to meet accreditation standards rather than an exercise of developing a common belief system within the department. The recommended and fairly common elements of a nursing philosophy include beliefs about man, the environment, health, and nursing.

Mission Statements

Healthcare organizations generally have mission statements. A mission statement describes in broad terms the reason for the organization's existence. It also describes the patient or client population, lists the services provided, and is oriented to the present rather than to the future. A hospital mission statement might be as short and concise as the following:

The mission of General Medical Center is to care for patients in Greater County. It is a private, not-for-profit organization. The medical center offers a wide range of primary, secondary, and tertiary services. The Medical Center has a tertiary emergency room and is the only trauma facility in the county. Additionally, a full range of medical and surgical services are offered. Pediatric and obstetric services are also available. The medical center is a referral center for both pediatric and neonatal intensive care.

A nursing department might have a mission statement as well. It would reiterate the general mission statement of the overall organization and expound on the available nursing services.

Vision Statements

A similar but different approach for organizations is to write a *vision statement*. The vision statement is more futuristic than either the philosophy or mission statements. It describes a desirable future and a statement about where energies should be focused. This statement provides a written, concrete guide for the people in the organization to quest for the future. However, the terms used in a vision statement are subjective, rather than precise, objective statements.

Generally, the vision statement includes information about patients or clients, nursing staff, management systems, and the relationship of the department to the organization, community, and society. Britton and Stallings (1986, 29-32) recommended that the vision statement include, at a minimum, the following elements:

- Statements of excellence and success. These statements may include financial objectives, such as cost-effective care or even a profit goal, but most importantly, the statement needs to consider the quality of patient care.

- A transcending purpose which focuses on the long term not the short term

- Statements that tap the talents and enthusiasm of all levels of employees

- Statements that reflect the organization's attitude toward humanness and fairness

- Statements that show that creativity and innovation are valued

- Wording to reflect the organization's acceptance of informality

- Organization and details.

The case study at the end of this chapter includes sample statements from a vision statement.

Often with a longer document there is a short logo or slogan that captures the essence of the message. The most popular examples of these slogans are found outside nursing and healthcare, such as Du Pont's "better living through chemistry" or Delta's "family feeling." For many companies, their use of slogans may be meaningless. However, in excellent companies, the leader believes deeply in the vision for the organization and reinforces it through management actions and systems.

Communication of and Commitment to the Vision

Once the vision is developed, the work of the leader-manager shifts to communicating and building a commitment to the vision. The written vision statement should be published and widely distributed. In meetings with staff, the leader-manager can discuss the statement. She should openly and honestly explore feelings and reactions to it. This process is educative since the articulation of a vision for a department is most likely new to everyone involved.

The discussions can include other aspects of the vision. First, they can be focused on the values inherent in the vision statement. For example, people can explore their definition of quality patient care or their use of the nursing process. Second, the human needs and aspirations of people can be examined. Concepts such as self-esteem, belongingness, a sense of importance, and meaningful work are generally not recognized and openly discussed. These meetings with staff provide the transformational leader-manager the opportunity to explicitly discuss these values and to increase the staff's consciousness of them.

The words used to communicate and sell the vision are also important. Bennis and Nanus (1985, 107) found that leaders used metaphors to clarify the vision and to keep people focused. For many nursing leader-managers, this is a new skill. Learning to communicate the vision metaphorically and with enthusiasm will take time and conscious effort.

Explaining how the vision statement differs from past management techniques and directives is important for building staff commitment. Specifically, the staff needs to learn that a vision statement focuses on the future. It is a hope rather than a truth. The leader-manager may want to compare the vision statement to a past practice with which staff is familiar.

For example, unlike in a system such as management by objectives, the vision statement promotes values and humanness, not tasks and processes. The staff should understand that a vision statement involves the entire organization, not just the managers. It has implications for everyone (Richards and Engel 1986, 202).

Communicating openly about her own feelings and beliefs about the vision is another important strategy leader-managers can use to gain commitment to the vision. This, also, may be a new behavior for some leader-managers. Many nurse managers have been taught to be logical and to keep feelings away from the work environment. However, it is important for the followers to have a true sense of the leader's feelings. One way to do this is to admit that the visionary process is new. She can acknowledge that it may not be a comfortable process for her, or that she will make mistakes. Further, she can ask the staff to challenge and question her so that she too can learn.

After these initial meetings, the leader-manager continues to communicate the vision persistently, consistently, and enthusiastically. Gaining the commitment of the nursing staff for a vision is a long, sometimes tedious, process. The leader-manager requires patience and persistence to sustain the necessary momentum. Face-to-face interactions between the leader-manager and staff are also desirable. People need to be able to test the sincerity and commitment of the leader-manager, and only personal discussions afford this opportunity. However, personal interactions are not always possible because of the large size of nursing departments. Thus, the nurse executive relies also on those who report directly to her. They, too, serve to help spread the message, both in words and in deeds. Thus, leader-managers need to gain a commitment for the vision first from middle managers.

However, it is the first-line supervisors and staff who translate the vision into action. Thus, they are the most important group from whom to secure commitment. Using other media, (e.g., videotapes and newsletters) to tell success stories is another way to build commitment for the vision.

Gaining commitment for a vision has many difficulties. One is that the vision statement is a "leading-edge" document. It does not describe what is, but rather what can be. Although it makes visible what was previously invisible, by its nature it is ambiguous. However, the leader-manager, by accepting and acknowledging this ambiguity, can help followers to accept and tolerate it as well.

The leader-manager should accept criticism of the vision statement. One hundred percent commitment of a large, diverse nursing staff is not realistic. It is very easy for a leader, who has developed a vision statement and who is personally committed to it, to overlook and ignore the reactions and feelings of others. But to build true commitment, the leader-manager listens to, reacts to, and openly explores criticisms and negative feelings about the vision. Further, the leader-manager, recognizing that people will resist change, handles the resistance so the vision is not abandoned as too difficult or impossible.

Implications for Nursing

By developing, adopting, and maintaining a visionary approach to leadership, the role of the nurse leader-manager significantly changes. Where once all energy and time were devoted to crisis management and daily problem solving, new approaches are adopted.

The actions of the leader-manager are vital to successfully develop and gain commitment to a vision. Some practical techniques to ensure consistency of action and vision are:

- When making decisions, each alternative should be reviewed to see how the solution is related to the vision.

- In times of crisis, the action taken by the leader-manager must be consistent with the vision. For instance, if the vision is autonomous staffing of nursing units, reverting to a system of floating, except perhaps in the case of a disaster, should be avoided at all costs.

- People in the organization should have an understanding of how specific tasks connect to and move toward the vision. Each morning the leader-manager could spend a short time reviewing how the planned events of the day relate to the vision.

- Produce "a miracle" or a sign. For example, the successful negotiation for a special benefit for staff can demonstrate a commitment to them.

- Task forces should be formed to study various items of the vision statement, such as a task force on creativity.

- Demonstration projects can be developed that are aligned with the vision.

- Successes should be shared during formal and informal meetings.

- How one's own actions and the vision are consistent should be explained. Sometimes what seems consistent to the leader-manager may not appear that way to the followers. By setting up an environment in which people can challenge perceived inconsistencies, they will emerge and can then be clarified.

Application to Nursing Practice: Case Study

The Setting

The current vice president of nursing has been in her position just over two years. Since her arrival, she has decentralized the nursing service, attained competitive salary and benefit packages for nurses, and implemented a comprehensive program for the development of head nurses. She is, however, concerned about the retention of qualified staff. She feels that this is her top priority, yet is frustrated that the head nurses do not express a similar concern. She believes that although there are things she can do as vice president of nursing to support staff, the major responsibility for retention rests with head nurses.

In the past, the vice president has conducted an annual goal-setting meeting for all nurse managers. The philosophy of nursing has not been revised for several years.

Current Situation

The vice president has decided to deal with the retention of staff in two ways. She is having two one-day retreats for the head nurses to identify issues and to develop individual retention plans for each nursing unit. Prior to these retreats, she decided to write and issue a vision statement for the nursing department. Figure 5-1 contains excerpts from the vision statement.

Figure 5-1 Sample vision statement (excerpts).

1. The mission of the nursing service is to provide care that assists patients in maintaining or regaining health, learning to live with disabilities, or dying with dignity and comfort. Nursing Service accomplishes this mission through human- istic and outcome-oriented programs that ensure effective patient care and provide nursing personnel with opportunities for professional satisfaction and growth.

2. Nursing service provides a practice environment that fosters excellence in practice by encouraging and supporting each employee's efforts to contribute to patient care to the maximum capacity possible and by stabilizing the nursing staff complement on each unit.

3. In an era of resource constraints, the nurse is challenged to establish priorities in the delivery of nursing care to ensure that the optimum quality and quantity of services are provided given existing resources. Thus, the nurse continuously assesses the fit of nursing care requirements and available resources, deter- mines priorities, selects and implements those nursing care activities that make best use of available resources, and evaluates outcomes in terms of established standards of care.

4. Eight key concerns—standards, quality assurance, patient advocacy, manage- ment systems, recruitment and retention, research, education, and image— form the basis for the identification, prioritization, and evaluation of Nursing Service goals and objectives and the activities designed to achieve them.

5. Registered nurses are identified as professionals who have selected nursing as a lifework and are committed to the profession and their own growth within it.

6. Nursing service recruits the highest caliber of professional and non-professional nursing personnel available; places those personnel in positions appropriate to their knowledge, expertise, and qualifications; and fosters individual growth and development in the employment setting.

7. Always cognizant of the ultimate goal of providing comprehensive nursing care for every patient, the nurse recognizes that flexibility and creativity are essential in selecting appropriate and achievable goals based on the patient's abilities and preferences and available time, materials, and personnel.

8. As key healthcare providers in a setting that is on the leading edge of technological advancement, nurses anticipate the need for and create the innovative care approaches necessary to respond effectively to constantly changing needs of patients.

9. As the leaders of nursing care delivery, registered nurses set the tone and standards for patient care.

10. Management systems within Nursing Service facilitate the work of patient care and create and maintain a climate which promotes job satisfaction.

11. The decentralized structure adopted for Nursing Service involves all levels of nursing personnel in not only clinical but also managerial decision making.

Case Study Discussion

In view of the vision statement given in Figure 5-1:

1. How will the nursing service ensure excellence and success?
2. How will nurses deliver patient care?
3. What is the definition of nursing and purpose of this nursing department?
4. How does the department ensure humanness and fairness?
5. What is the management system of this department?
6. How does the nursing service involve employees?
7. Is the system relatively informal?
8. What does the vision statement state about creativity and innovation?

References

Bennis, W., and B. Nanus. 1985. *Leadership: The strategies for taking charge.* New York: John Wiley and Sons.

Bradford, D. L., and A. R. Cohen. 1984. *Managing for excellence: The guide to developing high performance in contemporary organizations.* New York: John Wiley and Sons.

Britton, P. R., and J. W. Stallings. 1986. *Leadership is empowering people.* Lanham, MD: University Press of America.

Deal, T. E., and A. A. Kennedy. 1982. *Corporate cultures: The rites and rituals of corporate life.* Reading, MA: Addison-Wesley.

Kiefer, C. 1986. Leadership in metanoic organizations. In *Transforming leadership: From vision to results,* ed. J. D. Adams, 185-198. Alexandria, VA: Miles River Press.

Mintzberg, H., and J. A. Waters. 1983. The mind of the strategist. In *The executive mind,* ed. S. Srivastva and Associates, 58-83. San Francisco: Jossey-Bass.

Peters, T. J., and R. H. Waterman. 1982. *In search of excellence: Lessons from America's best-run companies.* New York: Harper and Row.

Richard, D., and S. Engel. 1986. After vision: Suggestions to corporate visionaries and vision champions. In *Transforming work: A collection of organizational transformation readings,* ed. J. D. Adams, 199-214. Alexandria, VA: Miles River Press.

6

Social Architecture

Chapter Objectives

1. Define social architecture.

2. Discuss the purpose of social architecture.

3. List the three types of social networks found in nursing organizations.

4. Explain how norms affect organizational behaviors.

5. Discuss three types of social architecture.

6. Describe a situation when participatory management should be used and one in which it should not be used.

7. List the advantages and disadvantages of managerial boards.

Introduction

Social architecture is an intangible, but it governs the way people act, the values and norms that are subtly transmitted to groups and individuals, and the construct of binding and bonding within a company (Bennis and Nanus 1985, 110-111).

Providing a vision for the nursing department is not enough. As an even more challenging task, the leader-manager next provides structure and processes so that the vision can be sustained. A leader-manager who only has a vision and does not support it with structure is merely wishing for change. Hoping dreams will come true without working toward a goal is unrealistic. Similarly, structure without vision is useless.

A popular synonym for social architecture is *organizational culture*. This is a term widely used in management literature. Deal and Kennedy

(1982, 4) are perhaps the most cited authors in the management literature on this topic. They have adopted the definition of culture from *Webster's New Collegiate Dictionary*:

> The integrated pattern of human behavior that includes thought, speech, action, and artifacts and depends on man's capacity for learning and transmitting knowledge to succeeding generations.

Deal and Kennedy then defined organizational culture as the way things are done in an organization.

The term *social architecture* is being used in this book because it is a term less vague than *culture*. It includes the structural elements of human resource management and implies having the ability to change the organizational environment. Further, the term is a good metaphor. As the social "architect" of the nursing department, the nurse leader-manager is not building a new structure from raw materials and an ideal design. She is, instead, undertaking a major renovation. New additions can be made and some "rooms" can be deleted. Some "walls" can be rearranged, but not the weight-bearing ones. The "electrical wiring" and "plumbing" can be updated. However, the basic foundation and the frame remain. In other words, the "blueprint" for remodeling a nursing department's social architecture is constrained by the past. The tools used by the leader-manager are an understanding of and an ability to redesign social networks, norms, and organizational structures.

The Function of Social Architecture

The purpose of building the social architecture is to generate commitment to the established vision and organizational identity. Social architecture also provides meaning to its members and presents a shared interpretation of organizational events so that people know how they are to act. Further, the social architecture provides a system for informal control. The traditional theories and prescription of management and leadership are largely focused on the methods of control. These methods include the budget; management information systems; the formalized, technical aspects of the reward and punishment systems; a system for performance appraisal; methods for division of labor; and job descriptions. However, none of these systems alone are capable of controlling organizational functioning. In fact, their overuse leads to rigidity and stifles creativity and innovation. In contrast, building and maintaining a social architecture provides "informal control" which ensures accomplishment of organizational goals.

Social Networks

Tichy and Devanna (1986, 186-202) describe social relations in organizations as *networks*. Organizations are a cluster of people joined by a variety of links. Social roles define who people are (manager, secretary, nurse), as well as who they are in relation to others in the organization (superior, subordinate, peer). People in the organization exist in networks. For example, there are networks of bosses, peers, subordinates, and friends. All these people expect certain behaviors of each other, depending on the assumed role. These expectations may, of course, conflict with one another, and these conflicts constantly face nurse leader-managers. The head nurse balances the demands of patients, staff, and her superiors. The nurse executive often must manage a similar disharmony of expectations. For example, her boss may frequently look for ways to contain costs while the nursing staff asks for increased benefits.

Further, each person in one's social network is a participant in another social network, thus connecting the networks with one another. Communications, influence, and affection flow among these networks. In her role as the social architect of the nursing department, the leader-manager develops an understanding of these networks in her organization. She manages them, and, if necessary reweaves the system of social relations and the flow of communications to realize meaningful change.

Formal and Informal Networks

Networks can be categorized into two groups. *Formal* or *prescribed* networks are those clusters of people who relate to one another as defined by the organizational design. They are easily identified by the organizational chart, policies and procedures, committee structures, and work groups. *Informal* or *emergent* networks are ones that have no organizational sanctions. They simply emerge out of the everyday activities of the organization. They have often been called the "informal organization" and have had a negative connotation, at least for managers. In fact, they are neutral. They take on desirable or undesirable characteristics depending on how they are managed.

Both prescribed and emergent social networks can have three purposes: *information, influence,* and *friendship. Information* networks determine the flow of information regarding the organization and its environment. They determine who exchanges information with whom. *Influence* networks describe who influences whom about what, using both formal orders and informal persuasion. *Affect* networks determine feelings of friendship among people. It is largely through the friendship networks that values and norms are disseminated and reinforced.

"Management By Wandering Around"

By having an understanding of the networks in the organization, the nurse leader-manager can then influence them. Obviously, it is easier to rearrange the formal networks than the informal ones. However, "management by wandering around" (MBWA), a term coined by Peters and Waterman (1982, 122), is an essential tool for assessing and managing the social networks. Talking to the right person in the hallway, providing on-the-spot positive reinforcement, and giving information are behaviors that can impact a variety of networks. This is true for both formal and informal networks.

The purpose of MBWA is to find out what is going on in the organization. It allows the leader-manager to observe what is causing problems for people—both staff and patients. Further, it is an opportunity to guide and direct others by posing questions that convey the leader-manager's values and vision. The first technique of MBWA is to listen to others and get first-hand information. Since the sharing of values can only happen in face-to-face interactions, the second technique is to use the interaction as a time to teach and share values, and to build the self-esteem of others. Thirdly, MBWA provides the opportunity for the leader-manager to facilitate work. Frequently, a problem that is currently hampering the productivity of the day can be brought to the attention of the leader-manager. She may be able to quickly resolve it. One shortcoming of giving on-the-scene advice and guidance is the tendency for employees to act on what the leader-manager says because she is "the boss." This may result in lowered employee self-esteem. The leader-manager can help reduce this tendency by talking last, asking people what they think, and asking people for detailed information in order to examine their reasoning (Peters and Austin 1985, 447-465).

Because nursing departments are not geographically contained, MBWA is an essential technique for the nurse executive and other nurse managers. Historically, when the nurse executive was the superintendent of nursing, she made frequent, probing rounds of the nursing units. She supervised and criticized patient care. Remnants of this approach remain today. Thus, there are some bad feelings by staff attached with the issue of supervisory rounds in nursing departments. Some nurse executives have dealt with this by avoiding rounds all together.

Visiting nursing units to see what is happening and to be accessible to staff is important. It conveys a message of caring and support. Unless presented with a dramatic problem, the nurse executive should withhold criticism. If she finds a problem, she can deal with it later and on more general terms. The nurse executive who makes rounds and closes all the medication doors as she proceeds through the hospital is not nearly as successful as the one who ignores the open doors. She can later analyze why doors are left open and what obstacles in the environment led to this problem. Thus, her rounds result in a facilitating change for staff, not a punitive approach with engenders guilt and lowers self-esteem.

Norms

Norms are habits of the organization. Like social networks and organizational structure, they have a strong influence on the behaviors of everyone in the organization. Norms are intangible. Without an attentive, objective analysis of norms, most people are not aware of them. The best way to understand norms is by example.

In some organizations, it may be acceptable behavior to "point fingers" and blame others. Doing this may result in the person successfully relinquishing responsibility for a task. In nursing, this can be seen at all levels. Because nursing has traditionally accepted responsibility for the coordination of patient care, nursing departments rely heavily on other departments. Many problems with these other departments may exist and many are left unsolved. Nursing managers can then blame other departments and not accept responsibility for solutions. A common example is the emptying of trash on the nursing units. Although the janitorial services are responsible for this task, many nursing employees complain about assuming the task of emptying of trash cans, particularly on the evening and night shifts. In some nursing departments, it is an acceptable norm to blame the other department, continue to empty the trash cans, and continue to complain. In other nursing departments, it is not acceptable to blame others, and the nursing department takes the lead in resolving the problem.

Norms may at times conflict with the organizational/departmental vision. The vision of the nursing department may be that quality care is expected of everyone. It is everyone's responsibility, not only to provide quality care to patients, but also to participate in the quality assurance program. However, the norm might be that quality assurance is really the problem of the quality assurance nurse and the designated staff nurse on each unit.

Organizational Structure

The use of the term *structure* here will mean:

the underlying interacting variables in a system that organize it in a particular and unique manner. This underlying structure consists of the prescribed organization (its stated goals, policies, procedures, and formal hierarchies), and the collective human attitudes (expectations, motivations, talents and interpersonal relationships). It is the interaction between the prescribed and the human elements of structure that tend to drive organizations toward or from their desired destination (Shandler 1986, 124).

Structure affects how people in the organization behave and in so doing can either accelerate or inhibit movement toward organizational goals. Human behaviors (in nursing) are affected by a number of organizational variables including recruitment practices, staff development procedures, the appraisal and control system, the nursing care delivery system, and the financial system. These variables may have either positive or negative influence on behavior.

Types of Social Architecture

Three types of social architecture classify 95 percent of all organizations (Table 6-1) (Bennis and Nanus 1985, 118-138). *Formalistic* organizations, the major organizational model of the industrialized world, combine decentralized operations with centralized policy and financial control. Decisions are made by people in positions of authority. Control is exerted

Table 6-1 Three styles of social architecture.

Values and Behaviors	Formalistic	Collegial	Personalistic
Basis for decision	Direction from authority	Discussion, agreement	Directions from within
Source of power	Superior	What "we" think and feel	What I think and feel
Forms of control	Rules, laws, rewards, punishments	Interpersonal, group commitments	Actions aligned with self-concept
Desired end	Compliance	Consensus	Self-actualization
To be avoided	Deviation from authoritative direction; taking risks	Failure to reach consensus	Not being true to oneself
Position relative to others	Hierarchical	Peer	Individual
Human relationships	Structured	Group-oriented	Individually oriented
Basis for growth	Following the established order	Peer group membership	Acting on awareness of self

by written rules, regulations, laws, and a formalized system of rewards and punishment. Power is vested in superior positions in the hierarchy. Employees are expected to comply with authoritative decisions. Promotion and growth are based on following the established order, "fitting in," and being loyal.

In *collegial* organizations, group discussion and agreement form the method of decision making. Controls occur through interpersonal relationships and commitment to groups. Power, influence, and status exist through peer recognition, not hierarchical position. Information exchange is verbal and face-to-face. In decision making, the group values consensus and avoids failure to reach consensus. Personal growth occurs through peer group membership.

Personalistic social architectures are found primarily in "young," high-growth organizations. They place emphasis on the individual. In personalistic organizations, decisions arise from within the individual. Control occurs from within the person; power is derived from the person. The desired end is self-actualization with growth occurring through acting on self-awareness.

Nursing organizations are most often characterized by the formalistic type of social architecture. Further, they most often exist within a healthcare facility with the same style. Thus, designing a new social architecture for an entire nursing department would be constrained by the willingness of the entire organization to change, not just the department. What follows is a proposed design for nursing organizations. It combines elements of both collegial and personalistic social architecture with a new concept: the semi-autonomous work group.

The Semi-Autonomous Nursing Unit

Lashbrook (1986, 127) succinctly described what he calls a "positive work culture" which serves as a worthy goal when considering the redesign of the social architecture of a nursing department:

A positive work culture is characterized by members of a work unit perceiving themselves to be satisfied with themselves, their jobs, their co-workers, and the way they are managed, and by using as evidence for their levels of satisfaction the norms of the work unit with respect to communication about mission, goals, feedback, rewards, and support.

Also in a positive work culture, the leader-manager wants to build a climate of success and excellence. In redesigning a nursing department's social architecture, the leader-manager considers not only what is good for the department, but also what is good for the overall organization. Permeating the entire design is a firm belief in the value of the nursing care rendered. This is true within the institution and is perceived by patients.

The elements of the following design may seem like a "brave new world" to some. The design is presented as a vision—one that is realistic and credible *over time*. It is hampered by many organizational and political constraints. On paper these constraints may seem simple and straightforward. However, in the real struggles to achieve this vision, they are not.

In the proposed design, each nursing unit in a nursing department is a *semi-autonomous work unit* with its own unique vision and goals. They are consistent with and contribute to the vision and goals of the overall organization. Each nursing unit is given as much freedom as possible to make decisions for itself in a democratic fashion. Staff nurses and other nursing personnel discuss and reach consensus on decisions affecting their practice and the services provided to patients. The decentralized design currently in place in many nursing organizations do not embrace this form of decision making. Generally, the head nurse retains the majority of the delegated decisions in most decentralized designs. Shared governance models have begun to embrace democratic decision making. Yet, for the most part these models are implemented on a department-wide basis rather than being unit-based.

The members of the work group can be solely nursing personnel. However, in some settings with good intradepartmental relationships and support from the chief executive officer, the work group could consist of others including physicians, social workers, secretaries, housekeepers, and dietary staff. Certainly, this second design is probably not as realistic as the first, but may be possible in the right institution.

Decentralization Versus Semi-Autonomous Work Units. Nursing is in a favorable position to develop a design of semi-autonomous work groups in that it is already organized into discrete units which provide care for a select group of clients. The idea of the semi-autonomous work group is, in fact, an extension of the present movement toward decentralized nursing organizations. However, in the decentralized design, nursing units are at the bottom of a hierarchical organizational chart (Figure 6-1). As semi-autonomous units, nursing units are better illustrated surrounding a core of

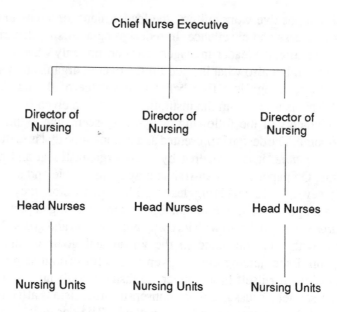

Figure 6-1 Traditional hierarchical organizational chart of a nursing department.

centralized leadership and staff functions. They absorb from this core the requisite support and resources. The units and the central core have mutual influence on one another (Figure 6-2). The work units—some being geographically remote from the organization (such as overnight surgical units, satellite ambulatory care centers, and patients' homes) and some being near the central core—would interact with one another and the central core via electronic connections. Each nursing unit should be integrated with others that serve a common patient population.

The New Role of Managers. Implementation of this design will lead to a reassessment of the number of and roles of middle managers. Computers and communication links that bind together the semi-autonomous work units and the central core will be cheaper than layers of middle managers in today's hierarchical organizations. Electronic technology will soon be replacing much of the communication, processing, and receiving functions of middle managers. What will be required instead are strong leader-managers for each work unit. In many settings, these leader-managers will

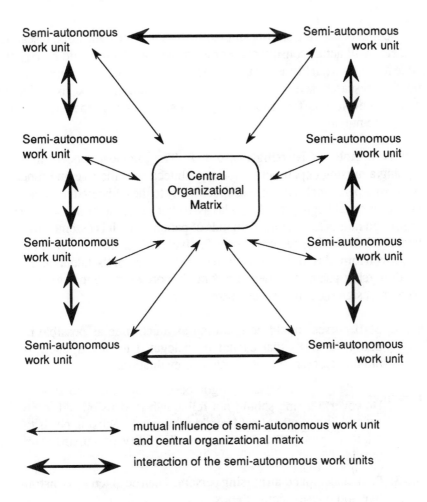

Figure 6-2 Organizational design of semi-autonomous work.

Figure 6-2 Organizational design of semi-autonomous work.

report directly to the nurse executive and will form a decision-making body for issues that affect the entire nursing department. With this change will come a redefinition of power in the organization. There will be an emphasis on empowerment of all, rather than power in he hands of the few managerial elite. This change entails a belief that power is not a limited resource, but rather grows when more people share it.

People occupying staff positions, such as nursing educators, researchers, etc., will act as consultants. For example, each unit would be responsible for its own quality assurance, infection control, staff development, and nursing research activities. However, these staff may be available to consult, develop staff, and to pull together statistics and broad policies for the entire nursing department.

The New Roles of Nursing Personnel. The foremost concern in redesigning a nursing department's social architecture is the role and function of nursing personnel. This relates specifically to the registered nurse as well as to other healthcare providers who assist her. Because of the shortage of registered nurses to meet the demands of patient care, it is essential that the talents of all nursing personnel be effectively utilized. Although there are no proven formulas for ensuring the best possible use of the talents and skills of all nursing personnel, there are some important guidelines to consider when redesigning a nursing department:

1. Staff nurses should be spending as much time as possible in doing the tasks that cannot be delegated to others, such as nursing assessment, planning, and evaluation.

2. The daily routine tasks might best be delegated to others. However, nursing should not relinquish responsibility for the supervision of other healthcare professionals. Nursing needs to retain responsibility for the overall quality of nursing care provided.

3. Personnel other than nursing personnel can be given administrative and housekeeping duties.

One of the major challenges in moving toward semi-autonomous nursing units will be to develop nursing staff. Decisions cannot simply be delegated. Supporting and developing the decision-making skills of all staff will facilitate thoughtful and wise deliberations and decisions at the unit level. Much emphasis has been placed on developing head nurses in decentralized systems, yet in many instances this has failed. However, even less emphasis has been given to the development of the entire staff to support their decision-making skills. The nurse executive needs to look closely at her commitment to the growth and development of head nurses and to the entire staff. This means that formal instruction in topics such as decision making, change, creativity, and innovation will be needed.

How Work Groups are Paid. Ideally, a semi-autonomous group receives pay and rewards based on the income generated by the work group. In some situations outside of nursing, such as in a sales department of a high-tech industry, this is possible. However, it is not possible in nursing given the current financial management system of hospitals; nursing is viewed primarily as an expense center. Major changes in health care financing would be needed for each work unit to be paid independently. However, a system of rewards could be based on profit sharing, incentives for quality care, and/or reduced length of stay.

Table 6-2 summarizes the elements of the social architecture of semi-autonomous work units. Comparing this to the elements of the three most commonly found social architectures (Table 6-1) further exemplifies how semi-autonomous units will function in the future.

Table 6-2 Social architecture of semi-autonomous work units.

Values and Behaviors	Semi-Autonomous Work Unit Style
Basis for decisions	Discussion, agreement, democratic, consensus, decentralization
Souce of power	Empowerment of the work group
Forms of control	Interpersonal, group commitments; individual and group rewards
Desired end	Alignment, creativity, innovation
To be avoded	Poor team functioning
Position relative to others	Peer, value of the individual within the work group
Human relationships	Group- and individually-oriented
Basis for growth	Peer group membership Acting on awareness of self

Specific Organizational Designs

In this section, three specific organizational designs will be considered. The first is *participatory management* which is becoming more and more popular in nursing services. This popularity mirrors a similar move in other organizations toward the involvement of workers in decision making. The second design is a particular form of participatory management in which groups are formed according to fixed guidelines. These are called *managerial boards*. The advantage of the boards is that they are structured to ensure vertical integration of decision making. The third design considered is *parallel organizations.*

Participatory Management

Participatory management has many definitions, but most of these definitions have a common element, i.e., participatory management involves the joint decision making of a team of two or more people. Decisions made by the team can involve setting goals, solving problems, making recommendations, planning, generating alternative courses of action, making changes, or producing a unit of work. Kanter (1982, 6) emphasized that the team in a participatory approach is fully informed and fully consulted.

Obviously, participatory management is not autocratic decision making. A finer distinction is that it is not delegation. In delegating, the manager keeps control over what is being delegated and the final goals of the delegated activity. Similarly, managers who canvass employees' opinions and consult employees are demonstrating a consultative management approach. But this is not participatory management (Kanter 1982, 6).

The basic principle of participatory management, regardless of its form, is that employees who will be affected by a decision have some formal way to contribute to the decision. This input is seriously considered and becomes part of the final decision.

Forms of Participatory Management. As stated, there are many forms of participatory management. It is not a single mechanism or a particular program. Programs such as *quality circles* are popular forms of participatory management. Quality circles, which were adopted from Japan, provide specific guidance for how employees at all organizational levels can participate in decision making, thus improving the productivity of their work units. The recent trend to decentralize nursing services is another example of a structural mechanism to enhance employee participation. Some informal processes such as the daily or weekly meeting of the management team to make a joint decision is yet another example.

In nursing, participatory management can occur at the unit level. Head nurses can form groups of nursing staff to make decisions about a variety of issues including the delivery of nursing care, quality assurance activities, and time scheduling policies. Participatory management can also occur at the level of the entire nursing department. In this case, it is difficult to have every employee contribute to every decision that is made in a participatory manner. Generally, a representative group of people affected by a decision makes the decision. For example, standing committees may make the decisions about nursing research efforts, new policies and procedures for employee and patient safety, or the direction of quality assurance programs. Task forces may be used to make decisions about smaller, more discrete, nonrecurring issues such as a revision of forms, setting goals for the year, or revising the philosophy. Although these particular situations are not ideal, they certainly represent an improvement over autocratic decision making, and given the size of nursing departments, they are realistic approaches.

The Propriety of Participatory Management. Participatory management is not a panacea for solving all organizational problems. The leader-manager needs to be sensitive as to when a participatory approach should be used. There are daily decisions that are made that will continue to be the responsibility of managers. Kanter (1982, 6-7) suggested that the use of participation is most appropriate in the following circumstances where the leader-manager needs or desires to:

- Gain new sources of expertise and experience;
- Get collaboration that multiplies a person's efforts by providing assistance, backup, or stimulation of better performance;
- Allow all of those who feel they know something about the subject to get involved;
- Build consensus on controversial issues;

- Allow representatives of those affected by an issue to influence decisions and build commitment to them;

- Tackle a problem that no one "owns" by virtue of organizational assignment;

- Allow a wider range of discussion/solutions than are available by normal means (for example, to get an unusual group together).

- Balance or confront vested interests in the face of the need to change;

- Address conflicting approaches or views;

- Avoid precipitate action and have time to explore a variety of effects; and

- Develop and educate people through their participation.

Likewise, there are situations in which participation is not appropriate such as when 1) one person is clearly the expert and those affected by the decision acknowledge this expertise; 2) the manager already knows the "right answer"; 3) the content of the participation is part of someone's job description and the participatory method was not their idea; 4) no one really cares about the issue; 5) no contribution would be made by a person's involvement in the product; 6) there is a need for quick action; and 7) when people are happier and more productive if working alone (Kanter 1982, 7).

Managing Participation. Participation needs to be well managed. Most importantly, there should be a clearly defined structure for participation. This includes the consideration of a number of elements. First, appropriate people should be involved; each situation will define who these people are. Leader-managers should seriously examine who will be affected by the results of the decision and include a representative number of these people. Second, a time frame for completion of work should be determined at the outset. This allows for less procrastination and creates an energy for moving toward an outcome. Third, defining who is responsible for what tasks lessens the possibility of later conflict. Fourth, to whom the team is accountable needs to be defined. For instance, in some cases a participatory group may report directly to the leader-manager. In another case, they may report directly to a standing committee and its chairperson. Fifth, expecta-

Figure 6-3 Managerial boards.

Chief Executive Officer

Chief Nurse Executive*　　Chief Nurse Executive

Directors of Nursing　　　Director of Nursing*　　　Director of Nursing

　　　　　　　　　　　　Head Nurses　　　　　　　Head Nurse*

　　　　　　　　　　　　　　　　　　　　　　　　Registered nurses,
　　　　　　　　　　　　　　　　　　　　　　　　licensed practical nurses,
　　　　　　　　　　　　　　　　　　　　　　　　and nursing assistants

*the chairperson of the board.

tions of the group need to be described and adhered to including the standards for group meetings, expectations for accomplishment of assigned tasks, and the methods of conducting their business. Lastly, at what point the team will dissolve, how it will be rewarded and recognized for its accomplishments, and how it will communicate its process and final results are best determined at the outset.

Managerial Boards

Ackoff, Finnel, and Gharajedaghi (1984) suggested a specific structure for participation in planning for effective integration and coordination of long-term plans. However, the design can be used for other purposes and for ongoing decision making in nursing departments. For the purpose of this text, they are called managerial boards. Each manager has a board consisting of a manager, the manager's immediate subordinates, and the manager's immediate superior.

Figure 6-3 illustrates these boards for a nursing department. By looking at this figure and using the position of Director of Nursing as an example, guidelines for the formation of managerial boards are illustrated. First, every board, other than those at the top and bottom of the organization, should be composed of three levels of management. For example, the nurse executive, the director herself, and the head nurses (who report to the director) all sit on the director's board. Secondly, all managers serve on the boards at three levels: their own, their bosses, and their immediate subordinates. The director sits on her own board, the nurse executive's board, and those of the head nurses who report to her. Thirdly, managers will interact with individuals at five levels in the organization: their own, two higher, and two lower. As an example, while serving on the nurse executive's board, the director of nursing interacts with the chief executive officer (CEO), and while serving on the head nurse's board, she interacts with staff nurses. Thus, she is in the position to share the concerns and feeling of the staff nurses with the CEO and vice versa. This assists in vertical integration of communications and decision making.

There are strict rules that guide this structure and ensure that decisions are made at the appropriate level: 1) a unit can make its own decisions without external approval about any plan or action that affects only itself if the unit has the required resources; 2) if a plan affects other units at the same or higher levels, the lowest level planning board to which all report has final decision-making approval; 3) plans should be reviewed at the next highest level to determine how a unit's plan does or does not affect others; and 4) a plan which affects lower levels must be reviewed by them and units must be given an opportunity to react.

For example, a head nurse's board could decide to initiate 10- and 12-hour tours of duty. Once the board decided to implement these time scheduling alternatives, the decision would be reviewed by the director's board (see Figure 6-3). This board would not rule as to whether or not the nursing unit could implement these time schedules. Their role would be to ensure that the implementation would not affect any other unit. The involved head nurse, her head nurse peers, and the nurse executive sit on the director's board. Thus, communications about the decision are vertically and horizontally integrated within the nursing department. However, if the nurse executive's board desired to implement a hospital-wide nursing pool, consideration of this would need to be sent to all other boards in the nursing department. Each of these boards would have the opportunity to review the proposal and have input before action would be taken.

This structure can be cumbersome; it involves many people and many meetings. However, to minimize this problem, clear guidelines can be established for what should be handled by managerial boards and for expediting feedback.

Parallel Organizations

Parallel organizations (Stein and Kanter 1980) may be another answer to the problem of how to reform organizations. Parallel organizations are flat, flexible, formal problem-solving and governance organizations which serve to supplement conventional bureaucracy. They exist side-by-side with the formal hierarchy but do not replace it. Parallel structures provide a means for managing change, flexibility, and responsiveness. Most importantly, they provide a source of opportunity and power above and beyond the sources of the bureaucratic structure. This source of opportunity and power is particularly important to people, such as staff nurses, in positions least characterized by those two properties.

The committee structure existing in most nursing departments is an example of a parallel organization. However, committees are only effective if they have the power to make recommendations which lead to action and improvement of the service. Vertical and horizontal integration can occur with the use of a defined committee structure. As shown in Figure 6-4, the nurse executive board (NEB) acts on recommendations of each of the committees. Further, the NEB establishes policies and procedures developed from the recommendations. This structure provides two benefits. First, it ensures that the committee's recommendations are implemented and not "forgotten" within the seldom read minutes of the committee. Second, it provides horizontal integration. The actions of each committee are known by and can influence the direction and action of other committees. For instance, if the Nursing Safety Committee recommends the use of a new system for needle disposal, the Nursing Practice Committee and the Nursing Education Committee would need to write policies and procedures and educate staff, respectively.

Implications for Nursing Practice

The effective nurse leader-manager understands the concept of social architecture to manage the social networks, norms, and organizational structure. She should be aware of how the organization is designed formally to enhance the participation of all nursing personnel in decisions that affect their work and patient care. Likewise, she should understand the informal networks and how she can positively influence them for organizational benefits. This includes understanding the norms of the organization and

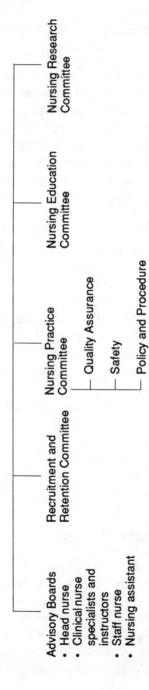

Figure 6-4 Committee structure of a nursing department.

participating in changing those which negatively affect organizational performance.

In designing the social architecture for today's organization, the leader-manager uses the principles of participatory management to address the needs of employees to participate and to achieve. There are many forms of participation which can be adopted depending on the norms and the overall organizational structure. In designing the social architecture for the future, the nurse leader-manager should consider the proposed design of semi-autonomous work units and begin slowly to incorporate elements of the design into today's nursing departments.

Application to Nursing Practice: Case Study

The Setting

The setting is a 500-bed medical center in the Northeast which offers medical, surgical, and psychiatric services on an inpatient and outpatient basis. The nursing service consists of 22 nursing units, including 3 ICUs, a dialysis unit, an operating room, acute and intermediate medical/surgical units, and a 90-bed long-term care unit.

Current Situation

The current organizational chart is displayed in Figure 6-5. Each nursing unit has one staff nurse who is responsible for quality assurance and one for infection control. Although these staff are responsible to the head nurse for these activities, they work closely with and receive support and direction from the nursing department's quality assurance nurse and infection control nurse.

The committee structure is illustrated in Figure 6-4. The membership of the nurse executive board, which the nurse executive views as the policy-making body of the nursing department, consists of the nurse executive, the directors of nursing, chairpersons of each of the four advisory boards, and chairpersons of each committee. For the most part, committee chairpersons are head nurses—those considered the "best and the brightest." Therefore, there is a great deal of representation of that group on the board. There are four advisory boards which consist of people in each of the job classifications including 1) clinical nurse specialists and nursing instructors, 2) head

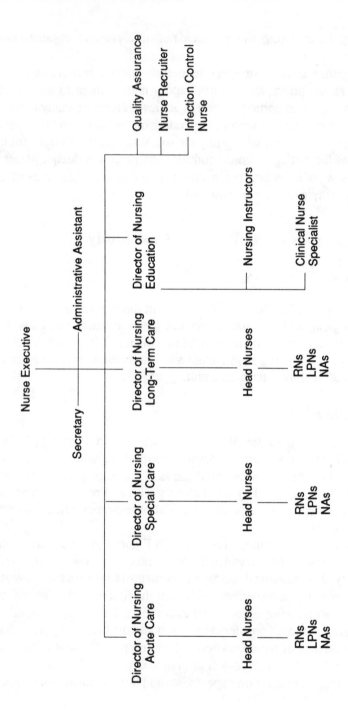

Figure 6-5 Organizational chart for case study.

nurses, 3) staff nurses, and 4) nursing assistants. Each of the chairpersons of the advisory boards meet monthly with the nurse executive.

In addition to committees, there are meetings at all levels in the department to share information. Task forces are commonly used to develop one-time programs or to solve a defined problem, such as implementation of a new computer system, nursing documentation, drafting of a new philosophy and annual goals, and implementation of nursing standards. Issues arising in meetings and the recommendations from task forces are also submitted to the nurse executive board.

Case Study Discussion

1. How would you describe the organizational structure of the nursing department? What is the social architecture?

2. What are the elements of participatory management found in the nursing department?

3. How could participatory management be further enhanced?

4. What are the benefits of the four advisory boards?

5. What is the norm which guides the decision about who chairs committees?

6. Should you describe the committee structure as informal or formal networks?

References

Ackoff, R. L., E. U. Finnel, and J. Gharajed-aghi. 1984. *A guide to controlling your corporation's future*. New York: John Wiley and Sons.

Bennis, W., and B. Nanus. 1985. *Leaders: The strategies for taking charge*. New York: John Wiley and Sons.

Deal, T. E., and A. A. Kennedy. 1982. *Corporate cultures: The rites and rituals of corporate life*. Reading, MA: Addison-Wesley.

Kanter, R. M. 1982. Dilemmas of managing participation. *Organizational Dynamics* 11(9):5-27.

Lashbrook, W. B. 1986. Management as a performance system. In *The leader-manager*, ed. J. N. Williamson, 125-136. New York: John Wiley and Sons.

Peters, T. J., and N. Austin. 1985. *A passion for excellence: The leadership difference*. New York: Warner Communications.

Peters, T. J., and R. H. Waterman. 1982. *In Search of excellence: Lessons from America's best-run companies.* New York: Warner Communications.

Shandler, M. 1986. Leadership and the art of understanding structure. In *Transforming leadership: From vision to results*, ed. J. D. Adams, 123-132. Alexandria, VA: Miles River Press.

Stein, B. A. and R. M. Kanter. 1980. Building the parallel organization. *Journal of Applied Behavior Science* 16:371-388.

Tichy, N. M., and M. A. Devanna. 1986. *The transformational leader.* New York: John Wiley and Sons.

7

Elements of the Social Architecture

Chapter Objectives

1. Differentiate between permanent and temporary objectives.

2. Cite five parameters of feedback and how each is used to ensure successful feedback in the organization.

3. Describe the primary purpose of performance appraisal systems.

4. List ways to manage both a monetary and nonmonetary reward system.

5. Discuss the importance of providing a supportive environment.

6. Discuss why the development of people in the organization is often neglected.

Introduction

To design, shape, and remodel the social architecture, the leader-manager is concerned with specific managerial tasks which are part of the overall social architecture. These elements are relevant to the social architecture of both today's and future nursing departments. These factors can be viewed as part of human resource management and include vision, goals, selection and placement of personnel, feedback, appraisal, rewards, support, and development.

These elements should be internally consistent; however, internal consistency seldom exists in any organization or department because each element is usually developed and revised in a piecemeal fashion, over time, and by different "players" with different philosophies and agendas. For instance, it is common for the appraisal system to be developed according to the guidelines of the human resource department. Thus, there may be criteria in the evaluation which do not help the nursing department realize its goals.

The purpose of the following discussion is not to present the technical aspects of each element such as writing objectives and developing performance appraisal systems. The intent, instead, is to present underlying concepts and beliefs about the need for, rationale for, and appropriate design of the specific elements of the social architecture. By using the presented information, the leader-manager can assess the social architecture of her own organization and see areas for improvement and internal consistency.

Vision

Chapter 5 presented a detailed discussion of organizational vision. It is important to understand that vision is the very foundation of social architecture. Without a firm vision for the organization, the social architecture will crumble.

Goals and Objectives

There has been a confusion in semantics regarding the terms *goals* and *objectives*. Some people refer to goals as longer-term aims or purposes; the written goals are broad statements which are not necessarily measurable. Objectives are then seen as short-term, measurable steps to achieve the broader goal. Some people define them oppositely with the objective being the long-term aim and goals being short-term.

Regardless of what terminology is used, a nursing department needs both a long-term purpose and short-term steps to achieve the purpose. Together they define the ends toward which a nursing department strives and which will contribute to overall organizational success. They are the next steps in the visionary process: concrete short-term and long-term plans for the department. If these plans are appropriately communicated and utilized, employees can see that their performance contributes to accomplishment of organizational purpose. Like vision, goals and objectives are held by all members of the work unit to provide a unifying force.

Long-term plans and short-term plans are differentiated in this book as *permanent objectives* and *temporary objectives* (Stevens 1985, 40). *Permanent objectives* are those which are ongoing, are achieved over and over, and are long-term in nature. Examples of permanent objectives might be to 1) recruit qualified staff that "fit" into the nursing department, have appropriate expertise, and a value system consistent with the organization; 2) utilize nursing research findings to improve patient care; or 3) provide opportunities for staff growth and development.

In contrast, *temporary objectives* are established to improve an aspect of nursing practice needing special attention. The improvement or change is usually one needed only temporarily (one year). Examples of temporary objectives might be to implement a case management method of delivery of nursing services or to determine the costs of nursing services based on DRGs.

Determining Objectives

Two opposite approaches to determining objectives have been taken. The first is that objectives are written by top management. They are then sent to each department to determine departmental objectives that contribute to the overall objectives of the organization. Next they are sent to each division and unit for objectives that contribute to the department's objectives. Using this approach, each manager in the chain serves to coordinate the objectives of the people under her in the organization. This ensures the fit and appropriateness of objectives at the lower levels in the organization with those at the top.

An example of this approach is a hospital which aims to provide quality care at the lowest cost possible in order to be competitive. The objectives in this case might be:

1. a. *Hospital Permanent Objective*: To deliver quality patient care in a cost-effective manner.

     b. *Hospital Temporary Objective*: To integrate the quality assurance, guest relations, and marketing programs of all departments.

2. a. *Nursing Department Permanent Objective*: To deliver quality nursing care in a cost-effective manner.

    b. *Nursing Department Temporary Objectives*: To revise the nursing quality assurance program to include a sensitivity to customer relations.

3. a. *Nursing Unit Permanent Objective*: To provide quality nursing care to the outpatient population within budgetary limitations.

    b. *Nursing Unit Temporary Objective*: To collect data about patients' perceptions of waiting times, nursing courtesy, and assistance in explaining procedures and medication instructions.

In contrast, another approach is to begin at the bottom of the organization, having each unit determine their objectives. Eventually, top management pulls together all the objectives into a common document.

For example, a nursing unit might have the desire to implement a patient teaching program. When asked to submit their objectives the process would be:

1. a. *Nursing Unit Permanent Objective*: To provide quality nursing care to cardiac patients.

    b. *Nursing Unit Temporary Objective*: To develop a patient teaching program for cardiac rehabilitation patients.

2. a. *Nursing Department Permanent Objectives*: To provide quality nursing care to patients.

    b. *Nursing Unit Temporary Objective*: To support the development of patient education programs on specific nursing units.

3. a. *Hospital Permanent Objective*: To provide quality care to patients in a cost-effective manner.

    b. *Hospital Temporary Objective*: To provide resources for the development of patient education programs.

The advantages of the first approach are standardization, consistency, and vertical and horizontal integration. However, this approach is not consistent with a decentralized philosophy. The major advantage of the second approach is that people at all levels, especially those with the best understanding of the activities of the unit, are involved in goal setting. In the example above, without a bottom-up approach to forming objectives, it would be unlikely that the overall hospital objectives would include a specific commitment of resources to patient education.

The best approach, in most situations, is one that combines both bottom-up and top-down planning. Top management can develop overall organizational goals and expect each unit in the organization to contribute to the goals. At the time of goal formulation, the involvement of as many people as possible improves the process. At the same time, each organizational unit can develop unit-specific and unit-generated goals. These goals are reviewed and approved by higher management, who is then obliged to support the goals of the unit, as well as overall organizational goals.

Selection and Placement

The aim when selecting and placing personnel is to achieve a fit between the technical skills, expertise, and values of the person and those of the organization. This is done with an eye toward the future. To achieve a perfect fit is not easy and most often not achievable. However, interview techniques such as preparing questions in advance regarding the person's philosophies, goals, and aspirations are important. Involving as many people as reasonably possible in the selection is also an excellent technique for screening and selecting people. This can be done by the use of search committees. A well selected search committee can bring a variety of perspectives to the selection. For example, the search committee for the selection of a head nurse could consist of head nurse peers, the nurse educator, clinical nurse specialists, the candidate's potential manager, and staff nurses from the unit. These individuals would bring a broad perspective to the process.

Feedback

Feedback is the information employees receive about their performance and it contributes to goal accomplishment. Feedback is not reinforcement by reward (the next element), but rather precedes reinforcement (Lashbrook 1986, 129-130).

Feedback serves to reinforce desired behaviors, helps to instruct employees in behavioral requirements of their jobs, provides information about what a leader-manager feels is important, influences the content and quality of work-related communications, and can increase job satisfaction. Feedback has five parameters (Fairbanks and Prue 1986, 338-341):

1. The *recipients* of feedback can be either individuals or groups. It is recommended that both group and individual feedback occur. This appeals to the paradoxical needs of people to be individuals while at the same time to belong to a group. Since so much of the work of nursing relies on group work, it is essential for the group to have feedback. Feedback can be given either privately or publicly. One study found that public feedback is generally more successful than private (Fairbanks and Prue 1986, 339). However, the leader-manager uses her judgment based on the individuals involved and the content of the feedback.

2. The *content* of the information is characterized by being accurate, relevant (tied to goals), and usable. The focus of the feedback can be on process (how the task was accomplished) or outcome (the results). Providing feedback on several areas of performance, if possible, avoids the tendency to focus too much attention in one area to the detriment of another.

3. *Temporal* characteristics include how often and when feedback is given. This involves two directions, i.e., employees should be able to ask for and receive feedback when they need it. Likewise, the manager needs to feel free to give feedback whenever she wants. Feedback can be provided immediately after an event or there can be a delay. Generally, feedback given as soon as possible after an event is preferred. Less frequent feedback may be given for overall performance of the individual or group.

4. *Mechanisms* of providing feedback can be verbal, written, or mechanical. Again, the use of a variety of feedback is best. Mechanical feedback, e.g., computer printouts, will be the wave of the future although it may not be used widely today.

5. *Sources* of feedback include all levels of managers, co-workers, subordinates, outside consultants, and clients. For feedback to be accepted, the recipient of the feedback needs to respect and trust the person providing the information. The more sources of feedback a person receives, the more likely the feedback will be accepted.

The leader-manager should use positive feedback to a much greater degree than negative feedback. Positive reinforcement is a better motivator and a better reinforcer of behavior because it enhances and protects self-esteem; negative feedback can damage self-esteem. Its use should be reserved for situations in which there is no other alternative but to give negative feedback and to situations that threaten the safety and well-being of others. Negative feedback should be preceded and succeeded by positive feedback whenever possible.

Appraisal

The ideal performance appraisal system is expected to accomplish the objectives of making satisfactory workers even better, rid the system of unsatisfactory workers, and improve the distribution of merit pay (Stevens 1985, 359). However, few, if any, performance appraisal systems achieve these objectives. One reason for this failure is that performance appraisal systems are seen as isolated entities. They are not viewed as one component of the entire social architecture.

Further, the failure of performance appraisal systems may rest with trying to achieve too many conflicting objectives such as both rewards and punishment. The primary purpose of the performance appraisal system should be to develop people. To do this, the leader-manager uses a goal orientation in performing the appraisal. This contrasts with the traditional approach of sitting in judgment upon and looking for weaknesses in others. People need goals for developing their knowledge and skills and for contributing to the organization. A goal orientation to performance appraisal has several benefits: goals can hold people accountable, empower them to act, and therefore increase their self-esteem.

Rewards

The successful nurse leader-manager needs to use the reward system effectively. To do this, she should remember that rewards are used to reinforce behaviors. For rewards to work, they *must* be tied to the desired behaviors of people. Behaviors are crucial in that they link the intended vision with actual outcomes. For example, if a nurse leader-manager is attempting to increase cooperation among staff regarding the coverage of the unit, she should use the reward system for this purpose. People who willingly cooperate with others to stay late or change their time in order for another staff member to have some special time off should be rewarded. As discussed below, the reward can be either monetary or nonmonetary.

Reward System Failures

In order to successfully design a reward system, it is helpful to look at why reward systems have not worked. Three reasons for the failure of reward systems include the following:

1. The links between rewards and behaviors have weakened. Thus, organizational reward systems have become a disincentive, rather than an incentive. If everyone in the organization is rewarded the same, whether or not their performance is equal, people adopt an attitude of "why work harder than anyone else." In a survey of American workers, about 50 percent of the respondents felt that there was no connection between their performance and how much they are paid (Yankelovich and Immerwahr 1986, 413).

2. Managers lack the skills or willingness to use the reward system to motivate others.

3. There is a mismatch between people's values and most organizations' reward systems. The emphasis of the reward systems has been on pay. This is important since it symbolizes material success and provides a higher standard of living. However, today's worker brings a pluralistic set of values to the workplace which can guide the choice of reward to use in a given situation (Yankelovich and Immerwahr 1986, 409-413).

Kerr suggested other reasons why the reward systems in organizations are not effective. His basic premise was that some systems reward a particular behavior while apparently hoping for an entirely different one. In other words, the professed desire to accomplish a goal or vision is not structured into and sustained by the reward system. In fact, the reward system may be directing behaviors in a different way. For example, the reward system in nursing might be based on the delivery of care in an efficient, cost-effective way—a worthy goal. Yet the leader-manager may be hoping for not only cost-effective delivery of care, but assessment, planning, and evaluation of that care as well. If the reward system does not reinforce these behaviors, they will not occur.

Kerr (1986) believed that the causes of this problem are threefold. First, there has been an overemphasis on objective, simple, quantitative criteria to measure and reward performance. Certainly it is easier to measure the quantity of nursing care given, for example, than the quality of nursing assessments. What results in goal displacement. Secondly, the emphasis on highly visible behaviors lessens the importance of those behaviors that are not visible. For example, team building and creativity are frequently not rewarded, simply because they are hard to observe. Lastly, there has been an emphasis on equity rather than efficiency. Inherent in this view is that everyone should be treated the same. This approach has failed. People are all different and have diverse needs and aspirations. Treating everyone the same leads to a dissatisfying, ineffective, dehumanizing work environment, and thus lowers employee self-esteem.

These reasons, combined with some practical issues surrounding the bureaucratic reward systems, point to further problems. Most nurse managers in large health care facilities have limitations on the use of rewards. There are rigid guidelines for when rewards can be given, the criteria for rewarding people, and limitations on the amount of money that can be given. The paperwork to recommend a reward often deters its use. Further, the time lag between the behavior and the receipt of the reward lessens its positive impact.

From this review of reasons why reward systems are failing emerges important concepts to consider when designing a reward system. Most importantly, rewards have to be meaningful to the employee. Money is still an important incentive because it improves one's standard of living. It cannot, however, be the sole incentive in a reward system. Herzberg (1968) suggested a new direction in managing reward systems. He recommended that rewards be restructured from extrinsic motivators such as salaries toward intrinsic ones such as the content of the work itself, hours of work, degree of control and responsibility, opportunity for achievement and recognition, and personal growth and learning.

Thus, in redesigning the reward system, the leader-manager should consider two distinct aspects. First, she should understand the issues surrounding money as a reward. Then she needs to consider nonmonetary rewards.

Managing Monetary Rewards

Monetary reward systems cannot reward everyone equally. Most employees will tolerate differential benefits, i.e., one person getting more than another. However, employees cannot accept a disproportionate use of the reinforcement process with only a few people receiving all the rewards (Lashbrook 1986, 131). This leads to a feeling of favoritism and mistrust of the leader. It can also cause employees to compete rather than cooperate with one another.

These issues should be considered when redesigning a monetary reward system:

1. Competent behavior which contributes to the organizational vision and goals should be rewarded.

2. Rewards should reinforce high performance not only improve low performance.

3. Staff involvement in designing the reward system results in a greater commitment to it.

4. Rewards should reflect a person's skills, educational background, and accomplishments. These can form the basis for determining starting salaries and promotions. If pay is attached both to quality of work and length of experience, the issue of salary compression can begin to be addressed.

5. The leader-manager should know how the reward system in the organization works. This ensures that the nursing department gets its full and fair share of the limited financial resources of the healthcare institution.

6. Ideally, each head nurse should have access to some money which she can use to reward individual and group accomplishments. This money should be used to reward behaviors that are consistent with the vision and goals of the nursing department and unit.

Nonmonetary Rewards

In a service industry such as nursing, tying pay to the performance is much harder than in manufacturing or sales. Thus, pay and individual performance become blurred. Pay is tied more to overall organizational performance than to individual performance. Thus, people want to have more input into policies and decisions that increase overall organizational performance. Listening to a person's idea and implementing it can be more satisfying and rewarding to an individual than money. Employees need to see that an increase in their productivity will cause an increase in the performance and productivity of the overall organization. They also need to know that they will personally benefit from organizational successes.

The issue of nonmonetary rewards has received little systematic attention and research. However, most scholars would agree that intrinsic elements need to be used to reward people. This is true for two reasons: 1) intrinsic rewards appeal to the values of people and a higher level of needs, and 2) because of scarce financial resources and the bureaucratic problems of administering a reward program, other forms of rewards need to be sought. Fortunately, most of these rewards can be used at the will and discretion of the nurse leader-manager.

Examples of Nonmonetary Rewards. Employee-of-the-month or nursing unit-of-the-month programs have been very successful in nursing and other organizations. The leader-manager may need a small budget to use for plaques, free dinners, or some other small recognition. Free, desirable parking spaces provide a meaningful recognition and a highly visible one as well.

To be most successful, the decisions regarding who is rewarded need to be participatory not autocratic. One way to achieve this is to permit anyone to submit a recommendation for deserving individuals. A small committee can review and make the decision for the monthly recipient.

The provision of positive, verbal feedback is cited frequently as an underutilized method of rewarding people. Leader-managers can assess their use of positive feedback and determine a goal for its use. Successful leaders who use this technique have to "work at remembering it." A written note to oneself is one external way to remember.

Promotion of people, delegation of tasks with increased accountability and responsibility, seeking advice, and providing opportunities for further growth and development can all be used to reward behaviors. The leader-manager needs to clearly state that the reason the person is being recognized in one of these ways is to reward their behaviors.

Support

Support is a critical management function that has not received much attention in the available literature on management until recently. *Support* means to guide and coach others while allowing them to stay in power. Employees need to know that they may seek help and will not be punished. However, the norms of the department should encourage employees to support one another as well. Support cannot threaten the self-esteem of others. If employees seek support and are met with a managerial response of 1) telling the employee what to do, 2) "I used to do it this way" solutions, or 3) doing it for the employee, employee self-esteem is destroyed.

In contrast, to protect employee self-esteem, the leader-manager can question the employee about what has been tried and elicit why the employee believes that something has not worked. By seeking ideas from the employee, helping her to see the strengths and pitfalls of each idea, and helping her to explore alternatives, self-esteem can be not only protected but enhanced.

Development

The development of people in the organization includes both formal teaching and informal guidance by helping people to learn from events and from mistakes. The importance of developing people, the greatest resource of service organizations, cannot be overemphasized. In healthcare, much money is spent in having the latest equipment at the cost of millions of dollars, but so little time and money are spent on developing people. In times of crisis, money for formal, personnel development is the first "perquisite" to be cut.

Development of staff through formal workshops is undervalued because generally, people cannot bring back what they've learned or implement it because of the constraints of the work environment. Further, the results of development are not concrete and are therefore difficult to evaluate.

Implications for Nursing

The tasks of the leader-manager are complex. By using the elements of the social architecture presented in this chapter, the leader-manager can thoroughly assess her organization and restructure those elements that require changes. The nurse leader-manager needs to establish a vision, determine goals and objectives, select and assign personnel, provide individual and group feedback, design appraisal and reward systems, and support and develop staff. At times, these tasks may seem overwhelming.

As mentioned, the first step in managing these elements of the social architecture should be to develop a vision statement. From the vision, all other elements should flow to provide internal consistency.

The importance of internal consistency cannot be overstated. Internal consistency helps everyone in the organization to think in a similar way. For example, most nursing departments have a written philosophy of nursing which states that nurses use the nursing process. The permanent goals of the nursing department should then include some statement regarding the use of the nursing process. Often this is not stated in the departmental goals. Further, rarely are staff nurse applicants questioned about or selected based on their understanding of the nursing process.

Feedback to staff regarding their use of the nursing process may or may not occur, depending on the head nurse. Many appraisal systems include an element for nursing care planning. Neatly written, completed care plans are relatively easy to observe and quantify. However, few appraisal systems truly emphasize the quality of nursing assessment and evaluation, for example. The reward system, which is tied to the performance appraisal system, loosely reinforces the nursing process. Yet, the instances in which nurses are rewarded for their expertise in applying the nursing process to attain positive outcomes for a patient or group of patients is virtually unknown. Support for assisting staff with the nursing process is negligible. In most nursing departments, nurses would not willingly ask for help in what is deemed to be basic knowledge and skill. Lastly, those few individuals who attend programs in nursing assessment, diagnosis, etc., seldom are able to implement what they have learned into practice.

Application to Nursing Practice: Case Study

The Setting

A 1,000-bed medical center which is part of a for-profit corporation is in the process of installing an integrated hospital information system (HIS). All departments will be connected to the system. Both clinical and management data will be stored, processed, and distributed.

An HIS coordinator, who will be in charge of the computer installation for the entire medical center, was recently hired. The CEO who interviewed and selected the HIS coordinator by himself was interested in hiring someone with computer expertise. The selected HIS coordinator is fully competent with computers and computer installation, but is not familiar with hospital operations. The coordinator has been assigned the responsibility of ensuring interdepartmental communications and coordination. Each department is responsible for implementing their software packages and the training of all staff who will use the package. For instance, the pharmacy, laboratory, and other departments will train nursing staff.

For the nursing department, the administrative assistant to the nurse executive has been delegated the responsibility of overseeing the installation of the computer system in nursing, including working with other departments and the HIS coordinator. This person was selected because of her expressed willingness to learn about computers and her proven competence in working with large programs. A nursing task force, chaired by one nurse educator, has been convened to advise the administrative assistant.

For nursing, the clinical component of the software application will include order entry and results reporting for diagnostic and therapeutic services such as laboratory, radiology, and dietetics. Nursing will not chart on-line; however, patient acuity will be computerized and information will be sent to the central nursing department once per shift. Administrative, budgeting, staffing, and electronic mail software packages within the hospital will be available. The nursing office will be able to communicate via the computer with administrative departments such as personnel and finance.

Current Situation

The first portion of the system is on-line with patients' files, admission data, and the bed control functions operational with some minor difficulties. Order entry/results reporting for the laboratory is now ready to go on-line. However, the HIS coordinator has failed to keep the administrative assistant aware of the progress in the laboratory. The nurse executive is suddenly faced with a request by the CEO to begin order entry for laboratory tests in three days without any nursing staff being trained. The laboratory has proposed several ways to train personnel, including reading the documentation, training everyone in three days between 10 A.M. and 2 P.M., and training five to 10 nursing personnel who would then be responsible for training the rest of the staff over a three-day period. The nurse executive wants the laboratory to train nursing personnel, as previously agreed upon, on all three tours of duty. She cannot guarantee that this can be accomplished in three days. The CEO wants the laboratory up and running in three days because he is being pressured by the corporate office.

Case Study Discussion

1. What might be included in the vision statement of the organization and of the nursing department regarding the installation of a HIS?

2. Write hospital and nursing department permanent and temporary objectives for the installation of a HIS.

3. How might the selection of the HIS coordinator have been better handled?

4. What support and development should be provided for the HIS coordinator and the nursing administrative assistant?

5. What type of feedback should be provided to the HIS coordinator and the administrative assistant about the current problem with implementation of the laboratory application?

References

Fairbanks, J. A. and D. M. Prue. 1986. Developing performance feedback systems. In *The leader-manager*, ed. J. N. Williamson, 331-354. New York: John Wiley and Sons.

Herzberg, F. H. 1968. *Work and the nature of man*. Cleveland: The World Publishing Company.

Kerr, S. 1986. On the folly of rewarding A, while hoping for B. In *The leader-manager*, ed. J. N. Williamson, 417-432. New York: John Wiley and Sons.

Lashbrook, W. B. 1986. Management as a performance system. In *The leader-manager*, ed. J. N. Williamson, 125-136. New York: John Wiley and Sons.

Stevens, B. J. 1985. *The nurse as executive.* 3rd ed. Rockville, MD: Aspen Publishers.

Yankelovich, D., and J. Immerwahr. 1986. Why the work ethic isn't working. In *The leader-manager*, ed. J. N. Williamson, 407-416. New York: John Wiley and Sons.

8

Organizational Trust

Chapter Objectives

1. Define trust from both a sociological and psychological perspective.

2. Describe three behaviors of trusting individuals which contribute to organizational effectiveness.

3. Describe eight sources of organizational trust.

4. List four stages of development of organizational trust.

5. List three assumptions which lead to organizational distrust.

6. Describe research findings which demonstrate the positive benefits of organizational trust.

7. Compare and contrast the effects of trust and distrust in a nursing organization.

8. Describe behaviors which build and maintain organizational trust.

Introduction

Although trust is a complex concept, the beliefs and behaviors of the leader-managers are the single most important determining factors of organizational trust. If the leader-manager is committed to trusting others and building a trusting environment, then trust will exist. If she does not trust others and believes that distrust is inevitable, there will be no organizational trust. For a leader-manager, trust is not an inherent part of her position. It must be earned and nurtured every day and in every situation. It takes time, patience, and unending attention.

The work of nursing involves a great deal of interdependence on others. Nurses need to rely on one another and on people in other disciplines to accomplish their goals of patient care. Trust is the foundation upon which individual and group relationships can flourish. Distrust, however, degenerates into conflict, wasted energy, paranoia, and hostility. Further, in future nursing organizations designed as semi-autonomous work units, trust will be essential for effective group functioning.

The Meaning and Characteristics of Trust

The Sociological Perspective of Trust

The sociological perspective of trust is grounded in role theory. According to this theory, organizations are social systems and the members of the organization assume roles within this system. The concept of expectations is the basis for understanding trust. There are two expectations which are specific to leadership: the expectation of competent role performance and the expectation that people will fulfill their fiduciary responsibilities to others (Barber 1983).

The first expectation means that people presume others to be technically competent in their role, bringing expert knowledge and skills to the activities of their role in society. For example, in nursing organizations the nurse leader-manager expects nursing personnel to be knowledgeable and skillful in their practice. Reversely, nursing staff expect the leader-manager to demonstrate competencies in nursing and management as she attempts to accomplish organizational goals.

Individuals fulfill their fiduciary responsibilities and obligations when they place the concerns of others above their own. This avoids misuse of power and makes honest use of knowledge and position in society. Fiduciary responsibilities are moral obligations which are placed more heavily on the individual with specialized knowledge, skill, power. For the individual nurse, this means that her concern for her patients' well-being overrides her concern for herself. Similarly, the leader-manager has more power and organizational resources for her use than do staff. Thus, in order to be trusted, she needs to place the concerns of staff and patients above her own. In other words, for organizational success, the nurse leader-manager acts in behalf of the interests of others, not in behalf of her own interests. This is not to say that the nurse leader-manager is disinterested in her own personal success. However, this success will be realized in the organizational context only when she does not take advantage of her position in the organization.

The Psychological Perspective of Trust

In contrast but not in conflict with the sociological perspective of trust is the psychological perspective which considers the behaviors of trusting and distrusting individuals. When a person trusts another person, their vulnerability to the other person is increased. The consequences one suffers if the vulnerability is abused are greater than the benefits one gains if the vulnerability is not abused. Trust, then, is the conscious regulation of one's dependence on another. This dependence will vary with the task, the situation, and the persons involved (Deutsch 1962).

For example, the daily occurrence of delegation of tasks involves both trust and vulnerability. The delegator trusts another person to complete a task on time and correctly, while at the same time her vulnerability is increased. For example, budget preparation is often delegated by the nurse executive to head nurses. If a head nurse abuses the trust placed in her and does not prepare the budget on time or prepares it incorrectly, the nurse executive will be forced to delay submission of the departmental budget. This may cause her to appear inept in the eyes of her boss and peers. However, if the head nurses carry out the delegated task, the benefit for the nurse executive will be the routine submission of the budget. Although this will increase trust between the head nurses and the nurse executive, it will not attain any special privileges for the nurse executive or the nursing department. Thus, in this situation, the consequence the nurse executive may suffer are greater if the trust is abused than the benefits gained if the trust is not abused.

A person's inner state of trust or distrust can be transformed into behaviors that are either trusting or distrusting. These behaviors are communications with others, exerting influence over others, and controlling others. Trusting behaviors beget trust and distrusting ones beget distrust. Relationships stabilize at either low or high levels of trust (Zand 1972).

Figure 8-1 displays a model, based on one by Zand (1972), in which trusting behaviors increase mutual trust. Because a trusting leader-manager is more willing to be open and vulnerable, she will communicate more fully, more accurately, and in a more timely manner. This openness of information

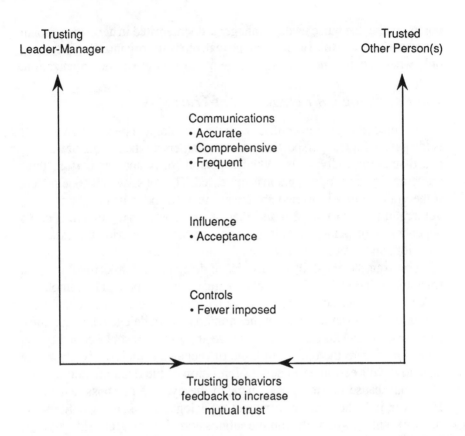

Figure 8-1 A model of trusting behaviors.

exchange feeds back to people who then see the leader-manager as someone who can be trusted. People, therefore, will likewise disclose more accurate, comprehensive, and timely information about facts, thoughts, and feelings. This interchange strengthens feelings of mutual trust.

This model holds true for mutual influence and control as well. The leader-manager who trusts others will accept more influence from others in goal setting, in selecting means to accomplish goals, and in evaluating progress toward goals. This willingness to be influenced feeds back to others. It increases mutual trust and the willingness to be influenced by the leader-manager.

Similarly, the trusting leader-manager accepts more interdependence on people and imposes less control over them. This shows confidence that they will do what was agreed upon.

Since the aim of the leader-manager is to provide a work environment in which people can contribute their talents and skills to the organization, it is clear that only if trust exists can people fully contribute. This is done through openness of information exchange, mutuality of goal setting, and empowering rather than controlling others.

The importance of trust to organizations becomes clear when viewing trust from this perspective. The true measure of success for nurse leader-managers is the wisdom and effectiveness of her decisions. These decisions can be those made by the leader-manager alone or ones made by a group. If information is not shared and if people are unwilling to set and work toward mutually agreed upon goals, organizational success will not occur. Trust is the ingredient that will ensure that information is shared appropriately and will enable the members of the group to influence and be influenced by one another.

The Effects of Distrust. If the leader-manager enters relationships not trusting other people, she will disclose less information, attempt to control them, and refuse to be influenced by others. If other people also enter the relationship lacking trust in the leader-manager, they will perceive the behaviors of the leader-manager as untrustworthy. Other people will respond by withholding information, refusing to be influenced by the leader-manager, and attempting to control the situation. The leader-manager will now believe that her initial impression that people cannot be trusted is correct. Likewise, others will also confirm their initial impression that the leader-manager cannot be trusted. Relationships will then settle at a low level of trust with each person attempting to minimize their vulnerability and maximize their control.

Distrust is devastating to organizational relationships and functioning and leads to feelings of anxiety and anger. These feelings prevent the effective utilization of one's talents and skills. Thus, the leader-manager's challenge is to develop an atmosphere of trust throughout the nursing department.

Development of Trust in the Individual

As a first stage of ego development, the roots of trust or distrust can be found in infancy as a result of the mother/child relationship. An inner sense of trust results if the infant learns that the mother will feed and comfort; the mother becomes both an inner certainty and outer predictability, providing consistency, continuity, and sameness of experience (Erikson 1950, 247-251).

It is important to have an understanding of the development of trust in infancy. However, the leader-manager cannot stop her understanding of trust at this point. She should understand the development of trust in adulthood, specifically in organizations. The nurse leader-manager cannot simply dismiss the presence or absence of trust to infancy and believe that nothing can be done to build trust. In organizations, leader-managers are constantly working with people and facing new situations. In each situation, people confront the issues of trust versus distrust, either consciously or unconsciously. Thus, the leader-manager needs to understand the sources, development, management, and maintenance of organizational trust.

There is evidence that trust may be an easier option to adopt than distrust. Distrust absorbs one's energy to explore and adapt to the environment in an objective and unprejudicial way, hence allowing one fewer options for learning and growing. It is easier for the human being to trust than not to trust because of this phenomenon (Luhman 1980, 71).

Sources of Trust in the Organization

In order for the leader-manager to generate trust in organizations, it is necessary for her to understand the sources of organizational trust. These sources of trust are behaviors which determine whether or not to trust another person. Observing superior/subordinate relationships over a period of three years, Gabarro (1978, 295-298) discovered eight sources of organizational trust. He categorized them into three groups: character-based, competence based, and judgment-based. These aspects apply both to the trust of the leader by subordinates and trust of subordinates by the leader. However, each group viewed the importance of each category differently. Table 8-1 summarizes the discussion that follows and suggests behaviors that enhance trust.

Character-Based Sources of Trust

These sources of trust are found in the character of the person and include 1) integrity, 2) intentions and motives, 3) openness and discreetness, and 4) consistency and reliability. The first and most important

Table 8-1 Sources of organizational trust.

Sources of Trust	Importance* to		Leader-Manager Behaviors
	Superior	Subordinate	
Character-based			
Basic honesty and moral character	X	X	Is honest Never lies Does not withhold information Acts in the interest of others
Intentions and motives		X	Has no "hidden agendas" Has intentions that are in the interest of staff and organization Is an advocate for staff
Openness and discreetness of communications		X	Is open and honest about organizational problems and employee performance Does not violate confidences Does not divulge personal, harmful information
Consistent, reliable behavior	X		Acts in accord with the vision and objectives of the organization Considers "past practices" but does not rigidly adhere to them Considers future implications of a decision
Competence-based			
Technical competence	X		Continues to learn and develop leadership, managerial, and professional skills Keeps abreast of clinical theory.

*The X indicates the three most important sources for each group.

Table 8-1 continued.

Sources of Trust	Importance* to Superior Subordinate	Leader-Manager Behaviors
Interpersonal skills		Nutures relationships Shows concern for both personal and professional issues
Business sense		Develops business knowledge and skills Knows economic trends and health policy
Judgement-based		
Ability to make good decisions		Is flexible but consistent Learns from experiences

Source: Gabarro, J. J. 1978. The development of trust, influence, and expectations. In *Interpersonal behavior: Communications and understanding in relationships*, ed. A. G. Athos and J. J. Gabarro, 290-303. Englewood Cliffs, NJ: Prentice Hall.

determinant of trust for both managers and staff is trust in the basic honesty and moral character of individuals, that is, their integrity. Without trust in the integrity of another, all other sources of trust are meaningless.

The second source for determining trust in organizations is trust in the intentions and motives of others. Subordinates perceive this source of trust as more important than do superiors because followers discern the manager to have control and dominance over their work lives. Thus, subordinates want to believe the manager's intentions are favorable to them, i.e., without a "hidden agenda." Clearly, the nurse leader-manager whose intentions and motives are truly in the best interest of her followers will promote organizational trust.

Along with integrity and intentions, subordinates view openness and discreteness of communications as an important foundation for trust. This third source of trust includes being open and honest about organizational problems and employee performance. At the same time, the leader-manager cannot violate confidences or divulge harmful information.

The last character-based source of trust is consistent, reliable, and predictable behavior. Although both superiors and subordinates base decisions about whether or not to trust another on this characteristic, superiors viewed it to be one of the most important bases of trust. The nurse leader-manager, whose task is to accomplish the goals of the organization through other people, needs to rely on staff to get their job done consistently and in a predictable manner.

Competence-Based Sources of Trust

These sources of trust refer to a person's competencies, skills, abilities, and knowledge. This category includes 1) technical competence, 2) interpersonal skills, and 3) business sense. One of the most important sources of trust for superiors is the expectation that staff will be technically competent to perform their assigned task. Competency in interpersonal relationships, i.e., the ability to work with others to accomplish the goals of the organization, is the second source of trust in this category. Since organizations rely on teams of people to work harmoniously, interpersonal relationships are important to organizational effectiveness and success. Trust in the general business sense of others, i.e., their common sense and wisdom about the procedures and workings of business, is the third source in this category.

Judgment-Based Sources of Trust

A person's ability to make good decisions regarding their work and behaviors more or less encompasses all the other sources of trust. For example, openness and discreetness are manifestations of both a person's character and his judgment.

In summary, four relationships for trust development emerge: 1) the leader-manager's trust of staff; 2) the staff's trust of the leader-manager; 3) the leader-manager's trust of her superior; and 4) the superior's trust of the leader-manager.

These four relationships can actually be viewed as two. What the nurse leader-manager looks for in her boss to determine whether to trust him or her are the same characteristics that the leader-manager's followers are looking for in her. The most important of these characteristics are integrity, the intentions and motives of the superior, and openness and discreetness. However, the leader-manager's boss is looking for the same behaviors in the leader-manager as the leader-manager looks for in her subordinates. These behaviors include integrity, consistency of behavior, and technical competence.

Development of Organizational Trust

Developing organizational trust starts with the leader-manager. In studies of organizational trust, the leader's behavior was more important than that of followers' in setting a trusting tone in the group (Boss 1978; Zand 1972). Common sense confirms this research. It is difficult to imagine a staff nurse being the pivotal developer of trust in a nursing organization. The responsibility starts with the top and filters down through all levels of nursing management. Although the formula for building trust is somewhat simplified (trust begets trust), trusting and believing in the trustworthiness of others is not always an easy task.

Building and maintaining organizational trust occurs over time. The nature of the trust becomes more concrete and differentiated as people come to know one another better. Four stages of trust development have been described:

Stage 1. Early in the working relationship there is initial impression making and mutual orientation with general clarification of expectations.

Stage 2. Stage 1 is followed by more intense exploration and learning with more specific, in-depth clarification of expectations, including the discovery of the other person's expectations and articulation of one's own.

Stage 3. During this stage of tacit testing of mutual expectations, the eight sources of trust are tested to determine in which specific areas a person can or cannot be trusted. For example, the leader-manager may learn that a particular subordinate is consistent and reliable in the technical aspects of nursing care, but that this person does not enjoy good relationships with peers. Thus, the individual cannot be trusted in this regard.

Stage 4. The relationship stabilizes unless some new or different information is presented to the parties in the relationship (Gabarro 1978, 301-302).

Managing Organizational Trust

Three Assumptions that Create Mistrust

Barnes (1986) described three assumptions which, acting together, can lead to pervasive mistrust in an organization. The first assumption, "either/

or" thinking, limits decisions to two options and stifles creativity. People therefore view an issue in only one of two ways and do not consider alternatives. A popular illustration of this is exemplified in the decision whether to centralize or decentralize a nursing organization. When there is a focus on centralizing versus decentralizing, the result might be that other alternatives are overlooked. In this case, two alternatives may be the modification of either design or a matrix design.

An even more serious effect of "either/or" thinking is that it places people on two sides of an issue with emotional overtones attached to each option. The two sides become marked as "good" and "bad," leading to a "we versus they" relationship. If the leader-manager then labels her choice as "good" and attacks and criticizes those who do not agree with her view, she sets up adversarial relationships. This leads to a climate of distrust.

Unfortunately, this climate is frequently a part of nursing organizations: labor versus management, nursing staff versus nursing administration, and nursing administration versus nursing education. However, in order for a nursing department to be powerful and strong and to successfully compete for organizational resources, the "we versus they" environment cannot exist. The nurse executive is only as strong and successful as the support, trust, and respect she receives from the rest of the nursing department.

The second assumption described by Barnes is the principle that hard facts and data are better than "soft" feelings and abstract possibilities. In order to defend an "either/or" choice, leaders may look for facts, figures, and short-term tangible results. In today's climate of cost containment, this tendency is particularly strong. For instance, bottom-line financial figures may guide many decisions..

Again, as a result of this assumption, people within the organization take sides—facts versus feelings. Consequently, leaders might adopt a nonproductive behavior style such as a "wheeler dealer" or "hard nose, shoot from the hip, buccaneer" approach in order to defend an "either/or" choice. These behaviors, combined with ignoring feelings and soft data, further contribute to organizational distrust.

The third assumption, that the world is a dangerous place, entrenches feelings of organizational distrust. People approach relationships with one of two views: to trust someone until they prove they cannot be trusted or not to trust someone until they prove they can be trusted. If the second view is adopted, as has been demonstrated, relationships settle at a low level of trust.

In order to develop organizational trust, the leader should first be aware of these three assumptions and how they operate within the organization. These assumptions should be replaced with alternative ones. The new assumptions should not be the exact opposites of the three that lead to organizational distrust. In fact, the three exact alternatives, ambiguity in decision making, soft feelings, and pervasive trust, are likewise not consistent with organizational success.

"And/Also" Thinking and Paradoxical Actions

By adopting a view that "things are not always what they seem" and style of "and/also" thinking and behaviors (such as listening, exploring, and confronting), the leader will be helped in a search for options and alternatives. At the same time, she will demonstrate a sense of care for the organization and concern for other people.

In order to be an "and/also" thinker, Barnes prescribed the use of *paradoxical actions*. A paradox is "any conclusion which at first sounds absurd but that has an argument to sustain it," although the arguments are often buried, ignored, or brushed over quickly (Quince 1976, 1). Paradoxical actions involve adopting a viewpoint where the elements in a particular situation are kept separate, but are not assumed to necessarily be in conflict. These actions also help the leader-manager cope with new information, confront important discrepancies, and care for individual people and issues.

In nursing management the leader-manager is often confronted with considering two concerns: the goals of the organizationa and those of nursing. The nurse leader-manager can view an issue solely from the nursing perspective or solely from the organizational perspective. This then becomes an "either/or" situation in which the leader-manager risks loosing the trust of either the nursing staff or her superior. To be an "and/also" thinker, the nurse leader-manager can seek solutions to issues that are best for nursing and also for the organization.

For example, what the nursing staff believes is a desirable new technology (e.g., the Clinitron bed) to provide good patient care and what the organization can afford may be totally different. To some nurses, the idea of systematically rationing this technology may at first seem absurd because only a few years ago third-party payors would assume the cost of the technology without question. But when sound criteria are developed for applying the technology, the solution becomes more acceptable and appealing. If managed appropriately, the needs of both the organization and the nursing staff can be satisfied.

Neither pervasive distrust nor pervasive trust is healthy for an organization; both lead to inflexibility. Organizations with too much distrust lack unity and people succumb to "either/or thinking" and prefer "hard versus soft" data. However, organizations with blind trust become overly integrated and people lapse into prolonged ambiguity and "soft is better than hard" behavior. Both extremes rely on emotions rather than on data and self-awareness. Barnes recommended adopting tentative trust by adopting these paradoxical actions: 1) viewing the elements in the organization as both certain and uncertain; 2) dividing and blending these elements; 3) seeing questions in answers; 4) viewing a situation from both inside and outside; 5) learning while teaching; and 6) finding unity in opposites and opposites in unity.

For example, in deciding about the use of the aforementioned Clinitron beds, the leader-manager should ask the following questions about the organization and about the nursing staff. What are the financial limitations on the use of the bed? Is this a real estimate of the resources or are there some additional funds available? Has the nursing staff accurately predicted need for the bed? Is there a danger the bed could be a substitute for basic nursing care? Is the bed as effective as the manufacturer states? If the nursing staff is correct in their estimate, what are the financial implications? Is there a way to meet the estimated needs through means other than the capital budget?

This line of questioning can continue until the nurse leader-manager has a firm grasp on all the elements in the situation. Through this thorough examination, the leader-manager can glean those elements which are certain and those which are not; blend the elements or pull them apart; continue to question and learn in the process; and find a unifying solution.

A Research Perspective on Trust and Organizational Effectiveness

It is evident from the following review of research findings that without trust organizations cannot be excellent. Trust affects many aspects of an organization including the individuals, the effectiveness of the leader, motivation and satisfaction of the staff, performance, decision making, and communications.

Individuals

Trustful individuals are more innovative and creative, more emotionally stable, and have more self-control than distrustful individuals. They are less likely to feel the need to psychologically defend themselves against real or perceived threats (Rogers 1961). A trusted person is highly influential. At the same time this individual has a low need to control others and is open to influence by others. A trusting person has high self-esteem, the single most important characteristic of successful leaders (Frost, Stimpson, and Maughan 1978, 107). There are additional positive characteristics of trustful people: they are more dependable, more likeable, and better adjusted psychologically than persons who do not trust (Rotter 1980, 35).

Leadership Effectiveness

A leader-manager cannot be a transformational leader unless she is trusted by followers. The leader-manager's ability to appeal to the values of followers is directly related to whether she is trusted by them. For example, her ability to define a vision and commit people to it cannot occur unless the leader-manager herself is credible and demonstrates the eight sources of trust (Table 8-1).

Motivation and Satisfaction

Organizational trust is the best predictor of overall job satisfaction and in satisfaction with participation in decision making. The environmental climate of the organization is more important in determining satisfaction than a person's background or than the individual's participation in decisions (Driscoll 1978, 50). When distrust exists in an organization, people need outside pressure to motivate them. When trust exists, people are motivated from the inside out by being self-directed (Tannenbaum and Davis 1969, 76).

Performance

Trust has a positive effect on both individual and group performance in organizations. High trust stimulates high performance. In turn, high performance reinforces trust. Generally, a subordinate will respond positively with high performance in response to a superior's genuine confidence in him. This high performance will beget a higher level of trust by the superior (Haney 1967, 12). Further, trust enhances the performance of groups. Groups in which members have a high degree of trust in one another are more effective than groups composed of distrustful individuals (Friedlander 1970, 397).

Problem Solving/Decision Making

Zand (1972) designed an experimental research project with two groups: one having low levels of trust and one having high levels of trust. He found that in groups with a high level of trust, problem solving was more effective. Specifically, the high trust group exchanged relevant ideas; searched extensively for alternate courses of action; exerted influence on solutions; were satisfied with the problem solving efforts; possessed motivation to implement decisions; saw themselves as a team; and had little desire to leave the group.

Communication

Both the frequency and accuracy of communications are functions of trust. Good communication leads to more consensus of opinion and to more accurate perceptions about one another's views. In the absence of trust, communications tend to exaggerate differences and to diminish consensus of opinion. Distortion of communication occurs if the transmitter of information is distrusted (Mellinger 1956).

Implications for Nursing

In this chapter, the important issue of organizational trust has been reviewed from a variety of perspectives. Trust is essential for organizational success. It is a vital ingredient for nursing departments to thrive. The task of developing and maintaining trust falls heavily on the shoulders of the nurse leader-manager. There are some practical leadership behaviors that will build, enhance, and maintain trusting relationships in nursing departments. However, there are no set formulas that automatically guarantee trust.

Trust is built every day and in every situation. It is developed through formal mechanisms such as meetings with groups or with individuals and through activities such as budget preparations, determining goals, or preparing reports and strategic plans. More often it is done during the day-to-day, routine interactions and decision making. In this setting, expectations are often made explicit and immediate feedback occurs.

Building trust starts with an awareness of its importance to organizational success and of the devastation caused by distrust. Trusting others is not trite, superfluous behavior. It involves deep soul searching about one's beliefs about others in the organization. The leader-manager can reflect on the question, "Do I trust others?" If the answer is no she should explore why she does not.

Trust, like other human behaviors, is enhanced by expectations. If the leader-manager believes others are lazy and not trustworthy, others will respond to her as such. However, if the leader-manager behaves in such a way to show that she expects trust from others, she will receive it.

Steps in Building Trust

The *first* step in building trust is to assess the strength of its presence in the organization. Figure 8-2 is an assessment questionnaire that can be used to do this. It is not only a useful tool for the leader-manager to use for her own purposes, but it can also be used to assess the level of trust in a group. Ironically, however, a leader-manager's comfort in using the tool to assess group trust may be a function of how trusting the group is initially.

The *second* step in building trust is to treat people with respect, courtesy, care, and concern. This advice is well worn, but often unheeded. Again, the leader-manager has to examine her personal value system and beliefs about people. Trust begets trust. The leader-manager is thus the first to trust and to adopt appropriate trusting behaviors.

Trusting behaviors are ones which support followers, peers, and superiors. Support means giving people both help and freedom in order for them to achieve. At the same time, the leader-manager should be cognizant of the need for people to maintain a sense of personal worth and self-esteem.

By supporting both cooperation among group members and the independence of the individual, the leader-manager further builds trust. To do this the leader-manager can use several techniques. She can support the individual and the group by giving them information and resources to accomplish goals. Although in some cases follow-up may be necessary to ensure that people do not get distracted from working on mutually agreed upon goals, the leader-manager balances this by stepping back and observing. Interfering inappropriately squashes initiative. By encouraging people

How much trust is there in the organization? In order to get an idea, circle your responses to these 13 questions on a scale of 1-5, with 5 indicating the highest degree.

1. How willingly is information shared among the group? (1 2 3 4 5)

2. How much do you trust others to use information that you share for the good of yourself as well as for themselves or the department? (1 2 3 4 5)

3. How free do people feel to be themselves even in competitive struggles? (1 2 3 4 5)

4. How much mutual support do you give one another? (1 2 3 4 5)

5. How much mutual respect does the group have? (1 2 3 4 5)

6. How much empathetic understanding of others' positions is there? (1 2 3 4 5)

7. To what extent do people reserve judgment while respecting complexity and subtlety? (1 2 3 4 5)

8. To what extent is there an openness to look at motives? (1 2 3 4 5)

9. How much are helpful (nonmanipulative) motives prized? (1 2 3 4 5)

10. How much of an attempt is there to flatten the traditional hierarchical line and staff structure? (1 2 3 4 5)

11. Are people and the mission of the nursing department seen as compatible? (1 2 3 4 5)

12. To what extent is stability of jobs a goal of the nursing department? (1 2 3 4 5)

13. How much bureaucratic inflexibility is there? (1 2 3 4 5)

Figure 8-2 Questionnaire to assess organizational trust. *Source:* Britton, P. R. and J. W. Stalling. 1986. *Leadership is empowering people.* Lanham, MD: University Press of America

to work together not only for the benefit of the organization but also for themselves will also build trust.

Delegating also demonstrates trust in a very concrete, measurable way. It is, in fact, an act of trust. By giving people power, authority, and responsibility, the leader-manager enhances another's self-esteem and places her trust in them.

The leader-manager's subtle reactions to others speak loudly. Negating others' viewpoints, criticizing others' work or behaviors, and nonverbal reactions of disapproval all send messages to others in the organization. If a particular employee is deemed to be "out of favor," she will have difficulty securing the cooperation and trust of others. Being sensitive to one's own subtle messages about others and sending only positive ones is another technique to use to build trust within the group.

Successful transformational leaders rarely use punishment and disapproval as techniques of control. They should be sparingly and thoughtfully used. If a person makes a mistake, look for something they did right and compliment them on that. Showing someone how to avoid the mistake in the future builds both trust and self-esteem of the other person.

A *third* step is to communicate openly and honestly. The leader-manager needs to communicate not only facts, but also feelings of both encouragement and disappointment. In other words, the leader-manager should show her humanness. The leader-manager should share all information except that which is confidential or harmful to divulge. Deciding what is harmful to divulge is not easy since each situation is different.

Within the group, people need to feel comfortable in exploring and expressing differences of opinion. Thus, the group norm should not be to criticize others who express unpopular ideas or bring out negative information. In fact, even poor ideas should not be penalized.

Fourth, one of the expectations of people in leadership roles is that they will fulfill their fiduciary responsibilities. This means that one cannot take advantage of her managerial position. There should be a sense of fairness for all.

A *fifth* technique to build trust is to be consistent. This can be achieved by keeping the vision of the department always in mind and using it in decision making and when taking actions. By clarifying expectations and giving people a clear sense of goals, the leader-manager ensures consistency and competency.

Sixth, by always being genuine with people, the leader-manager maintains her integrity and honesty and therefore the trust of her followers. Some popular ways of not being genuine are to test people by withholding information or setting up an event to see their reactions. Another way is to spy on people rather than getting information directly from the source.

These steps to build organizational trust in nursing departments are neither new nor inspirational. However, the leader-manager needs to consistently apply these techniques. To do this she needs to take the time to think before acting and to consider how her words and behaviors will convey to others her trust in them.

Application to Nursing Practice: Case Study

The Setting

The setting is a 500-bed medical center in the Northeast which offers medical, surgical, and psychiatric services on an inpatient and outpatient basis. The medical center is a public facility serving patients from a lower socioeconomic background within a 100-mile radius of the medical center. The medical center is affiliated with a nearby prestigious medical school.

The nursing department consists of 21 nursing units including two ICUs, a dialysis unit, an operating room, acute medical surgical units, and acute psychiatry. Additionally, ambulatory care services are provided. The major problem facing the department is low morale with an RN turnover rate of 35 percent.

The nursing department is centralized. The current organizational chart is displayed in Figure 8-3.

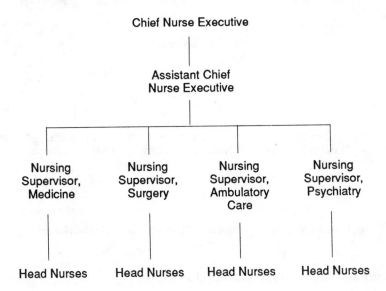

Figure 8-3 Current organizational chart.

The chief nurse executive (CNE) is new to her position, having assumed the role six months ago. This is her first position as a top nurse executive. The previous CNE was rigid and believed in a centralized structure. She seemed to have little influence in the department; the nursing education department and the assistant chief had the most influence.

The CNE firmly believes in a decentralized structure, a belief she has expressed since beginning her new position. She is concerned about the large turnover of staff and the 20 percent vacancy rate. She feels these situations are due to poor leadership in the past.

Current Situation

After six months, the CNE has determined that it is time to flatten the hierarchical chart. She is proposing the organizational chart picture in Figure 8-4. She has hired one person to fill the current position of Supervisor of Critical Care with the intention of promoting her to the position of Director of Nursing Services in the new structure. This new supervisor and the CNE worked together in a previous hospital. They are seen by the assistant chief and nurse educators as having a close friendship as well.

At a meeting of the nursing management staff, the CNE proposed the new organization chart. Positions for all displaced current supervisors had

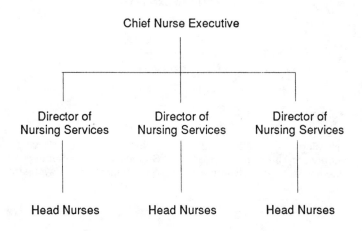

Figure 8-4 Proposed organizational chart.

been previously discussed with the people affected. In the meeting the nursing educators were very vocal about decentralization. They voiced many concerns about the head nurses and felt that they were not capable of assuming additional, more sophisticated responsibilities including budgeting, hiring staff, and overtime approval. They cited many problems, especially poor clinical care.

The CNE countered these concerns stating that the new structure would improve communications, strengthen the head nurses, and ultimately improve satisfaction. Citing the large turnover and vacancy rate, the CNE stated firmly, "Something has got to change." She suggested that the nursing education department would have to assume responsibility for head nurse development along with the directors of nursing.

The meeting ended with two clashing sides evident: the new guard striving for decentralization and the old guard striving to maintain the status quo.

After the meeting, the CNE talked to the new critical care supervisor about what had occurred. The CNE said that she did not trust the nursing educator and believed they would attempt to undermine any changes.

Case Study Discussion

1. How would you assess the level of trust in this situation?

2. Using the assessment tool in Figure 8-2, answer questions 1, 3, 5, 6, 8, 10, 12, and 13 for this situation.

3. Assume you are one of the nursing education instructors. How would you rate the CNE in each of the eight sources of trust, i.e., integrity, intentions and motives, openness and discreetness, consistency and reliability, technical competence, interpersonal skills, business sense, and judgement?

4. What "hard" facts or figures did the nurse executive use to support her argument? In contrast, what "soft" information did the nurse educators use?

5. How could the CNE have avoided the "we versus they" confrontation?

6. What can the CNE do to repair the damage?

References

Barber, B. 1983. *The logic and limits of trust.* New Brunswick, NJ: The Rutgers University Press.

Barnes, L. B. 1986. Managing the paradox of organizational trust. In *The leader-manager,* ed. J. N. Williamson, 465-478. New York: John Wiley and Sons.

Boss, R. W. 1978. Trust and managerial problem solving revisited. *Group and Organizational Studies* 3:331-332.

Driscoll, J. D. 1978. Trust and participation in organizational decision making as predictors of satisfaction. *Academy of Management Journal* 21(1):44-56.

Deutsch, M. 1962. Cooperation and trust: Some theoretical notes. In *Nebraska symposium on motivation,* ed. M. R. Jones, 275-320. Lincoln, NE: University of Nebraska Press.

Erikson, E. H. 1950. *Childhood and society.* New York: W. W. Norton and Company.

Friedlander, F. 1970. The primacy of trust as a facilitator of further group accomplishment. *Journal of Applied Behavior Science* 6:387-407.

Frost, T., D. V. Stimpson, and M. R. Maughan. 1979. Some correlates of trust. *The Journal of Psychology* 99(5):103-108.

Gabarro, J. J. 1978. The development of trust, influence, and expectations. In *Interpersonal behavior: Communications and understanding in relationships,* ed. A. G. Athos and J. J. Gabarro, 290-303. Englewood Cliffs, NJ: Prentice Hall.

Haney, W. V. 1967. *Communication and organizational behavior: Text and cases.* Homewood IL: Richard J. Irwin, Inc.

Luhman, N. 1980. *Trust and power.* New York: John Wiley and Sons.

Mellinger, G. D. 1956. Interpersonal trust as a factor in communications. *Journal of Abnormal Psychology* 52:304-309.

Quince, W. V. 1976. *The ways of paradox.* Cambridge: Harvard University Press.

Rogers, C. 1961. *On becoming a person: A therapist's view of psychotherapy.* Boston: Houghton Miffin.

Rotter, J. B. 1980. Trust and gullibility. *Psychology Today* 14(15):35-40, 104.

Tannenbaum, R., and S. A. Davis. 1969. Values, man, and organizations. *Industrial Management Review* 10(2):67-86.

Zand, D. E. 1972. Trust and managerial problem solving. *Administrative Science Quarterly* 17(2):229-239.

9

Leadership and Self-Esteem

Chapter Objectives

1. Define self-esteem.
2. Discuss how self-esteem is developed.
3. Utilize visualization and affirmations to enhance one's self-esteem.
4. Discuss ways that self-esteem is damaged.
5. Discuss how to develop the self-esteem of others.
6. Cite an example of a self-fulfilling prophecy.

Introduction

The next three chapters discuss the most important tool the leader-manager has available for transformational leadership—herself. Although leader-managers seldom think of themselves as tools, they are. Like any other tool, the more a person knows about it, the more effective they will be in achieving results. Thus, a vital element of leadership is self-awareness and self-development.

Definition of Self-Esteem

The most essential personal trait of successful leaders is having a positive self-regard (Bennis and Nanus 1985, 57). Defining this is difficult. Maslow's (1970, 45-46) classic definition of esteem needs is a useful way to look at positive self-regard. Self-esteem is a stable, firmly-based, usually high evaluation of self, or self-respect. It includes the need for achievement, mastery, competence, confidence, independence, and freedom to act. Satisfaction of self-esteem needs results in feelings of self-confidence, worth, strength, capability, adequacy, and being useful and necessary.

Maslow warned that it is dangerous to base self-esteem on the opinions of others. Rather, it must generate from real capacity, competence, and adequacy of task performance. These competencies and achievements must come from one's inner self. They do not occur out of sheer will power or determination to satisfy someone else's demands. A simpler definition of self-esteem, proposed by Waitley (1978, 17), an expert in the area of self-esteem and the psychology of success, is "a deep down, inside the self feeling of your own worth."

There are two methods to quickly diagnose one's self-esteem. First, the leader-manager can recall her internal response to making mistakes. If the most common response to a mistake is one of berating the self and telling the self, "I'm stupid" or "I can never do anything right," the person's self-esteem may not be at its optimum. A person with high self-esteem might respond much differently: "I goofed this one time, but I learned from it." A second technique to assess one's level of self-esteem is to think about interactions with other people. If a person continually kids others about their weaknesses, their own self-esteem is usually low. A person with high self-esteem looks for the strengths in others and compliments and "strokes" them (Rinke 1988).

Self-esteem is not ego self-centeredness, cockiness, or self-worship. It is a common misconception that "great leaders produce big results, and to produce big results you must have a big ego." Ego, in that context, means an overemphasis on self and personal self-aggrandizement. People with this type of ego development use the organization and the people in it for personal gain, whether it be financial or emotional (Ritscher 1986, 68).

A leader who has a positive self-regard greatly benefits the organization for whom she works. Leaders with positive self-regard create an atmosphere of excellence and greatness, but the most significant result of positive self-esteem in a leader is a positive regard for others. This is a pivotal factor in the ability of the leader to lead. A positive regard for others creates in them a sense of confidence and higher expectations. Confident employees can better use their talents and skills for organizational success.

Development of Self-Esteem

How people think about themselves has its foundation in the repeated thematic messages they receive from significant authorities. This is true particularly in the first 12 years of life. These authorities may be parents, teachers, other family members, ministers and other religious leaders, friends, and so forth. Some of the messages received are positive and some are negative, but they all provide the premise for how one feels about oneself. In one study of children who were tape recorded for several days, the psychologist investigators found that over 90 percent of what children were told was negative—either what they could not do or how what they were doing was wrong (Fritz 1986, 163). These negative messages are unwittingly programmed into one's mind. To counterbalance these negative messages accumulated over time, the leader-manager can tell herself positive ones to enhance her self-esteem. In other words, the leader-manager (and, in fact, anyone) can act or think as if a different premise about herself is true.

Affirmations and Visualization

The subconscious mind records everything one experiences and has been told. It cannot distinguish between images, perceptions, or actual experiences. It also cannot distinguish between right and wrong. In other words, if a person tells her subconscious that she is good at some particular task, the mind cannot distinguish if it is true or not. However, if a person assumes that she is unable to do something, she will most likely be unable to do it.

To counteract negative ideas and thoughts, the leader-manager can "reprogram" her subconscious using affirmations and visualization. Exactly how these techniques work is not known. However, much of people's actions are subconsciously motivated. Stated another way, people's behavior is a result of their thinking. Therefore, what a person affirms or visualizes becomes a part of their consciousness. This helps them bring about what they think about.

Affirmations. These are positive messages about oneself which, when repeated over and over again, the subconscious mind believes are true. Positive affirmations can become reality and govern behaviors in positive ways. One leader-manager used this technique to remember names. Over and over again, she told herself, "I can remember people's names." In a relatively short period of time, she was able to overcome her bad habit of forgetting people's names.

Visualization. This is the natural power of the brain to create an idea or mental picture. Unlike verbal images, the human mind can recall visual images with a great deal of accuracy. To maximize this human potential, images can also be used to reprogram the brain. It is often culturally unacceptable to fantasize and dream, especially in the workplace. However, the use of and the importance of visualization is becoming widely recognized. It is being used for may purposes such as the treatment of disease, weight loss, and developing athletic skills. In management, visualization can be used for increasing one's self-esteem, making decisions, and managing time.

Real visualization is not daydreaming, but rather it is picturing and imagining a future event. When visualizing, the use of all five senses is recommended. First, the leader-manager pictures an event that she desires. The desired end should be a realistic, credible goal, but one that may seem slightly out of reach, something for which to strive.

For example, the nurse leader-manager may wish to be the driving force behind a new program to enhance the quality of patient care throughout the hospital. She can use visualization to "rehearse" her argument to the chief executive officer and other department heads. While visualizing the scenario, she would use all five senses, picturing the setting, hearing her voice, smelling the air, feeling the upholstery of the chair and even tasting the coffee. She should further visualize the successful acceptance of her proposal by the others.

Other Methods to Develop Self-Esteem

Three further methods for developing a high self-regard are to: 1) recognize one's strengths and weaknesses and learn ways to compensate for weaknesses; 2) nurture one's talents and skill with discipline, and set high goals and objectives for oneself; and 3) recognize the fit between one's perceived talents and what the organization requires (Bennis and Nanus 1985, 58).

Having positive self-expectations is another key factor in the development of high self-esteem. A phenomenon called the *Wallenda Factor* illustrates this. Carl Wallenda, a successful tightrope artist for many years, fell to his death during a performance in San Juan as a result of focusing too much of his attention on the upcoming feat and worrying about possible failure. The Wallenda Factor is the capacity to embrace positive goals, to expect success, and to pour one's energy into the task. It discounts the value of looking back at past failures or believing one will fail (Bennis and Nanus 1985, 69-71).

Damage to Self-Esteem

One of the biggest detriments to one's self-esteem is the perceived need to be perfect and the avoidance of making mistakes. Since no one is and can be perfect, this is an unrealistic standard against which to measure oneself. The perfectionist never lives up to her own expectations, and so often feels a sense of failure which then lowers her self-esteem.

People with high self-esteem do not want to fail. However, when they do fail, they recognize that failure is sometimes inevitable. In fact, people who never experience failure are probably not trying hard enough and are not taking enough risks. People with high self-esteem are able to capture the energy from failure to reach higher goals.

In nursing, our heritage and socialization often demand perfection. Florence Nightingale, in order to counteract the negative stereotype of nurses, demanded that nurses were of good character and rigidly adhere to procedures. Although this demand is lessened in today's environment, there remain remnants of this belief within the profession. Although nursing must maintain high standards, rigid enforcement of procedures and expectations of perfection can damage individual self-esteem.

Further, nurses encounter negative messages about the profession and their work almost daily. The nursing shortage results in the recitation of a long list of woes. Words such as "powerlessness" and "handmaiden" damage the self-esteem of nurses. Nurses themselves perpetuate this list of negatives. Further, the media, especially television, continues to portray a negative image of nursing. Nurses on television are generally portrayed as handmaidens to physicians, sexual objects, or "battle axes." To counteract this negativity, nurses can adopt visualization and affirmation techniques to tell themselves positive messages about nursing.

Developing Self-Esteem in Others

The leader-manager has an awesome responsibility. As the leader of others, she has the task of enhancing the self-esteem of the people she supervises. Obviously, since self-esteem begins early in life, the leader-manager is not totally responsible for others' level of self-esteem. She can, however, play an important role in either diminishing or enhancing the self-esteem of people, particularly in the area of their work competency and mastery. For organizational success, the leader-manager can create in others a sense of confidence and high expectations.

There are two positive outcomes of enhancing the self-esteem of followers: increased productivity of people and enhancement of the leader's self-esteem. People with high self-esteem who feel good about their work will be more productive. Secondly, when a leader-manager treats others with respect and expects success, their self-esteem will increase. As previously discussed, people with high self-esteem have a high regard for others. If the followers' self-esteem is increased, this will result in their having a higher regard for the leader. This feeds back to the leader and increases her self-esteem (Rinke 1988, 14).

One technique used to enhance the self-esteem of others is to look for people who are performing well and to publicly recognize them for accomplishments (Rinke 1988, 14). This technique is opposed to the traditional management practices which focus on negative performance and discipline, rather than on positive performance and rewards.

Self-Fulfilling Prophecy

The Pygmalion effect, or self-fulfilling prophecy, was named after a Greek sculptor who molded a beautiful statue named Galatea. Pygmalion fell in love with the statue and willed her to come alive. Later, George Bernard Shaw wrote the play, *Pygmalion*, which was later made into a Broadway show and movie, *My Fair Lady*. In one scene, Eliza Doolittle best explains the Pygmalion phenomenon:

> You see, really and truly, apart from the things anyone can pick up (the dressing and the proper way of speaking, and so on), the difference between a lady and a flower girl is not how she behaves, but how she's treated. I shall always be a flower girl to Professor Higgins, because he always treats me as a flower girl, and always will; but I know I can be a lady to you, because you always treat me as a lady and always will (1948, 270).

The essence of the Pygmalion effect is that a person, by his will and effort, can transform another person through one person's expectations of another. People live up to the subtle, at times unconscious, expectations of others. It is called a self-fulfilling prophecy because one person's expectation of another person's behavior, quite unwittingly, becomes a more accurate prediction of behavior, simply by having been made (Rosenthal and Jacobson 1968, vii).

Stated another way and applied to management, if the leader-manager sets high, realistic, and achievable expectations for productivity and performance, people will live up to them. Yet, when the leader-manager has low or negative expectations of others, they will have great difficulty in maintaining their self-esteem. Thus, to avoid further damage to their self-esteem, people will avoid situations in which they might fail. This becomes the self-fulfilling prophecy—low expectations and damaged self-esteem lead people to behave in a manner that fulfills the expectation or prophecy.

Livingston (1969) suggested that there is scientific evidence to support the existence of this phenomenon in business organizations. In his research, he found that:

- The expectations that a manager has of subordinates directly affects their organizational performance and career progress.

- Superior managers have a unique ability to be able to create high-performance expectations for subordinates. This characteristic seems to spring from the manager's confidence in her own skills to develop others.

- Conversely, less effective managers fail to expect the same level of high performance. Consequently, people do not perform as well. These managers have less confidence in their own abilities to set high expectations.

- Subordinates, most often, will behave in the way they think they are expected to behave.

It is the behaviors, not the verbal communication, of the leader-manager which transmit feelings of positive or negative expectation. Merely hiding negative feelings will not work to avoid transferring negative expectations.

Implications for Nursing

The promotion of one's self-esteem and the self-esteem of others is important to organizational success. Specific techniques to enhance one's self-esteem—affirmations and visualization—should be practiced. The techniques, although not time-consuming, need to become a part of one's daily routine. The more they are used, the easier and more effective they are.

Self-esteem is a key element in the theoretical framework of transformational leadership and in the design of the leadership strategies previously discussed. Some techniques may not directly develop self-esteem in others; however, they do not damage self-esteem. Such techniques include listening to people, giving people credit for their ideas and accomplishments, and using rewards appropriately.

Most importantly, the leader-manager must make a conscious effort to focus on the positive, the innovative, and the creative. Practicing this approach is important. The leader-manager needs to focus not only on positive individual performance, but also on the positives of the entire department and the nursing profession. Further, giving people sincere, warm complements is important. That is, telling people that they did a good job will make them feel good, but telling them that they are enjoyable to work with will make them feel even better.

Seemingly simple decisions might give subtle, unconscious, negative messages to people. This possibility presents a real dilemma for the nurse leader-manager. Often only a few people can be given responsibility for a particular desirable task or inclusion in a prestigious event. Sharing the perquisites and including everyone in a manner that is equitable and not damaging to people's esteem takes thoughtful consideration. When making decisions about these issues, the leader manager should have a clear understanding of what is and what is not viewed as desirable and prestigious by the staff.

Application to Nursing Practice: Case Study

The Setting

Recently, Barbara Atkinson was selected as the new vice president for nursing in an active, urban healthcare center in the Northeast. When she was interviewed for the position, she became concerned about the center's nursing recruitment activities. Considering herself an expert in this area, prior to reporting to her new position, Barbara wrote the nurse recruiter asking her for information about recruitment efforts, statistics on hires, sophisticated turnover data, budgets, and a recruitment plan.

Current Situation

On the day Barbara started in the position of Vice President of Nursing, she received a resignation from the nurse recruiter who left two weeks later. The vice president immediately began recruitment for the position. Five internal applicants who held head nurse positions applied for and were interviewed by Barbara for the job. All five candidates were excellent in their role and were looking for advancement.

After interviewing the five candidates, Barbara discussed each applicant with the three directors of nursing, one of which had been the acting vice president. Although the directors of nursing supported one individual for the position, Barbara chose another person who had actively been involved in recruitment in the past. The decision came as a surprise to the directors. At that time, the directors expressed their concern that the person chosen to be the nurse recruiter was not organized and could not handle the massive paperwork appropriately.

Case Study Discussion

1. How could Barbara perhaps have prevented the resignation of the first nurse recruiter?

2. How can she explain her choice to those people not selected without damaging their self-esteem?

3. What might be a self-fulfilling prophecy in this situation?

References

Bennis, W., and B. Nanus. 1985. *Leaders: The strategies for taking charge.* New York: Harper and Row.

Fritz, R. 1986. The leader as creator. In *Transforming leadership: From vision to results,* ed. J. D. Adams, 159-182. Alexandria, VA: Miles River Press.

Livingston, J. S. 1969. Pygmalion in management. *Harvard Business Review* 47(3):81-89.

Maslow, A. 1970. *Motivation and personality*, 2d ed. New York: Harper and Row.

Rinke, W. J. 1988. Maximizing management potential by building self-esteem. *Management Solutions* 33(3):11-17.

Ritscher, J. 1986. Spiritual leadership. In *Transforming leadership: From vision to results*, ed. J. D. Adams, 61-80. Alexandria, VA: Miles River Press.

Rosenthal, R., and L. Jacobson. 1968. Pygmalion in the classroom. New York: Reinhart and Winston.

Shaw, G. B. 1948. Pygmalion. In *The selected plays of Bernard Shaw*. New York: Dodd Mead, and Co.

Waitley, D. 1978. *The psychology of winning*. Chicago: Nightengale-Conant.'

10

Thinking and Decision Making

Chapter Objectives

1. Differentiate between the functions of the left and right side of the brain.

2. Describe three mental abilities involved in decision making.

3. Discuss methods to improve one's analytical, synthesizing, and intuitive skills.

4. List five steps in the decision-making process.

5. Explain the pitfalls of each step.

6. Discuss the relationship of thinking and decision making to actions.

Introduction

Effective decision making is a key leadership skill for transformational leaders to be successful and to achieve excellence. Thinking and decision making are paired processes that lead to action:

Thinking   ⟶   Decision Making   ⟶   Action

Thus, effective decision making entails both effective thinking and effective action which is measured by the contribution of the action to the achievement of organizational success. In this chapter, all three components of this model—thinking, decision making, and acting—will be discussed.

Thinking

The brain has many powers such as logical thinking, sensing, judging, creativity, and intuition. The abilities of the brain that are specifically related to decision making, i.e., analyzing, synthesizing, and valuing, are examined in this section.

Understanding Brain Functioning

Current research on the "split brain" provides insight into how people think. The two sides of the brain, the right and left hemispheres, perform different types of mental activities. The right hemisphere functions in the recognition of visual patterns, remembering faces, rhythm, control of large motor movements, music, and imagination. The left hemisphere is involved in analytical processes such as logic, reasoning, mathematics, and the use of language. Physically, the two sides of the brain are connected by a four-inch long, pencil-shaped bundle of complex nerve fibers called the *corpus callosum*. The corpus callosum functions to integrate information from the two sides of the brain. How people use each side of the brain, how the two sides interconnect, and how people can develop both sides of the brain are the subjects of ongoing research.

People differ in how predominant one side of their brain is over the other. For example, when confronted with similar problems, some managers use an intuitive process and some a more analytical approach to problem solving (Dokter and Hamilton 1978). However, people can intentionally focus on the development of the functioning of either the right or left side of their brain. Research indicates that all areas of mental performance are enhanced by this focused development of the brain. (Buzan 1983, 14-15). For example, a person who wishes to develop the capacity of the right side of the brain for visualization may also find increased capacity for recalling events.

The work of cognitive scientists and the use of artificial intelligence have also contributed to the understanding of thinking and problem solving. Cognitive science involves the use of a "psychological laboratory" to observe human behaviors. Cognitive scientists propose that the memory holds information in patterns or sets, called *chunks*. Further, the memory stores these chunks of information in relationship to other stored chunks of information. The work done with artificial intelligence confirms this research. Digital computers are used to model human thought patterns and to perform problem-solving/decision-making functions at expert levels. Artificial intelligence has been used successfully in the areas of medical diagnosis, chemistry, and electronics. Artificial intelligence uses an analytical process that works in "if-then" pairs. The "if" is a set of conditions or patterns to be recognized by the computer. The "then" is a body of information associated with the "if." For example, in medical diagnosis, "if" the patient exhibits symptoms a, b, and c "then" the diagnosis is x. The "if-then" sequence of reasoning appears to be a universal scheme of thought and can be readily applied to management sciences (Simon 1987, 59-61).

Mental Abilities for Decision Making

As stated previously, the abilities of the brain that are used in decision making are analyzing, synthesizing, and valuing. These are all abilities that occur in the conscious mind. The work of Adair (1985) forms the basis for the following discussion of these abilities.

Analyzing. This mental ability enables a person to break the "total picture" into its parts. The following activities require analytical skills: 1) establishing the relationship of the parts (specifics) to one another and to the whole (general); 2) determining the causes of problems; 3) identifying issues upon which a decision rests; 4) discovering laws in nature; or 5) searching for the principles behind experiences.

Analytical skills are developed in school through academic work and are the skills most often taken for granted. However, because one's analytical skills can decline, the leader-manager is encouraged to continue to develop these skills in order to make sound decisions. To develop analytical skills, the leader-manager needs to question herself and others about the elements of the particular decision-making situation. First, she can ask the basic questions of who, where, when, why, how, which, and why not? These questions will lead to others that will help the leader-manager get to the heart of the problem.

Writing down the pros and cons of alternate courses of action is a visual way to organize facts and facilitate analytical thinking. By having information in writing, one can rearrange and restructure facts to realize the full scope of each option.

Knowledge of logic and logistical methods also helps the leader-manager to develop analytical skills. The science of logic is a prescribed method of drawing proper conclusions from information or premises. One of the major problems in managerial thought is basing logic and analysis on a false premise. Thus, understanding the logical method can assist the leader-manager to understand the importance of her premises.

There are two types of logical processes: inductive and deductive. Inductive logic is the process of deriving generalizations from specific data; this type of logic would be applied in nursing research. Oppositely, deductive logic is the process of drawing particular inferences from general information. The following is an example of deductive logic:

All coins are round. (major premise)
You have a coin in your pocket. (minor premise)
Your coin is round. (conclusion)

In this example, the major premise is wrong, i.e., all coins are not round. Yet the logic used could mislead one to believe that the conclusion is correct. Understanding the basic premises upon which her analytic processes are built will strengthen the leader-manager's analytical skills and the quality of any decisions.

For example, if a leader-manager bases her actions on the following premise, she will not realize success in accomplishing goals:

All nurses are powerless. (major premise)
I am a nurse. (minor premise)
I am powerless. (conclusion)

Synthesizing. This mental skill is the opposite of analyzing. It is the ability to see things as a whole by combining parts. Behind this mode of thought is the belief that the whole is greater than the sum of its parts. It may also be called *holistic thinking.* This type of thinking is not well understood. It involves conceptual thinking, imagination, and intuition. Intuition is the only mental skill discussed in this chapter which occurs in the subconscious part of one's mind.

Holistic thinking, balanced with analytical thinking, is important for the leader-manager. In order to avoid a too narrow view of the organization, she needs to view the nursing department and the organization as a whole.

One type of holistic thinking is *conceptual thinking.* A concept is something conceived in the mind to which the person attaches attributes. Conceptualization involves taking something concrete and making it more general. A person develops concepts by making them whole through life experiences. For example, people attach certain qualities and attributes to the concept of leader. *Boss* and *commander* are two synonyms for *leader* which do not fully portray the concept of leadership. Because of life experiences with leaders, bosses, and commanders, each concept has different meaning to the individual.

Another form of holistic thinking or synthesizing is *imaginative thinking*. This is a vital mental ability for innovation and creativity in management. Imagination has five components:

1. *Recall.* This is the ability to bring back to mind an idea of something not actually present to the senses, such as remembering one's twenty-first birthday.

2. *Visualization.* As discussed in the previous chapter, this is the ability to see or form a mental image of something which does not presently exist in its entirety.

3. *Creating.* This is the ability to form a mental image of something that has never existed, such as a new way to deliver nursing services.

4. *Foreseeing.* This is the ability to mentally see an event or result before it happens.

5. *Fantasy.* This is the ability to create a fanciful design or invention. It is done by altering or combining the elements of reality in a particularly unrestrained and extravagant way.

Holistic Thinking and the Leader-Manager. To develop the skills of holistical thinking, the leader-manager first develops an awareness of its importance. She then deliberately thinks about a situation holistically, i.e., she purposefully views the situation, the nursing department, and the organization as a whole. At the same time, she may also use some analytical skills to review the specifics of the situation.

Ideally, all the leader-managers within a nursing department should have similar concepts about nursing, quality, the nursing process, assessment, patient education, etc. Although this is not generally possible, it is important for all the leader-managers to discuss their concepts of the organization and the nursing department and their individual missions, strengths, and weaknesses. If they have similar concepts about the organization and the nursing department, decision making will be easier to accomplish as a team. Developing a vision statement as a group would be one excellent approach to stimulate discussion at the conceptual level.

To develop imagination, one must purposefully use it. For any problem situation, the nurse leader-manager can imagine ways of solving it. When purposefully using her imagination, she should refrain from using a solution that she can recall or one she read in a textbook. The technique of visualization can be used to develop imagination and strengthen thinking and decision making.

Valuing. This is a dimension of all thinking rather than a discrete entity. Valuing involves having a perception of the value, worth, or significance of something. It includes such mental abilities as judging, criticizing, and evaluating. Valuing helps to ensure the quality of thinking. It establishes the truth or reality of the situation and ensures consistency of values within the organization. As stated previously, thinking precedes action and for the action to be effective, the value of the thinking must be correct.

The Subconscious Mind

Until recently, the significance of the subconscious mind had not been intellectually respected. This was due to society's reliance on science and the highly rational scientific method. This attitude is now changing. Very few of a person's mental activities take place in the conscious level. Most of these activities such as reflexes, habitual behaviors, and psychological defense mechanisms take place at a subconscious level. Unconscious beliefs and values about oneself and one's environment affect behaviors. These beliefs can limit or strengthen capacities for success in every aspect of one's life including leadership abilities, relationships with others, the ability to heal illnesses, and effectiveness of communication.

Intuition

Intuition is the constant, "behind-the-scenes" processing of information and imagination. It is the power or faculty of the mind to immediately grasp that something is the case, without the intervention of any reasoning process. It manifests itself consciously as a "hunch" or "gut feeling." People also experience intuitive moments when something forgotten suddenly "pops" into their consciousness. Unfortunately, people seldom tap into their intuition and use it wisely.

How this inner mind works is not known. But what is known is that the more a person uses it and trusts it, the better it seems to perform (Harmon 1986, 107). Leader-managers can appeal to their intuition when developing their vision, when establishing relationships with people, when dealing with the complexities of designing the social architecture and when making decisions. Listening to and using one's intuitive mind should be balanced with rationality and logic. Checking an intuitive thought with common sense before acting is one technique to avoid misusing one's intuition. Intuition can be negatively affected by strong emotions and mental or physical stress. Thus, if the leader-manager wishes to follow her intuition, she needs to be feeling well and not under undue stress.

There are a variety of recommended techniques to access one's intuition and subconscious (Buckley and Steffy 1986, 235-240). These include the following:

1. If one's skills are rational thinking and logical thought processes, the leader-manager can take up a creative venture such as music or poetry. If the rational side of the brain needs developing, learning to use a computer or taking a logic course will strengthen left brain abilities.

2. *Nondesk thinking* is a term used to describe a break from left brain activities. This is done by being in a relaxing environment and pursuing a relaxing activity such as exercise. Following this interlude, leaders have reported more precise thinking, clearer vision, and even a pronounced sense of smell.

3. Consciously making a request of one's intuitive, subconscious mind is another technique. It can be used when the problem to be solved is clear and reduced to its most basic level. For example, the leader-manager can ask her subconscious who to select for a particular job once the options have been limited to two or three candidates. Following such a request, engaging in nondesk thinking is recommended. Sometimes the answer will just come into one's mind. At other times, the answer might be

found unexpectedly somewhere in the environment. For example, something someone says or an article in a magazine might trigger an idea that leads to the solution.

4. A similar technique is to ask the subconscious to work on a problem while sleeping. Sometimes the answer may come in a dream and at other times upon waking. As soon as the answer comes into the consciousness, the leader-manager should write it down or the thought may be lost.

5. Experimenting with inner listening is a technique which stops the left brain and starts the right one. This five-step framework facilitates inner listening:

   a. Let go of answers that one "thinks" is right.

   b. Empty the mind, quieting internal noise.

   c. Ask oneself a simple, specific question.

   d. Listen, do not pass judgment. (Steps a-d can be repeated several times).

   e. Examine the information rationally and act.

6. Self-talk or affirmation, reviewed in the previous chapter, is "reprogramming" a belief about oneself which is held in one's subconscious.

7. Self-suggestion is a similar technique which can be used to repeatedly remind oneself to refer all choices to the subconscious mind.

Reflective Thinking

One reason organizations are plagued with bad decisions may be that managers do not take time out for reflective thinking. Ritscher (1986, 65) proposed that:

The power of quiet and solidity cannot be overemphasized. The single largest problem in organizations is a kind of anxiety and low-grade confusion. Leaders often make decisions based on anxiety, ego, insufficient experience, and the slightly crazy atmosphere that frequently accompanies group decision-making. Such decisions are no match for ones made by going to a quiet place, steeping oneself in the nature of the problem, and using clarity of mind to uncover the right solution.

The value of reflection is that it slows down action and thus makes subsequent actions more thoughtful (Weick 1983). The nurse leader-manager needs to take time to reflect on the nursing department, the organization, and the profession. These moments of reflection can influence her decisions and improve their quality. The daily work of the nurse leader-manager seldom allows for this time. Further, often one wishes to "leave the work behind" when at home with family and friends. Yet the time used to reflect can be invaluable and should be scheduled into the leader-manager's time.

Decision Making

Levy and Loomba (1973, 169) defined decision making as:

the conclusion of a process by which one chooses among available alternatives for the purpose of achieving a set of desired objectives. Decision making involves all the thinking and activities that are required to produce a choice among alternative courses of action; it is the central activity of all human beings.

Decision-Making Models

Although there are a variety of decision-making models presented in nursing and management literature, they all have common elements which form the model proposed below. Some are presented as five- or six-step models; they differ according to how each activity is categorized. The following is a typical decision-making model:

1. *Identify the Problem.* Be aware that a problem exists in the organization that requires some action, i.e., recognize the need for a decision. This process involves the collection and assessment of data; an examination of facts and the opinions of others; identification of possible causes of the problem; and recognition of time and other resource constraints.

2. *Define Objectives.* Define a goal and develop standards to assess the options.

3. *Develop Alternate Courses of Action.* At this stage ideas for possible options are generated; the pros and cons of each alternative are listed; the consequences of each are examined and measured against the objective.

4. *Make a Decision and Implement It.* Select the best course of action and follow it through with action.

5. *Evaluate Results.* Monitor the results based on predetermined criteria and the objective; revise the decision, if necessary, by repeating Step 1.

A Closer Look at the Decision-Making Model

The model presented above is simplistic; the decision-making process does not necessarily proceed from Step 1 to Step 6. Often in real situations there is overlap and some steps are eliminated completely. Moreover, the model is seldom consciously used by managers in real life situations. However, effective decision making is the hallmark of good management and leadership. Therefore, even if the realities of the situation dictate not following a textbook prescription, the leader-manager needs to understand the pitfalls of decision making that lead to poor decisions.

First, there is no such thing as a perfect decision. An effective decision, or best decision, is one in which the leader-manager uses the resources available to her that enable her to best achieve the desired goals of the organization. The leader-manager is cognizant of this especially when searching for solutions and evaluating results of the decision.

Problem Identification. The first step, sensing a problem and giving it form, involves a great deal of skill and time. How the problem is eventually defined is the foundation upon which the entire process lies. If the problem definition is not correct then the solution will not be either. For example, if a nurse executive sees rivalry and fighting between two members of the department, she might label this as an interpersonal relationship problem. She might attribute the cause to the different educational backgrounds of the two. By defining the problem in this manner, her solution may be to call in a third party to mediate their differences. However, the real problem may be that one of the involved parties does not trust either the other person or the nurse executive. She may, in fact, be jealous of their relationship. This situation requires another type of intervention. In this case, the solution will need to involve the direct intervention of the nurse executive.

Stevens (1985, 173) used Dewey's approach to problem solving, viewing problem definition as the key to effective decision making. The following hypothetical situation illustrates the process of accurate problem definition.

On one nursing unit, there is exceptionally high turnover of registered nurses. The nurse executive has explored the environment to get an initial sense of the problem. Is the turnover related to the initial selection of people for the unit? Are the nursing care demands too strenuous? Is the problem the nursing leadership, the patient mix, or the way the medical staff treat the nurses? The first statement of the problem could be that the workload is too heavy and the time schedule too demanding of rotation. Based on this, the nurse executive resurveys the environment to see if these are truly the causes of the problem. This process of tentatively defining the problem, surveying the environment, and redefining the problem is repeated until the true cause of the turnover is determined.

In the example, it may be that the workload and time schedules are definite problems. (However, they may be symptoms of the problem rather than the problem itself.) The nurse executive, at this point, may have one or more solutions to the problem: close beds on the unit or hire two people for nights. Solutions are continuously suggested as the problem is defined and refined and as various solutions are implemented into the environment. A tentative solution may be tried and fail to correct the problem; this indicates that either the solution is wrong or the problem needs redefinition.

Defining Objectives. If there is a vision and goals to guide the process, defining objectives is one of the easier steps in decision making. In the above example, the objective of the decision may be to stabilize staffing on the unit as an indicator of high staff morale.

Developing Alternate Courses of Action. Generating ideas, developing alternate courses of action, listing pros and cons, and examining the consequences of each course of action form the core of the decision-making process. However, the process is fraught with difficulties. It is not possible or necessary to develop every possible course of action to a problem. It is more appropriate to develop *feasible* alternatives, i.e., those actions which are possible and realistic in view of available resources. Eliminating unfeasible alternatives helps the leader-manager to scan realistic options and evaluate them quickly (Adair 1985, 109).

However, the decision maker needs to search widely for feasible alternatives. By narrowing possibilities too soon, the leader-manager may inadvertently eliminate better, more creative options. Rather than limiting herself to one obvious "tried and true" alternative, the leader-manager should make a determined effort to come up with more than one alternative to any problem situation. Using one's imagination to construct assumptions is a good technique to generate options. For example, the leader-manager could imagine that there were more financial resources available or that the union would agree to an unusual scheme.

Brainstorming. Limiting options to feasible ones does not mean that *brainstorming* should not be used, but it should be used thoughtfully and in more complex situations. Brainstorming usually involves a group of people who suggest many different options and scenarios for a solution. In brainstorming, everyone involved in the decision-making process is able to contribute both extreme and moderate options. The essence of brainstorming is that judgments on each proffered option is suspended until there are sufficient options available. Each person should have the opportunity to explore and understand all the options. Consequently, elements of one idea may be combined with those of another to produce a third, even more creative solution. This is a good technique for solving complex problems, such as the design of a method of nursing service delivery to ensure quality care or to define the future role of the registered nurse in the nursing department. Its usefulness for more routine decisions, such as the problem of high turnover of a unit due to poor leadership, may result in delaying a vital decision that needs to be made quickly.

Functional Fixedness. The decision maker also needs to avoid *functional fixedness* which is the tendency to see things in association with a given function (Adair 1985, 112). Use of the imagination can overcome this tendency by letting one's mind roam freely. In hospitals, inpatient nursing units are 24-hour-a-day, 7-day-per-week operations. One creative nurse leader-manager came up with the cost-saving idea for a 24-hour, 5-day-a-week operation for short-stay surgical patients. In presenting this alternative work week, she was not fixed on the traditional assumption that all nursing units need to be operational 7 days per week.

In generating ideas, the decision maker(s) should avoid negative talk. The danger in this is that good alternatives will be dismissed before they can be fully explored. Frequently heard statements such as, "We tried that before and it didn't work"; or "Theoretically it's a good idea, but in practice it is impractical"; or "That option will cost too much," can shut down exploration or worthwhile alternatives.

One problem in considering options is that there may not be a desirable alternative available. When this happens, decision making is delayed which may cause more problems than if an undesirable decision is acted upon. If this is the case, reaching a decision and taking action as quickly as possible is recommended.

One option that might be considered is not to make any decision at all. This may be a viable alternative on some rare occasions. However, its use should be limited. Deciding not to decide may cause inertia. It is most often better to be wrong than to make no decision at all.

Consequences. The consequences of each option cannot be determined or predicted precisely. However, the more familiar the manager is with the situation, the better she can judge the consequences. In situations that are not familiar to the leader-manager and/or the decision-making group, the use of someone else's expertise is important. Another danger in predicting consequences lies in unraveling so many and such extreme possible outcomes that the group or individual becomes immobilized.

Evaluation and Implementation. Once a decision is reached, it should be evaluated before it is implemented. Questions to help this evaluation are:

- Does the decision meet the objective?
- Will the decision move the organization toward its vision and mission?
- Has someone been overlooked in the decision-making process?
- Are there resources available to implement the decision?
- Does the decision "feel right?"

Action and decision making mean taking risks, but taking risks does not mean being reckless. Good risks are ones taken only after careful consideration. To assist in assessing risks, both imagination and quantitative methods may be helpful. In management literature, there are mathematical formulas and methods to diagrammatically calculate risks. Although their practical use is doubtful, there may be times when they could be valuable tools. In implementing a decision, planning and foresight can help to minimize the risk. Questions to ask are: What is the worst possible outcome? Are we willing to accept this outcome, if necessary?

The next step is implementation of the decision. Implementation can range from the simple to the complex depending upon the scope and breadth of the decision. The more people who are involved and affected by the decision, the more complex the implementation will be. For decisions that affect the entire nursing department, such as a new system of care delivery, the implementation might progress on a step-by-step basis over the course of many months. Often demonstration projects are used to implement a decision and evaluate it before implementation on a wide scale basis occurs.

Evaluation of the Results of the Decision. Once a decision has been implemented, the leader-manager needs to evaluate it. This is done by evaluating the results against the objectives and standards determined in the second step of the process. If the implementation does not achieve the intended objectives then the entire decision-making process is again initiated.

The Myth of Rational Decision Making

Nicholas Nicholaidis (cited in Adair 1985, 6) found that emotions, organizational politics and power, and the values of people play a large role in decision making. Managers seldom consciously use the steps of the decision-making process that were previously discussed. Further, they do not choose prescribed textbook solutions when reaching a decision and taking action. Instead, these factors influence decisions:

- The individual's values, interests, and needs

- The standards of their superiors

- The acceptance of those people affected by the action and those who have to implement it

- The reasonableness of the decision

- If the decision contained a "built-in" protection which could provide an excuse if the actual results differed from the expected ones.

Experienced managers also use intuition to make decisions because they have a large amount of knowledge gathered from their experience, training, and education. They organize this information in their minds into recognized chunks and patterns. In this case, intuition is seen as making thoughtful leaps from one chunk of information to another. Experienced managers are able to do this because these patterns and chunks of information are contained in their memory (Simon 1987, 60).

Bhaska (cited in Simon 1987, 61) researched a "thinking aloud" protocol with business school students and experienced businessmen. Both groups reached similar decisions. However, the experts, using intuition, arrived at solutions quicker. The novices, however, used a more conscious analysis to arrive at the solution. Thus, knowing and learning the steps of the decision-making process is also valuable for developing decision-making abilities.

In complex decision-making situations, it seems that solutions are obtained by combining conscious deliberation and intuition. Decision-making styles can be seen to exist on a continuum with the nature of the problem to be solved and the predominant decision-making style of the decision maker deciding what process will be used (Simon 1987, 61).

Acting

Weick (1983, 223-236) argues that when managers act they also think. Thinking is not a separate and distinct activity, occurring in isolation. Acting is continuous and thinking is woven into it. Thoughtful acts are characterized by attention, intention, and control. When a manager acts thinkingly, attention is paid to what is happening, order is imposed, and action is corrected when it strays from a predetermined set of standards. Thus, managerial actions are significant and have important consequences. In contrast, actions that are done unthinkingly are acts of impulse, mindlessness, or rigidity, done without sensitivity to the environment or others.

The following example illustrates thinking and unthinking actions in decision making:

The Situation: A staff nurse is requesting two months off during the summer to take a European honeymoon. The nursing service policy limits vacations at this time of year to two weeks in order to allow everyone to have vacation during this time. Because the nurse has been with the department for five years and is considered to be outstanding, the head nurse has petitioned the nurse executive to waive this policy in this case.

Response 1: To act thinkingly, the nurse executive would pay attention to the facts such as the seniority of the nurse, the likelihood of her resigning if the request is denied and the feelings of the head nurse and staff. She would then look at the available options and outcomes: losing the nurse forever versus not having her services for two months, and the effect of each on the other staff's morale. With careful consideration, the nurse executive decides that she will approve the request only if the nursing staff agree to it and understand the implications for their vacation time, if any.

Response 2: In contrast, to act unthinkingly, the nurse executive would simply state, "The policy says only two weeks, I will not approve this request."

Acting with thought is important for another reason. There is, in reality, a sparsity of discrete decision making in managerial actions. Decisions seldom occur by people meeting at the same time and using a model similar to the one presented. Rather, decisions occur through small, gradual actions that tend to limit other alternate courses of action and possibilities. In other words, decisions are made without anyone realizing it. Therefore, the leader-manager needs to act thinkingly in small actions (memo writing, correcting policy drafts, in meetings, etc.) because these small actions help mold decisions (Weiss 1980).

Implications for Nursing

There are three general types of conscious mental abilities involved in decision-making: analyzing, synthesizing, and valuing. There is also a large realm of unconscious mental activities which has been labeled *intuition*. The effective thinker needs to know which of these skills or combination of skills to use in any given situation. The leader-manager should balance intuition with rationality, analysis with synthesis, conceptualization with imagination, and valuing with all these processes. For example, in developing alternate courses of action, analytic skills are used to view the whole situation and break it into its parts. However, when deciding on the course of action to take, synthesizing skills are used to perceive how the action fits with the overall organization. Further, the effective thinker is sensitive to her intuition and unconscious mind and knows when to listen to them.

The best way to become an expert decision maker is to make many decisions. After reaching a decision, the leader-manager can study the differences and similarities between this decision and various decisions made in the past.

Application to Nursing Practice: Case Study

The Setting

The hospital is a 500-bed, not-for-profit facility offering tertiary care services in a large city on the West Coast. The entire city is experiencing a shortage of nurses. There is an active surgical service with a 10-bed ICU and three surgical units. The hospital would like to open a small ambulatory surgical center, but no one has initiated any specific plans for one.

The nursing department is decentralized. Reporting to the vice president of nursing are four directors of nursing, one of which is the director for surgical nursing.

Current Situation

One of the surgical units, 5 North, is experiencing major staffing problems. It is a 40-bed unit with an occupancy rate of 80 percent over the last three months. There are eight RN vacancies out of a possible 20 positions. Three nurses have requested transfer to the surgical ICU which has five RN vacancies. The head nurse of 5 North has been in the position for three years. Although it is generally believed that she is part of the problem of a high vacancy rate, there are no formal plans to support her development or to remove her from the position.

A second surgical unit, 4 North, has no vacancies and enjoys the reputation of a good unit on which to work. Whenever a nursing vacancy occurs positions are filled with in-house transfers. The unit is small, having only 25 beds. The occupany rate of the unit has been 50 percent for about three months. Staff on the unit are frequently floated to other units which is causing dissatisfaction. The head nurse of 4 North has been on the unit for 10 years and is well respected by nursing administration, physicians, and her staff. It is widely believed that the low turnover of staff is a direct result of her superior leadership abilities.

The third surgical unit is 4 South which is a 35-bed unit. The occupancy rate of this unit is also 50 percent. There are currently four RN vacancies out of 18.5 positions. The head nurse of the unit has been in her position just over one year and has been slowly trying to stabilize the staff by improving morale.

The staffing crisis on 5 North has reached the point in which the director of surgical nursing is recommending to close a surgical unit. She has calculated the average daily census on each unit for the past year and has determined that the same number of patients can be cared for on two versus three units. She has recommended closing 4 North which is the smallest unit. Staff from 4 North could be reassigned to the two surgical units and the three nurses wishing to transfer to the ICU could then do so. The director has presented her plan to the vice president of nursing.

The vice president of nursing has agreed to think about the plan. However, something doesn't "feel right."

Case Study Discussion

1. How can the vice president use (a) analyzing, (b) synthesizing, and (c) valuing to think about this situation?

2. How should the vice president use the steps of the decision-making process to reach a decision about closing a unit?

3. What would be one acceptable solution to this problem? Support your decision.

References

Adair, J. 1985. *Management decision making.* Hants, England: Gower Publishing.

Buckley, K.W., and J. Steffy. 1986. The invisible side of leadership. In *Transforming leadership: From vision to results,* ed. J.D. Adams, 233-243. Alexandria, VA: Miles River Press.

Buzan, T. 1983. *Use both sides of your brain.* New York: E.P. Dutton, Inc.

Dokter, R.H., and W.F. Hamilton. 1978. Cognitive science and the acceptance of management science recommendations. *Management Science* 19:884-894.

Harmon, W.W. 1986. Transformed leadership: Two contrasting concepts. In *Transforming leadership: From vision to results*, ed. J.D. Adams, 11-23. Alexandria, VA: Miles River Press.

Levy, S., and N.P. Loomba. 1973. *Health care administration: A managerial perspective*. Philadelphia: J.B. Lippincott.

Ritscher, J. 1986. Spiritual leadership. In *Transforming leadership: From vision to results*, ed. J.D. Adams, 61-80. Alexandria, VA: Miles River Press.

Simon, H.A. 1987. Managing management decisions: The role of intuition and emotions. *Academy of Management Executives* 1(1): 57-64.

Stevens, B.J. 1985. *The nurse as executive*. 3d ed. Rockville, MD: Aspen Publishers.

Weick, K.E. 1983. Managerial thought in the context of action. In *The executive mind: New insights on managerial thought and action*, ed. S. Srivasta, 221-242. San Francisco: Jossey-Bass.

Weiss, C.H. 1980. Knowledge creep and decision accretion. *Knowledge* 1: 381-404.

11

Time Management

Chapter Objectives

1. Explain the importance of time management for effective leadership.

2. Assess one's time management skills.

3. Distinguish between boss-, system-, and self-imposed time.

4. List 10 guidelines for setting goals.

5. Discuss the importance of planning and delegation as techniques for managing one's time.

6. List tasks which can and cannot be delegated.

Introduction

The most traditional view of time management, and an important one, is that time is a precious resource. As such, time needs to be managed in order to effectively and efficiently achieve intended results. But the importance of time management transcends this conventional view. The nurse leader-manager who has control over her time can have a clear, calm mind when confronted with multiple demands. Unfortunately, a clear vision and articulated objectives often get forgotten in the confusion and muddle of daily events and crises. If a leader-manager is not composed and is struggling to accomplish daily tasks, her actions and decisions tend to become reactions to events; she will not have the time or peace of mind to act thoughtfully and proactively. The most important step in achieving clarity of mind is to gain control over one's time.

Time is also a reflection of personal energy and how it is consumed. A leader-manager, no matter how spirited, has a limited amount of energy to use for herself and for the organization. There are many possible demands on the personal energy of the leader-manager including daily routine tasks and crises, vision and goal accomplishment, personal and professional activities, and home and family obligations. The goal of time management is to minimize the number of demands facing the leader-manager at any one time. This management will ensure that she has adequate energy for the tasks that advance the vision of the organization and her personal goals and purpose.

Further, how the leader-manager spends her time is important because it sends messages to others. Ideally, the leader-manager should be spending most of her time in activities that move the nursing department toward the vision and objectives. If the nurse executive becomes involved in all daily, routine situations, she sends the message that the vision and objectives are not really important.

For example, a vision statement may purport a "decentralized" management philosophy and structure. However, if the nurse executive does not delegate to others, allow others to participate in decision making, or permit others to act independently, she is signalling that she really prefers a centralized approach to management. Even though the vision statement avows "decentralization" and trust, the real message (the leader-manager's behavior) is "centralization" and distrust.

Effective time management also contributes to feelings of well-being and happiness. Personal success is measured by spending time in endeavors in which the individual wants to spend time. This is true for both personal and work time. In other words, the way one spends time brings joy and satisfaction to one's life.

From the opposite view, there are serious consequences of poor time management. Most importantly, managing one's time is managing oneself. If a leader-manager is incapable of managing herself, then it is doubtful that she can manage others. Further, a leader-manager's difficulty in managing time can result in delays of completion of projects. Consequently, the entire organization is negatively affected and can be immobilized. Superiors, subordinates, and peers rely on the leader-manager to complete reports, provide information, make decisions, and take actions in a timely fashion. The inability to be timely on a consistent basis does not help the organization progress towards excellence and success.

This chapter will explore techniques that can be used by leader-managers to organize and therefore make the best use of available organizational time and personal time; to maintain her peace of mind, the leader-manager needs to realize a balance between the two. Both the amount of time available for an activity and how this time is spent are important considerations when searching for effective use of time.

Assessing Time Management

There are three ways to assess a person's skills in managing time. First is the appearance of her work space or office. Despite the popular saying, "A cluttered desk is a sign of a genius," a clear desk and a neat office symbolize control over one's time and responsibilities. Developing a system to file papers and to present an uncluttered front to the world is important. Some other visible signs of not having control of time are rushing from meeting to meeting, being late for appointments, and not taking time to fully discuss and consider issues.

Secondly, many people seem to measure their success and importance by the number of hours they devote to their job. Frequently, people "complain" or even "brag" about the hours spent on their jobs. This may be the result of a need for increased self-esteem, a need to be needed, or a belief that one is indispensable. Consistently spending time in excess of the officially designated hours may signal both ineffective time management and an unfulfilled need.

Nurse managers often give conflicting messages regarding hours to be spent on work. Frequently, they will implore staff nurses to determine priorities and to not stay past the end of their shift, yet, the managers will take work home, stay late every night, and can be seen on the weekend doing paperwork.

Similarly, in some organizations one's dedication and loyalty is measured by the number of extra hours devoted to the organization. If this is an organizational cultural belief, people will burn out. The nurse leader-manager is responsible for ensuring this is not the norm in her department.

Time Logs

A third, more systematic way to assess one's skill in time management is to use a time log. Some experts believe that people, on the average, waste two to three hours per day as a result of ineffective use of time (Davenport 1982, 52). A time log will help a person to be aware of this wasted time, to determine how effectively time is used, and to assess other factors of time management.

Generally, a log is kept for a typical week. However, the leader-manager may decide to keep a log for a longer period of time if she has a particular need. Keeping a time log on a periodic basis will help the leader-manager to see her progress in managing her time and to identify new areas for further growth. If the leader-manager changes positions, a time log can be kept to assess if there are new areas of concern after several months on the new job. Because the leader-manager's primary reason for time management is to seek clarity of mind, it is helpful to keep the log for both organizational and personal time.

A sample of a time log format is found in Figure 11-1 and a partially completed log is found in Figure 11-2. (Some people may prefer to keep an ongoing narrative diary instead of using this form). In column 1 of the time log, the activity and the length of time spent on the activity are recorded; the purpose or objective of the activity is indicated in column 2. For example, the purpose of a phone call may be to get information, give information, make a decision, or to procrastinate.

The purpose of the third column is threefold: to identify time wasters, to categorize the time, and to assess one's energy level. Time wasters are activities that engage the time of the person which are not important or vital to the accomplishment of organizational or personal goals (Ferner 1980). Time wasters can be both internally and externally generated. In a comprehensive, international survey of executives, LeBoeuf (1980, 41) reported major time wasters experienced by them:

> telephone interruptions; drop-in visitors, meetings (scheduled and unscheduled), crises; lack of objectives, priorities, and deadlines; cluttered desk and personal disorganization; ineffective delegation and involvement in routine and detail; attempting too much at once and estimating time unrealistically; lack of, or unclear communication or instruction; inadequate, inaccurate, or delayed information; indecision and procrastination; confused responsibility and authority; inability to say no; leaving tasks unfinished; and lack of self-discipline.

Also in the third column, for those hours spent in organizational activities, the leader-manager categorizes the type of time. Oncken and Wass (1974) describe three categories of managers' time:

Time and Activity	Purpose of Activity	Assessment	Effectiveness of Time Spent
Indicate activity and length of time spent on the activity.	Prior to beginning the activity, write down the purpose or objective.	Identify time wasters.	Assess each task by asking:
Make entries every 15 minutes unless some activities extend for a longer period of time.		Categorize the time as boss-, system-, or self-imposed time.	Did the task contribute to goal accomplishment?
		Assess energy level.	Could the task have been done in a better way?
			Was the task performed at the right time?
			Could the task be delegated?
			What were the benefits of completing the task?
			Was it enjoyable or unpleasant?
			Were there many interruptions?

Figure 11-1 Sample time log format.

Time and Activity	Purpose of Activity	Assessment	Effectiveness of Time Spent
7:30-8:00 Nursing Report	Get information regarding 24-hr. status of patients and administrative concerns	Interrupted 3 times by staffing problems; much useless details; system- and boss-imposed time; energy level high	Meeting could be 15 minutes; must do this myself
8:00-8:15 Report to CEO	Give information and receive information from other departments	Boss-imposed time; Meeting seems to be a gripe session and not useful; energy level still high	Cannot delegate; meeting not useful but have no control over this
8:15-8:30	Returned to office	Stopped by 3 employees with payroll problems; sub-ordinate-imposed time	I volunteered to take care of problems; could have redirected them to payroll
8:30-9:00	Get and give informal information	This is discretionary time which could be better spent; procrastination	Enjoyed! Some of information is useful in understanding the social networks. Could be twice per week

Figure 11-2 Sample completed time log.

Time and Activity	Purpose of Activity	Assessment	Effectiveness of Time Spent
9:00–10:00 In box	Time set aside for routine correspondence	5 phone calls interrupted time; only 2 were important; energy level high	Resented 3 phone interruptions; task does not demand energy thus move this to a late afternoon function and use this time in personal meetings
10:00–11:00 Nursing executive board	Get and give information regarding new quality assurance policy	Discretionary time	Goal accomplished; Enjoyed task completion
11:00 Solved payroll problem	Resolve problem for the 3 employees	Subordinate-imposed time; time waster	Could have delegated this task

Figure 11-2, continued.

1. *Boss-imposed time* is time spent in activities required by one's superior. These may include attendance at organizational meetings, preparation of reports, development of policies and procedures, participation on special task forces, presence at ceremonial events, and communication with the boss. Gaining control over this time may not be possible. However, there are some activities, such as preparation of reports, that may be delegated. The leader-manager needs to know how much of her time fits into this category and to recognize that managing some of this time more effectively may not be possible. At the same time, she has the opportunity to assess what can be delegated to others or eliminated by negotiating with the superior.

2. *System-imposed time* is time spent in activities which support organizational peers. This includes activities similar to those mentioned above, but the purpose of the activity is different. For example, time spent receiving information and passing it on regarding changes in the laundry service is system-imposed time. As with boss-imposed time, the leader-manager can assess this time and determine ways to decrease time spent in these activities.

3. *Self-imposed time* is time spent doing things the manager initiates or agrees to do. It has two components. *Subordinate-imposed time* is spent in activities requested by subordinates; *discretionary time* is time for doing what a manager initiates and wishes to do. The true purpose of time management is to increase this discretionary time. An increase in discretionary time can be achieved by improving control over subordinate-imposed time.

For example, in Figure 11-2, the leader-manager agreed to follow up on a problem with paychecks for three employees. This activity could have been handled by the timekeepers. She could have referred these staff directly to payroll while offering support if the problem was not resolved at that level. Instead, the leader-manager spent one-half hour communicating with payroll and getting back to the employees.

Lastly, the third column can be used to analyze one's emotional status and energy levels. One leader-manager found that she was spending her most productive time, midmorning, in doing her least important, least demanding tasks. Consequently, she was doing her most important work when her energy level was lowest. By rearranging her schedule, she was able to give the most energy to the most important tasks.

In the fourth column, the effectiveness of the time spent can be analyzed. This should be done as soon as possible after completing a task, but must be done at least at the end of each day. This analysis has both an emotional and objective component.

At the end of the week, the entire log can be analyzed for time wasters and for ways to more effectively use time. Questions to consider when analyzing the time log include:

- What were the most significant accomplishments of the week?

- How many activities were enjoyable or detestable?

- If you continue spending time the way you did the past week, where will you be in five years?

- Are the most important tasks being accomplished during periods of high or low energy?

- How much time is spent in each category: boss-imposed, system-imposed, and self-imposed?

- How can discretionary time be increased?

- How much time was spent in moving forward the vision and goals of the organization and nursing department?

- How does wasted time affect the overall nursing department?

- How does subordinate-imposed time affect time management?

Goals and Goal Setting

Goals give people purpose in life—reasons to pursue daily routines and tasks with energy and enthusiasm. Further, goals help the leader-manager to avoid wasted efforts and to utilize time most effectively. Most importantly, goals provide focus in one's life which contributes to clarity of mind.

Goals work because they set up a discrepancy between what a person desires and current reality. This generates creative tension and personal energy which help motivate a person toward the goal (Harmon 1986, 107).

There are a number of guidelines for goal setting:

1. Determine holistic goals that include all aspects of one's life: professional, organizational, family, social, financial, spiritual, physical, and psychological or self-improvement.

2. Choose goals which open doors of opportunity such as meeting new people who can assist and support the attainment of the goal. Determine goals that force one to leave one's "comfort zone."

3. Determine goals which are measurable, concrete, achievable, and challenging.

4. Consider organizational constraints, resources, and personal strengths and aptitudes to determine realistic goals.

5. Develop goals that fit one's life purpose. This means that the goal will assist the individual toward self-actualization. Thus, well designed goals benefit not only the self, but are also in the service of others.

6. Set time frames for completion of goals. By having realistic time frames, tasks and activities seem less overwhelming. Appropriate time frames do not allow for procrastination, but should be realistic. It is not always easy to achieve such a balance. When a goal is not reached by a specific deadline, the date can be changed. The leader-manager should not feel that she failed if a date was not realized.

7. Periodically, reassess movement toward goals and set new deadlines if appropriate.

8. Reward self upon completion of goals.

9. Spend time each day, even if its only five minutes, on tasks that move toward goal accomplishment. Decide each morning what is the most important thing to be accomplished that day toward achieving a goal.

10. Enjoy working toward goals. In many cases, the pursuit of the goal is more fun than its actual achievement.

11. Visualize goals.

12. Pursue a goal with enthusiasm, even if the enthusiasm is a pretense.

13. Periodically, evaluate progress toward goal achievement. In this process, some goals may be dropped and new ones added.

Time Management Techniques

There are many practical time management techniques. Some of the most common techniques include managing time spent in meetings, controlling and minimizing interruptions, masterful use of phone conversations, and eliminating nonessentials such as reading "junk" mail. The focus of this section is on two of the most important techniques: planning and delegating.

Planning

The foundations of planning are based on goals, both organizational and personal. Writing down goals, carrying them around, and referring to them daily places the goals firmly in the leader-manager's subconscious mind. This creates sensitivity to opportunities which can lead to goal attainment. Without this subconscious awareness, a person might miss opportunities for reaching goals.

In Chapter 7, the use of positive reinforcement as one technique for rewarding people was suggested. This is a commonly recommended, yet frequently forgotten behavior. The leader-manager can write a goal to give one person positive reinforcement every day. If she refers to this goal daily, she will be less likely to miss an opportunity to give positive reinforcement to others.

The leader-manager determines both organizational and personal goals. If time management is a problem for the leader-manager she can choose time management goals as well. Figure 11-3 illustrates the goals for a hypothetical nurse executive. These goals are concrete, measurable, and include time frames for completion. It is recommended to carry these goals in a commercially designed calender and appointment system such as Daytimers. Either at the end of the day or the beginning of the day, the leader-manager should refer to her goals. She should plan activities for the day based on them, determining the priority of the day. Next, she should write down three to five activities to be accomplished. These tasks are to be done before anything else is done.

Personal Goals	Work Goals	Time Management Goals
1. To walk 30 minutes everyday. (ongoing).	1. Consciously work on building trust every day. (ongoing)	1. Spend 10 minutes every morning planning the day. Write down 3 to 5 things to accomplish and do these first.
2. Buy a new car by March 1.	2. Develop a vision statement by July.	
3. Entertain friends at least monthly.	3. Follow up on recruitment and retention retreat monthly with all staff for the next 6 months.	2. Negotiate with CEO to decrease the length of the morning meeting by defining exactly what information is needed by him. Complete in one month.
4. Develop a system to remember birthdays, etc. by January 1. Buy all the cards for one year by January 15.	4. Initiate a formal head nurse development program by September.	
5. Practice visualization and affirmations twice per day to remember people's names. Reevaluate in one month.	5. Start case management on one nursing unit by January.	3. Rearrange schedule so that the most taxing tasks are completed in the morning. Complete in two months.

Figure 11-3 Sample goals for a nurse executive.

Work seems to expand to fill the amount of time allotted for it. Thus, setting realistic time frames for daily tasks, without allowing for procrastination, is an important skill. It can be frustrating to set too many goals for the day and then leave some unfinished. However, from a time management perspective, it is better to err by having too many daily goals than to not have enough. Setting unrealistic goals every day can increase frustration and stress levels. Thus, the leader-manager should learn how long it realistically takes to accomplish tasks.

In planning time, the leader-manager should ensure that she has adequate discretionary time. One of the most helpful techniques is to set aside a block of time for completion of routine, nonpriority, "must do" paperwork. How much time and when the time is set aside are determined by other organizational demands and by the energy level of the leader-manager. However, at least two hours at any one time is recommended for discretionary time. An entire day per week can be set aside, or a morning or afternoon once or twice per week. This block of time can also be used for activities that move the vision, leader-manager initiated meetings, or nonroutine activities.

Delegation

Knowing how to effectively delegate is essential for organizational and personal success. There is both a science and an art to delegation. The science involves first assessing what can be delegated. To do this, the leader-manager decides what activities will provide the most return on her time investment. She then delegates those which do not. In general, the leader-manager's time is best spent on activities that advance the vision, mission, goals, and objectives of the department and in building trusting relationships within and outside the department.

Jenks and Kelly (1985, 56-63) categorized tasks that should and should not be delegated. Tasks which can be delegated include:

1. *Routine Tasks.* These tasks are done repeatedly and can be delegated without difficulty. The organizational chart is, in reality, a preplanned system of delegation. Responsibility and authority are delegated to people based upon this system of hierarchy. Periodic evaluation occurs when dissatisfactions are expressed or people change positions.

An example of delegation can be seen in the handling of the mail in a nursing department. This can be a cumbersome and time-consuming task. Secretaries can be taught to screen mail by 1) identifying "junk" that can be immediately discarded; 2) separating correspondence that provides information from that which requires action; 3) taking actions that are routine in nature; 4) signing some paperwork for the leader-manager; 5) sending some mail directly to other people; and 6) attaching routing slips to information that needs to be distributed to several people.

2. *Boss or System-Imposed Tasks.* Even tasks that are deemed absolutely necessary and which may involve decision making can be delegated as well. Usually, the nurse executive retains responsibility for those tasks which involve a high degree of evaluation and judgment. For example, approval of overtime can be delegated to head nurses, yet decisions about how to trim overtime costs may still preside with the nurse executive.

3. *Trivial Activities.* These tasks have little impact on the results that one is trying to achieve. They may include presiding over a meeting about the facility picnic, dealing with a repairman, or giving information to someone about a minor matter. These activities take a great deal of time and usually do not require the skills of the nurse executive.

4. *Tasks Involving Special Expertise and Skills.* These tasks can easily be delegated. For example, the quality assurance nurse would be the most qualified to prepare a quality assurance report.

5. *Chores.* Chores may be categorized under any of the categories above, but they are tasks which one does not enjoy doing. A chore for the boss may be seen as a reward for the "delegate." At the nursing unit level, time scheduling can be easily and efficiently delegated. If the head nurse is freed of this responsibility, she gains a significant amount of time to fulfill her other responsibilities. For the staff, there are added benefits as well. With a peer responsible for time schedules, there may be more willingness to cooperate and negotiate. At the same time, there may be more chance for input from everybody on the staff.

Further, it is possible that the staff might do the job better. Since the schedule involves their own time, they have a greater vested interest in its timely completion and equity.

6. *Pet Projects.* Although it may seem paradoxical, the tasks enjoyed by the leader-manager might better be delegated to someone else. For example, a nurse executive may thoroughly enjoy working with figures and preparing budgets, yet this may not be the best use of her time.

Just as some tasks or activities can be delegated, others cannot. Some leader-managers err by delegating too much or the inappropriate activities. As with everything a leader-manager does, a sense of balance is important. Jenks and Kelly suggested those tasks that should *not* be delegated:

1. *Ritual Activities.* Tasks which would be ineffective without the influence of the position, prestige, and title of the leader-manager should not be delegated. They may include both internal and external events. For example, Nursing Week activities and ceremonies should be presided over by the nurse executive and not delegated to other individuals.

2. *Decisions Affecting Nursing Department Policy.* These include both informal and formal policy. For example, the nurse executive may choose to use a search committee for selecting a head nurse. The search committee can help screen and interview applicants, yet the nurse executive retains ultimate authority for hiring. Prior to the work of the search committee, guidelines for the selection or rejection of a candidate are determined by the nurse executive.

   The nurse executive accepts final authority and accountability for formal policies. Staff can and should have input into the policy and several people may actually write it. Even if the policy is designed in a truly participatory manner, final authority and accountability for the policy rests with the nurse executive.

3. *Personnel Matters.* The nurse leader-manager needs to assume responsibility for the evaluation of direct subordinates. Further, she must adhere to the disciplinary routines and practices of the organization and play her defined role in order to avoid costly

technical mistakes for the organization. Also, any delegation that involves divulging confidential information is inappropriate.

The knowledgeable leader-manager will not delegate conflict resolution or the handling of crises that call for her direct involvement. Judging what does and does not call for her direct involvement is not always easy. However, once the leader-manager decides that intervention is needed, she cannot delegate the task to someone else.

Praise and positive reinforcement is strongest when given directly by the leader-manager. Second-hand praise loses its meaning. It signals that the task and the person are not important enough to be given direct feedback.

4. *Delegation Itself.* The delegate needs to have direct contact with the leader-manager to understand the parameters and standards of the task. The direct contact builds trust and mutual respect as well.

The Delegation Process. The leader decides to whom to delegate specific tasks. Jenks and Kelly (1985, 63-68) provided guidelines for making this decision. In a sense, this is an intuitive decision that involves fitting the best person with the right job. Most importantly, the leader-manager should know the expertise, strengths, knowledge, interests, aptitudes, and attitudes of the followers. These factors should be matched with the job to be delegated. The attitudes of individual followers are also important considerations. For example, if the delegated task is an innovative, nonroutine, boss-imposed task then an enthusiastic, eager delegate could be chosen. If the matter is routine and trivial, another person might be more appropriate.

Secondly, the leader-manager should assess the current workload of the delegate. She should consider whether the person can handle the duties along with their current responsibilities. In delegating to an individual with a high workload, the leader-manager might wish to help the person delegate other activities. She can also reassess workload and deadlines and relieve the person of certain tasks.

Another consideration in choosing the right person for the job is the reason for delegating. Most often the reason for delegation is the completion of a task. However, a leader-manager may choose to delegate in order to assist someone's development or to evaluate someone's performance.

Once the person is chosen, the process of delegation becomes the focus. First, the person needs to be aware of the relative importance of completing the task. The leader-manager then secures the commitment of the person for completion of the activity, outlines the requirements of the task, and provides the necessary information and resources. At this time, standards should be set, however, expectations of perfection are as inappropriate for others as they are for oneself. The assignment needs to be explained in terms of the organizational vision and should appeal to the values of the individual. Compare the following two approaches:

> *Leader A:* "JCAHO requires that this quality assurance report be completed. I really don't agree with it, but it has to be done. Do you think you can pull something together by Friday?"

> *Leader B:* "Our patients are concerned with the quality of care they are receiving and I want to be able to assure that we are delivering the best care possible. We therefore need to complete a survey of IV infection rates; that seems to be a major concern in the press right now. In today's health care environment it is really important to have a reputation for quality care."

In the first response, the leader minimizes the importance of the task by stating her disagreement with it. Since JCAHO accreditation is important to the hospital's long-term survival, the task is an important one to the mission of both the organization and the nursing department. In the second approach, the leader emphasizes the societal value of the survey in ensuring quality healthcare. This approach will have more success than the first since it appeals to the value of nurses to provide safe care.

Results should be the emphasis of the assignment, not the means. The person to whom the task is delegated is given the flexibility to decide on the means, as long as they are consistent with the department's vision. The delegate is free to ask for advise, support, and guidance from the leader-manager. Firm deadlines and points of evaluation, if determined, assist in ensuring that the task is completed on time.

For effective delegation, once the task is completed, rewards should be given. Rewards that are used will vary depending on the scope and breadth of the delegated task. However, it is vital to give the person recognition and credit for the task.

Many leader-managers are aware of these scientific principles of successful delegation outlined above, but they still fail to delegate because of an inability or unwillingness to apply these principles. The art of delegation involves the leader-manager's personal attitudes toward delegation including:

- Her receptiveness to other people's ideas and ways of doing things. This includes supporting others, praising their efforts and accomplishments, and accepting differences in approaches.

- Her willingness to let go of tasks and not to be "in control."

- Her willingness to let others make mistakes. Usually these mistakes are minor. Serious, repeated mistakes can be avoided through counseling, supporting, being available for questions, asking discerning questions, and providing thorough explanations of expectations.

- Her willingness to trust.

- Her willingness to establish and use broad controls rather than rigid, inflexible standards (Koontz and O'Donnell 1976, 382-384).

Implications for Nursing

Many demands are made on the time of the leader-manager. In order to have clarity of mind in dealing with these demands, management of time is necessary. Managerial time is characterized by variety, fragmentation, and brevity. This means that the leader-manager can easily get caught up in superficiality and be all action and no thought (Mintzberg 1973).

It is, therefore, important that the leader-manager assess her own time management skills. She can do this by asking herself a number of questions:

- Am I spending many hours over and above my regularly scheduled ones completing my work?

- Am I delegating appropriately?

- Do I allow too many interruptions?

- Do I take time out everyday for planning and thinking?

- Do I set daily goals and accomplish them?
- Have I determined my long-term professional and personal goals? Do I work on them each day?
- Am I able to say no when appropriate?

Application to Nursing Practice: Case Study

The Setting

The nursing department is located in an unoccupied patient care unit with 15 people occupying 12 offices. The offices are contained on two separate hallways forming an "L" shape. Most of the rooms are small—approximately 100 square feet. Thus, only one person is assigned to most offices. Because the space was a patient care unit, there are no connecting doors between offices.

The chief nurse executive's secretary occupies an office next to the CNE's. The office is approximately 220 square feet and one of two large offices. The CNE and secretary enjoy a positive relationship and the CNE is protective of the secretary. Other members of the department do not agree with the CNE's positive assessment of the secretary's performance.

Current Situation

Secretarial responsibilities have recently been realigned and the nurse recruiter has been assigned a full-time secretary. The secretary and nurse recruiter are in different hallways. Thus, the secretary cannot easily greet applicants nor communicate with the recruiter. The nurse recruiter asked the CNE to reassign rooms. In response, the CNE asked the recruiter to submit a plan for reassignment of offices.

The offices affected include those of the nurse recruiter, two administrative assistants, the infection control nurse, the secretaries to the CNE and the recruiter, and one other clerk typist. Because several offices are cold and do not have windows, some conflict is inevitable. The recruiter worked with all the people involved. An initial plan was discussed and agreed upon which involved moving just the infection control nurse and the nurse recruiter's secretary. Later, this plan was abandoned after the infection control nurse decided that she did not want a windowless office.

After several weeks of considering different options, the nurse recruiter met with the nurse executive and stated that he could not work out any mutually agreeable plans. He asked the nurse executive to make a decision. The nurse executive stated, "This is not acceptable. You are asking me to make a decision that will cause some people to be upset without your being part of the decision yourself. Come back to me with a proposal."

Several hours later the nurse recruiter reluctantly presented a plan which involved moving the CNE's secretary to a much smaller, windowless office across the hall from the nurse executive. This plan was accepted and implemented.

Case Study Discussion

1. For the CNE, is the initial request for office reassignment boss-, system-, or self-imposed time?

2. Was the decision appropriately delegated?

3. What category of activities for delegation does this decision fit?

4. Was the task delegated to the appropriate person?

5. Could the task have been delegated to someone else?

6. Did the nurse recruiter have appropriate guidance in making the decision?

References

Davenport, R. 1982. *Making time, making money: A step-by-step program for setting your goals and achieving success.* New York: St. Martin's Press.

Ferner, J. 1980. *Successful time management.* New York: John Wiley and Sons.

Harmon, W.W. 1986. Transformed leadership: Two contrasting concepts. In *Transforming leadership: From vision to results,* ed. J.D. Adams, 105-110. Alexandria, VA: Miles River Press.

Jenks, J.M., and J.M. Kelly. 1985. *Don't do. Delegate!.* New York: Franklin Watts.

Koontz, H., and C. O'Donnell. 1976. *Management: A systems and contingency analysis of managerial functions.* New York: McGraw-Hill.

LeBoeuf, M. 1980. Managing time means managing yourself. *Business Horizons* 23: 41-46.

Mintzberg, H. 1973. *The nature of managerial work.* New York: Harper and Row.

Oncken, W.O., and D.L. Wass. 1974. Management time: Who's got the monkey? *Harvard Business Review* 52(6): 75-80.

12

Leadership and Groups

Chapter Objectives

1. Define working groups.
2. List the advantages and disadvantages of working in groups.
3. Discuss a descriptive model of group theory.
4. Describe the five stages of group development.
5. Discuss practical techniques to facilitate group work.

Introduction

Throughout this book, it has been seen that the nurse leader-manager spends all of her organizational time in one of three ways. She is involved in tasks alone, with one other person, or with a group. This book has provided discussions of her role in each of these activities. Because group theory and dynamics are more complex than working alone or with one other person, it is important for the nurse leader-manager to have additional information about groups.

Although nurses are often engaged in activities in which they act on a one-to-one basis with patients, they also become involved in activities as members of various groups. In nursing, there is a great reliance on groups to reach organizational goals, but group activities frequently have not been valued in nursing. They are considered a "waste of time" or another "useless committee." Groups have also been denigrated for being expensive or leading to "group think." This means that groups make bad decisions because of distortion in the group process (Janis 1972).

This negative attitude toward groups is unfortunate and hurtful to organizational functioning and success. There are valid reasons that groups should be used in nursing and are necessary for the accomplishment of goals. Groups help to secure commitment, bring together a wide range of skills and expertise, give individuals a sense of belonging, and allow people a forum to express their views. It is also true that "two minds are better than one." In fact, there is a phenomenon called a *third mind* or *master mind.* This mind is the "coordination of knowledge and effort, in a spirit of harmony, between two or more people, for the attainment of a definite purpose" (Hill 1960, 168-169). In other words, energy springs from two or more people who think and work together toward a goal; this energy is not present when a person works in solitude.

The leader-manager needs to structure, value, and manage groups appropriately so that people recognize the usefulness of groups. This chapter will consider group theory by focusing on what the leader-manager needs to know to assess a group. She may be a member of the group, the leader of the group, or the composer who forms the group and to whom the group is responsible.

Work Groups

The primary characteristic of work groups is that they are composed of three or more individuals who are working together for an expressed organizational purpose. The group may be formally constituted as are committees, task forces, formal meetings, boards, councils, etc. The tasks of such formal groups may be to make a decision, develop policies and procedures, determine goals and objectives, or plan organizational change. Work groups may also be informally constituted such as the gathering of people to solve daily problems. The focus of this chapter will be the formally constituted group.

A Model for Group Assessment

The following model proposed by Ephross and Vassil (1988) is a descriptive one. It defines and describes concepts that are useful for the leader-manager to assess nursing work groups. This understanding can enhance a leader's skills for using groups to accomplish organizational tasks.

Temporary versus Permanent Groups

In nursing organizations, both temporary and permanent groups are formed. Temporary groups, usually task forces, ad hoc groups, or search committees, are formed to complete a time-limited, discrete task. In these groups, people may behave differently and bring a different set of expectations than in permanent groups. Members of temporary groups may take more risks and be more tolerant than members of permanent groups. This is due to two reasons. First, the temporary group is motivated by a set deadline. This means that the work of the group may need to proceed quickly. Thus, people will be more vocal and more tolerant. Secondly, in temporary groups, the members usually make less emotional commitment and investment in the group, knowing it is going to disband (Ephross and Vassil 1988, 29-30).

Permanent groups have the opposite characteristics of temporary ones. They are formed for fulfilling some ongoing purpose. Permanent groups may be committees, boards, advisory counsels, etc. Because group members must work together for an indefinite period of time, they are more likely to be tolerant of one another. Because they may not be motivated by deadlines, permanent groups are likely to progress slowly through the stages of group development. Because reputations may be determined by the outcomes of the group, people make more commitment and psychological investment in permanent groups than in temporary ones.

Structure and Process

Group *structure* can be defined as the stable characteristics of the group including roles, norms, subgroups, affection ties, and patterns of conflict management. In contrast, group *process* can be seen as ever-changing characteristics such as giving opinions, suggesting ideas, seeking cooperation, making plans, responding to ideas, expressing feelings and responding to them (Ephross and Vassil 1988, 30-31).

Stages of Group Development. The structure of groups includes *phases* or *stages* of group development. Various authors of group theory define between four and six phases. The phases adopted for this book contain four stages of group development with some stages having substages (Ephross and Vassil 1988, 56-73).

Pregroup Stage. This stage, initially described by Hartford (1972), is a preparatory stage in which members are chosen, expectations are defined, and goals and objectives are determined. The better the preparatory phase is thought out and planned, the more likely the group will succeed and be productive.

In her role as either a group leader or group composer, the leader-manager should consider the following list of questions. Although these questions can be used when forming a group, they can also be used when re-evaluating an existing group:

- Who should the members be?
- What is the purpose of the group?
- How long will the group exist?
- What are the expectations of each individual in the group? of the group itself?
- What is the formal structure of the group?
- How will the group relate to other groups, the nursing department, and the organization?
- What are the deadlines for task completion?
- What are the expected outcomes? (Shulman 1984).

Also, members should be selected for the contributions they can make to the group. Likewise, the membership of the group should be representative of the people who will be affected by any decisions the group makes. At times, the membership of groups may only be nursing staff, but at other times, the membership may include other health care professionals.

When selecting members and asking them to serve on a group, the leader's expectations of them should be made clear. One universal expectation is that as a member of a group, the individual is expected to contribute to both the group process and the outcome. By knowing expectations, individuals can contribute to the group more fully and in a timely way.

Formation Stage. This stage includes the *exploration* and *involvement* subphases. Once the group has formed and members are working face-to-face, they begin to interact. They explore with one another their understanding of what the task is, their expectations of one another, and the commitment of each other. Once this exploration is completed, the group members begin to become involved with one another. To do this, they begin to take risks by expressing their ideas and feelings.

Power and Control to Problem Solving. During these two subphases, the conflicts within the group become evident. As the struggles are played out, a sense of solidarity and group cohesion develops. Group cohesion is a sense of attachment to one another and sense of pride and investment in the group and its accomplishments. At this point, people are able to participate in the group and to express their opinions.

Termination. When a group has completed its task, people may withdraw from the group or have ambivalent feelings about the group. In this phase, the group should be helped to recognize what they have learned. This will enable them to transfer the learning to another setting. The group should also be rewarded for its accomplishments.

Public versus Private Sentiments

Members of the group may express themselves publicly about an issue, but what is stated may not reflect everyone's feelings. An individual may have private thoughts, feelings, and beliefs which are not expressed publicly within the group (Ephross and Vassil 1988, 31-32). The sensitivity of the nurse leader-manager to the private feelings of group members versus what is spoken publicly can assist her in better understanding and managing the group.

Molar/Molecular Characteristics

The molecular and molar characteristics of a group are the parts of the group and the relationship of the parts to the whole, respectively (Ephross and Vassil 1988, 33-34). The leader-manager can use both analytical and synthesizing thinking skills (see Chapter 10) to assess how individuals relate to one another, to subgroups, and to the entire group; how subgroups relate to each other and to the group as a whole; and how the group as a whole functions. By doing this, she can detect problems which can occur such as competition for resources among different groups or within groups.

Leadership

As with leadership theory in general, there is no universally accepted theory about group leadership. However, the elements of transformational leadership can be applied to group leadership. Group leaders need to appeal to the values, motives, and aspirations of the members to define the group's collective purpose. In a formal group, the collective purpose is often defined during the formation of the group. The group leader needs to show how the purpose of the task relates to the broader perspective. To do this, she can define how the task fits the vision and mission of the organization. The group leader also needs to:

- *Understand the Internal Workings of the Group.* She can do this by using information in this chapter to assess the group. By allowing the group to fully explore issues, by asking questions, and by expressing her own feelings and allowing others to express theirs, the leader-manager can better understand the dynamics within a group.

- *Plan the Work of the Group.* Planning enables group activity to flow well and ensures that deadlines are met. Efficient planning involves the use of agendas, recording of minutes, assignment of tasks, etc.

- *Be a Visionary.* By showing how the task of the group relates to nursing, the organization, and even society, she can achieve the role of visionary. If the task is quality assurance, then the leader can discuss how the group tasks relate to nursing, to the healthcare environment, and to societal trends such as consumerism.

- *Manage Interpersonal Relations.* When deciding who is assigned which tasks, the leader-manager is attempting to manage interpersonal relationships. She also may find herself mediating conflict and working toward group cohesiveness.

- *Be Proactive.* The leader need not be controlling and talkative, but she should provide guidance, resources, and support. The concepts of empowerment are as important to groups as it is to the individual in the organization.

Work

Both task accomplishment and satisfaction of members' needs comprise the work of groups. Despite conflicts and differences of opinion, ultimately a group is judged by its ability to become cohesive and accomplish the assigned tasks (Ephross and Vassil 1988, 35-36).

Learning

Although the purpose of work groups is not to change a person's attitudes or behaviors, learning can and hopefully does take place in groups. Through the exposure to other people and their ideas and through full discussion of issues, group members may experience a change in attitude brought about by new knowledge and understanding (Ephross and Vassil 1988, 36-37).

Participation in a group may be a particularly valuable way for people to understand various organizational constraints. For example, when a staff nurse, nursing instructor, or clinical specialist works on a group, they may become more familiar with constraints facing nursing managers such as union contracts and limited financial resources. The opposite can occur when a manager works with a group concerning clinical or educational issues. Further, by having the experience of working with a group, the members may gain skills which they can transfer to other settings.

Organizational Setting

Factors such as where the group reports within the organizational hierarchy, to whom it reports, and its tasks form the organizational setting for the group. Ephross and Vassil (1988, 104) hypothesized that the higher a group is in the organizational structure, the broader their field of reference and the greater their concern for the entire organization. At the same time, those groups who report at lower levels in the organization may be more innovative and creative.

In nursing departments there are two types of groups to consider. The first group is composed primarily of members with line responsibility and authority. The tasks of this group may be promotion and selection of people or safety issues. The other type of group would be groups that are assigned staff responsibilities such as nursing research, quality assurance, staff development, etc.

Democratic Microcosm

A democratic microcosm is the ideal for which to strive when managing group activities. Although democracy as a concept may have varying connotations from anarchy to total equality, there is one definition most suited to groups—the concept of democracy as shared participation. Democratic groups are more creative, more productive, and appeal to the human need to belong.

In a democratic group, 1) members should have some voice in who the leader of the group will be; 2) each person can express their ideas and participate in the decision-making process; 3) formal and informal procedures for participation exist; 4) there is an agreed upon and used method of making decisions; 5) members agree to support group decisions or dissent in a particular defined way; and 6) the individual accepts responsibility for his or her own actions, respects other group members, and accepts responsibility for the group (Ephross and Vassil 1988, 43-54).

Decision Making and Groups

Groups function according to the same decision-making model as do individuals. This process was presented in Chapter 11. The difference between individual and group decision making lies in how the decision is reached. Schein (1969) stated that groups can reach decisions by any of the following six ways:

1. *Lack of Response.* This can take several forms. The group may simply not be interested in a particular issue or the dynamics of the group may not allow for full participation. Further, the group itself may be designed to be a "rubber stamp" committee or the issue at hand dictates that the committee "rubber stamp" another person's or group's decision.

2. *Authority Rule.* In this case, the leader makes the decision.

3. *Majority Rule.* In reaching a decision, the sentiments of the majority serve to make the decision.

4. *Voting or Polling.* This technique is often used in very formal groups and search committees. Although voting may be neces-

sary and useful at times, voting tends to polarize people. Thus, in setting up a group, it may be useful to decide under what circumstance a vote can be called for. The purpose of this is to limit voting to a minimum.

5. *Consensus.* This is what every group should strive for. It is a sign of group strength. Consensus means that although some group members do not fully agree with the decision, they are willing to support the decision and give it a chance to succeed.

6. *Unanimous Vote.* Decision making seldom happens with everyone in total agreement. In fact, if there is never disagreement, this may be a sign of too much group cohesion or group think.

Self-Esteem and Groups

As with decision making, the basic principles regarding self-esteem discussed in Chapter 9 can be applied to self-esteem and groups. Also, the leader-manager should understand that individuals can join groups to enhance their self-esteem. If they are allowed to contribute in a meaningful way and if the group affirms the principles of a democratic microcosm, members' self-esteem can be enhanced. However, if the group does not allow for the respect of and contributions of each of its members, self-esteem can be damaged.

Further, the self-esteem of the group as a whole needs to be considered. The group needs to have a sense of accomplishment. This will lead to confidence in the group and its processes. Simply by acting on the decisions and recommendations of the group, group self-esteem can be promoted.

Implications for Nursing

Whether a member, a leader, or composer of a group, the leader-manager has an obligation to ensure that nursing work groups are supported and effective. There are some relatively simple, well known techniques for facilitating the work of groups. Often these mechanism are forgotten and put aside. Yet the effective leader-manager should expect that groups utilize them in order to accomplish their tasks.

Agendas for meetings should be prepared ahead of time and distributed to members in advance of meetings. Having a specific format for agendas will ensure that items are not forgotten and "fall through the cracks." One suggested format includes 1) announcements, 2) old business, 3) new business, and 4) additions. Under "old business," the person preparing the agenda can review previous minutes and list those items needing further discussion or follow-up. If this is done faithfully, the person preparing the agenda will need only to review the minutes of the previous meeting.

All group meetings should have *minutes*. The minutes can follow the same format as the agenda. One of the most useful ways to keep minutes is to have a routine format to label recommendations and further action separately. If recommendations and actions become part of a narrative discussion, they often get lost and forgotten. There are two approaches to keeping minutes. One is to use three columns with one column listing the topic, the next the discussion, and the third the recommendations or follow-up action. Another format is to have the topic and discussion in one narrative paragraph followed by a second paragraph marked "Recommendation/ Action." This will make agenda preparation easier as well.

To whom recommendations are set, either an individual or another group, should be clearly defined. If the group has the authority to act independently on their recommendations, this should also be known. Most importantly, the leader-manager should ensure that the recommendations made by the group are heeded and acted upon or implemented.

Attendance at meetings in nursing departments is often a major problem. Upon its formation, expectations about attendance should be clearly defined. Guidelines should be developed for how many meetings can be missed before a person is removed from a group. Attendance should be listed at the beginning of each minutes. There should also be a system of excused and unexcused absences and this should be noted in the minutes as well.

Application to Nursing Practice: Case Study

The Setting

In order to enhance participation in policy development, the nurse executive formed a nursing executive board. The board reviews the minutes and recommendations of each committee and management meetings in the department. From this review, the board issues policies and procedures and empowers either a committee or an individual to take action.

The membership of the group is:

- The nurse executive, chairperson

- Four nursing directors who report to the nurse executive

- Five head nurses. A head nurse chairs the Nursing Safety Committee, the Nursing Practice Committee, the Nursing Education Committee, the Selection and Promotions Committee, and the Head Nurse Advisory Council.

- One clinical nurse specialist who chairs both the Nursing Research Committee and the Clinical Specialist Advisory Council.

- One nursing instructor who chairs the Nursing Staff Development Committee.

- The quality assurance nurse who chairs the Quality Assurance Committee.

- The infection control nurse, nurse recruiter, and administrative assistant to the nurse executive are members but do not chair committees.

- One staff nurse who chairs the staff nurse advisory council.

- One nursing assistant who chairs the nursing assistant advisory council.

An agenda is prepared and distributed about one week prior to the meeting. Each committee chairperson is asked to report on their committee during the monthly board meetings.

At the first meeting, the nurse executive asked each person to introduce themselves. Each member was asked to explain their perceived role in the group and to describe the committee they chair. Committee chairpersons were asked to discuss the goals, objectives, and current activity of the committee. Following this, the purpose and objectives of the board were discussed. The nurse executive advised the membership that the board was not to be pro forma and merely ratify recommendations of the committees. However, the board was cautioned not to usurp the authority and responsibility of other committees.

At the second meeting of the board, two head nurses expressed their concern that the board would become a rubber stamp committee. They felt the board was possibly a waste of time and would prove to be cumbersome.

After about six months it became clear that one director of nursing, Nina P., was frequently asking for the opinion of another director, Mary K. Nina had been in her position one year and Mary had been in hers for 15 years. When Mary would express her view, Nina would defer to her.

Current Situation

The current issue before the group is a recommendation from the Nursing Practice Committee that nursing assistants be trained to use the electronic blood sugar monitor. The five head nurses are in favor of this action because of the need to transfer the responsibility away from registered nurses. To justify their position, they state that patients are taught to use the machine in their homes. The quality assurance nurse feels that there are still too many problems with the accuracy of the machine to concur with the recommendation. The nursing instructor is opposed because of the training that will have to take place. The nursing assistant quietly states that she is opposed to agreeing to new responsibilities for nursing assistants without an increase in their salaries. After heated discussion, a vote is called for with the results being 13 agreeing to accept the recommendation and 5 opposed.

Case Study Discussion

1. Is this a temporary or permanent group? Is it a formal or informal group? What are the implications of this for the nurse executive?

2. Are there biases in the composition of the membership of the board?

3. What was the purpose of the executive introducing members at the first meeting?

4. Were the concerns expressed by the two head nurses at the second meeting healthy?

5. How could the board's work be better facilitated?

6. Is the interaction between Nina and Hilda an example of structure or process?

7. Which subgroups are evident in the case and how do they relate to the whole?

8. How was the decision to allow nursing assistants to electronically monitor blood sugars reached? Could a better approach have been taken?

References

Ephross, P. H., and T. V. Vassil. 1988. *Groups that work: Structure and process.* New York: Columbia University Press.

Hartford, M. E. 1972. *Groups in social work.* New York: Columbia University Press.

Hill, N. 1960. *Think and grow rich.* New York: Fawcett Crest.

Janis, I. 1972. *Victims of groupthink.* Boston: Houghton Mifflin.

Schein, E. 1969. *Process consultation: Its role in organization development.* Reading, MA: Addison-Wesley.

Shulman, L. 1984. *Skills of helping individuals and groups.* 2d ed. Itasca, IL: F. E. Peacock.

Epilogue

This book has presented contemporary leadership and management theories along with a futuristic approach to nursing. It can be concluded from this examination of present and future nursing management approaches that the leader-manager must have the ability to balance many things simultaneously. This requires sensitivity, judgment, and flexibility. This book is meant to help the nurse leader-manager refine these attributes: sensitivity to tasks, people, and the future; judgment for what can be accomplished and how to get there; and flexibility to understand that there are no easy answers.

To maintain a balance of the many complexities of nursing management, the nurse leader-manager needs to 1) appeal to the paradoxical needs of followers to belong to the group, while at the same time be recognized as individuals; 2) design the environment to enhance the work of the group and the individual; 3) be concerned about tomorrow and act today, but be ever mindful of the past; 4) make rational decisions, but also use intuition; and 5) trust others and be trusted.

Also, the leader manager must be a visionary, i.e., optimistic and hopeful for the future. Being a visionary involves having expectations, and because people get what they expect, the leader-manager needs to expect the best from herself, from others, and from the future.

Stated throughout this book is the belief that collective aspirations and goals will result in success for nursing and the organization. But what is the true purpose of nursing leadership? Is it merely for the financial survival of the organization and the people in the organization? The purpose of nursing leadership transcends organizational survival and bottom-line financial success. The fundamental reason for the existence of the nursing profession is for the health and welfare of society. It is because of this fundamental purpose that transformational leadership in nursing today is so necessary.

Appendix A

Answers to Case Study Questions

Chapter 1

1. *What traits does this nurse leader have? Do these traits ensure leadership success?*

The nurse leader exhibits the personality traits of intelligence, insight-fulness, and flexibility. Although these traits seem important to effective leadership, there is no conclusive evidence that they will ensure effective leadership. Further, there is no evidence that without these traits someone cannot be successful.

2. *Does this letter indicate the leader's ability to attend to both the tasks of the nursing department and the people with whom she works (i.e., consideration and initiating structure)?*

Yes, the information indicates that the nurse executive is a "doer." At the same time, she enjoys good relationships with others.

3. *How would you classify her leadership style using the Blake and Mouton managerial grid? Using theory X and theory Y?*

The letter indicates that the nurse executive is a team manager, scoring high both on relationships and tasks. The leader is a theory Y manager.

4. *What characteristics does this nurse leader exemplify that are not included in the theories discussed thus far?*

The letter states that the nurse executive is a visionary, a characteristic not yet identified as necessary for leadership in the theories presented. This characteristic will be discussed in detail later. The letter also indicates that the nurse executive is flexible, a thinker, a risk taker, innovative, and has good judgment. All these characteristics will be discussed in this book.

5.   *How do you think this nurse leader might motivate staff?*
The letter states that when the leader leads others want to follow. Exactly how this is accomplished is not stated. However, this ability indicates that this nurse executive is a visionary who can determine future directions and inspire others to work for a common goal. It also indicates that this nurse leader has established an environment of trust.

6.   *Does this letter reflect the nurse leader's skill in dealing with the list of dissatisfactions of nurses with their practice? Why or why not?*
Not directly. This may be because the writer of the letter is not a nurse. To truly measure the effectiveness of this nurse executive, it would be important to know how she addresses these issues. One statement, "You have made a difference," implies that she has made changes.

7.   *Does this letter reflect the nurse leader's ability to use different leadership styles in different situations?*
No.

Chapter 2

1.   *Describe one positive and one negative outcome of computerization on nursing.*
Computerization of many routine nursing tasks is on the horizon. One such example is the development of miniature computers which can be inserted in an IV catheter. This computerized monitor can monitor blood pressure, temperature, and pulse, thus eliminating the need for one of the "time-honored" tasks of nursing. This means that fundamental redefinitions of the roles of nurses are going to be needed in the immediate future.
One negative aspect may be a decrease in the frequency of nurse-patient personal contact. The need for human contact and interaction will always be important to people. In restructuring and redefining nursing, the quality and quantity of time spent with patients need to be thoughtfully considered.

2.   *What are possible benefits of improved global communications for the nursing profession?*
With interactive communications and satellite communications, it may be possible for nurses to communicate with expert nurses and other health

professionals throughout the world. Or there may be an "electronic nursing library" in which a nurse, confronted with a patient care problem, can from the bedside ask for and receive appropriate guidance from the literature.

3. *What opportunities do cost containment and the growing elderly population open to nursing?*

Nursing prides itself in being less expensive and more caring than physician counterparts. Both of these traits can be useful to society as there is a search for cost-effective, quality alternatives to long-term care.

4. *Are semi-autonomous work units in healthcare a credible future reality?*

These units do seem to be somewhat of a "pipe dream." It is not likely that they will be commonplace in the healthcare industry in the near future. However, the changing values of people and the need to be competitive may force bureaucratic healthcare facilities to search for alternative organizational structures in the future. Semi-autonomous units seem to be the answer.

5. *What will be the characteristics of future nurse leaders?*

Most importantly, the future leader's primary concern will be matching and maximizing the talents and skills of the nursing staff with those of the organizational goals. This will mean that the leader will need to be flexible, creative, innovative, and caring. She will have to balance people and tasks.

Chapter 3

1. *What is the value conflict in this situation?*

There is value in having each nursing unit be responsible for staffing itself, i.e., for the unit to be autonomous. This means that no one floats out of or into the unit. This striving for autonomy permits staff to feel competent and expert in their practice and to know the patients, the other staff, and the clinical problems. However, to achieve this goal, the usual trade-off is that staff must agree to cover the unexpected absences of their peers, sometimes at relatively short notice. This practice conflicts with another personal value—the need for control over and freedom of personal time.

2. *Would you describe this nurse executive as a transformational nurse leader? Why or why not?*

Although there is not sufficient information from which to draw a conclusion, the nurse executive has demonstrated one important transformational leadership strategy. She and the staff have identified a collective goal—to eliminate floating. This is the first step toward improving the work environment in this hospital.

3. *What should the nurse executive do?*

The role of the nurse executive in this situation is to identify the values apparent in the situation. She then would make staff consciously aware of these values and how they conflict. To do this, the leader first identifies her own values. In this case, the nurse executive's value is to have autonomous staffing of units. This is based on her belief that decreased floating from area to area will increase staff morale and decrease turnover. This is a desirable purpose that espouses the aspirations and goals of both the leader and the followers. The leader then assesses the followers' values in this conflict and discusses them openly with staff. The leader uses a variety of skills in this situation: 1) expresses the conflict in the values; 2) assesses the character and intensity of the followers' willingness to act and ability to act; 3) clarifies and shapes the values by identifying the sources of dissatisfaction; 4) sees and articulates the contradictions in values; 5) arouses dissatisfaction; and 6) ultimately forces a choice between autonomous staffing of the units or continuation of floating. Throughout this process, the leader will have to negotiate between clusters of followers, between nursing units, between individual staff members, and between middle managers and staff.

Chapter 4

1. *Did the nurse executive recognize the need for change? What measure did she use?*

Yes. She used turnover data as her quantitative indication of the need for change.

2. *Why was the nurse executive not successful the first time in negotiating for a tuition reimbursement benefit? Why was she later able to achieve this goal?*

At that time, by building trust and decreasing floating, the turnover rate of nurses had decreased. Later, with increasing turnover and closure of beds, a sense of urgent dissatisfaction occurred. The CEO thus agreed to implement a tuition reimbursement package.

3. *What high-control, high-speed tool of change did the nurse executive employ?*
The retreat served as a high-control, high-speed tool.

4. *What "mundane" tools of change did the nurse executive use?*
At the retreat, the nurse executive was present and included many staff nurses. This is an example of the mundane tools listed as settings for interaction. Following the retreat the nurse executive used meetings, agenda, and memos as mundane tools of change. The fact that the nurse executive spent so much of her time on this issue signalled its importance.

5. *How would you classify the nurse executive's response to the external problem of the nursing shortage. Why?*
The nurse executive responded with resilience. She also helped others to do so by having the retreat and by encouraging people to cope with the shortage of nurses constructively.

Chapter 5

1. *How will the nursing service ensure excellence and success?*
As stated in paragraph 2, the nursing department fosters excellence through encouraging individual contributions to patient care and by stabilizing staffing.

2. *How will nurses deliver patient care?*
As stated in paragraph 3, the nursing department proposes to use a resource-driven model of care.

3. *What is the given definition of nursing and the purpose of this nursing department?*
As shown in paragraph 1, the definition of nursing is to help others to maintain or regain health, learn to live with disability, or die with dignity and comfort.

4. *How does the department ensure humanness and fairness?*

In paragraph 6, it is stated that the nursing service fosters individual growth and development and places people in positions appropriate to their knowledge.

5. *What is the management system of this department?*

In paragraphs 10 and 11, decentralization, involvement of others, and promotion of job satisfaction are mentioned.

6. *How does the nursing service involve employees?*

In paragraph 5, it is stated that the nursing service views nursing as life work and acknowledges the commitment of professionals to their own growth.

7. *Is the system relatively informal?*

Yes, as stated in paragraph 9, registered nurses, not formal authority, set the tone and standards of patient care.

8. *What does the vision statement state about creativity and innovation?*

In paragraphs 7 and 8, it is stated that flexibility and creativity are needed in a resource-driven model of care. Because the nursing department is on the leading edge of technology, innovation is needed.

Chapter 6

1. *How would you describe the organizational structure of the nursing department? What is the social architecture?*

This is a decentralized organizational structure with only one managerial layer between the head nurses and the nurse executive. It is an example of a formalistic social architecture.

2. *What are the elements of participatory management found in the nursing department?*

The committee structure with the four advisory boards is an example of parallel organizations. The membership of each committee is a representation of people who are affected by decisions made by the committee. The assignment of a quality assurance and infection control nurse for each unit is another form of participatory management.

3. *How could participatory management be further enhanced?*

More representation of staff nurses and nursing assistants on committees and task forces would enhance the committee functioning. The quality assurance and infection control nurses should be part of the decision making regarding these programs. They should not merely be delegated the tasks of data collection and analysis for these programs.

4. *What are the benefits of the four advisory boards?*

The four advisory boards provide staff who do not have managerial power as a means to communicate directly to the nurse executive about issues and concerns. Further, by reporting to and sitting on the nurse executive board, there is a formal mechanism for acting on recommendations of the four advisory boards.

5. *What is the norm which guides the decision about who chairs committees?*

Head nurses who are considered "the best and the brightest" are selected to chair committees.

6. *Would you describe the committee structure as informal or formal networks?*

The committee structure is an example of formal networks or prescribed networks which are groups of people who relate to one another as defined by the organizational design.

Chapter 7

1. *What might be included in the vision statement of the organization and of the nursing department regarding the installation of a HIS?*

The vision statement of the hospital would include the use of advanced technology to enhance both the clinical and administrative functions of the organization. It should also mention that this technology can better utilize valuable human resources. For the nursing department, the visionary statement would be consistent with that of the hospital. In addition, it could mention the use of technology to enhance the role of nursing personnel by allowing them more time to interact with and help patients.

2.   *Write hospital and nursing department permanent and temporary objectives for the installation of a HIS.*
Example of objectives might be:

- To utilize advances in technology to provide quality, cost-effective patient care (hospital permanent objective)

- To implement the hospital information system for pharmacy and laboratory within the next 12 months (hospital temporary objective).

- To utilize technological advances to provide quality, cost-effective nursing care (nursing permanent objective)

- To support the development of the laboratory and pharmacy applications (nursing temporary objective)

- To develop the computer skills of nursing personnel (nursing temporary objective)

3.   *How might the selection of the HIS coordinator have been better handled?*
The selection of this individual could have been accomplished easily by a search committee. The CEO could have appointed a committee that was comprised of staff for those services which would be implementing the largest software applications, both clinical and administrative. The CEO would advise the committee that his major concern was to find someone with experience in computer installation. The committee might have been better able to also screen applicants and find someone with a knowledge of hospitals as well.

4.   *What support and development should be provided for the HIS coordinator and the nursing administrative assistant?*
The HIS coordinator should spend time learning about each department and observing work activities. Particular emphasis should be placed on intradepartmental communications and cooperation. He should learn how to coordinate the implementation of applications with each department so that needs can be anticipated in advance.

In contrast, the nursing administrative assistant should be trained in computer literacy and in hospital information systems. She should spend time at the computer company and in a hospital currently implementing a system and one with a computer system fully operating.

5. *What type of feedback should be provided to the HIS coordinator and the administrative assistant about the current problem with implementation of the laboratory application?*

Feedback should be provided to the HIS coordinator, appropriate laboratory personnel, and the administrative assistant in order to prevent the recurrence of the problem. The information provided should review how the current situation occurred and show how the lack of coordination is not consistent with organizational goals. Both the process and the outcome should be discussed. This is feedback that should occur now in order to correct the current situation. Later, once the laboratory is operational, further feedback and review can be provided.

Chapter 8

1. *How would you assess the level of trust in this situation?*

The level of trust is very low. It is effecting the ability of the group to make decisions regarding organizational structure, the ability of the CNE to lead, and communications.

2. *Using the assessment tool in Figure 8-2, answer questions 1, 3, 5, 6, 8, 10, 12, and 13 for this situation.*

The assessment should rate the nursing department below 3 on every question except 10 and 12. The CNE is attempting to flatten the organizational structure while ensuring positions for those displaced by the reorganization.

3. *Assume you are one of the nursing education instructors. How would you rate the CNE in each of the eight sources of trust, i.e., integrity, intentions and motives, openness and discreetness, consistency and reliability, technical competence, interpersonal skills, business sense, and judgment?*

Integrity—There is no evidence that the CNEs integrity is questionable.

Intentions and motives—As a nurse educator, I would be concerned that decentralization might change my role. Thus, I would have less say in decisions regarding the department. Therefore, the CNE's intentions may not be in my best interest.

Openness and discreetness—Before discussing the new organizational structure in an open forum, the CNE discussed it with those individuals displaced.

Consistency and reliability—Although I may not agree with her goal, the CNE has been clear about the move toward decentralization for her entire tenure in the facility.

Technical competence—There is no evidence in the case study regarding this source of organizational trust.

Business sense—There is no evidence in the case study to evaluate the CNE's business sense.

Interpersonal skills—The CNE is having difficulty in establishing good relationships with the nursing educators and the assistant.

Judgment—The CNE did not prepare adequately for the arguments presented in the meeting. She seemed to be caught unprepared.

4. *What "hard" facts or figures did the nurse executive use to support her argument? In contrast, what "soft" information did the nurse educators use?*

The CNE used information about turnover and vacancy rates to support her arguments. The educators expressed concern about quality of care and the leadership effectiveness of the head nurses. This is an example of a hard versus soft fact polarization.

5. *How could the CNE have avoided the "we versus they" confrontation?*

The CNE should have trusted the educators, considered their feelings, and addressed their concerns. The CNE also could have acknowledged their input and their skills.

6. *What can the CNE do to repair the damage?*

This situation may never be characterized by complete trust. The CNE is desiring change that will take power from this group of educators. However, by trusting them and delegating appropriate tasks some trust can be established.

Chapter 9

1. *How could the vice president perhaps have prevented the resignation of the first nurse recruiter?*

The vice president should not have written the first nurse recruiter the letter. Since recruitment was a major concern, there was evidently some problems with this program. The vice president should have talked with and explored the problems with the nurse recruiter rather than impersonally writing a letter. The vice president could also have assessed the situation first hand before "jumping."

2. *How can the vice president explain her choice to those people not selected without damaging their self-esteem?*

This is a very difficult situation. Most importantly, the vice president should meet personally with the candidates not selected. This displays her concern for them as individuals. Since the vice president's decision was made because of the selected individual's activity in recruitment in the past, this should be emphasized. When telling people they did not get a job, the vice president could explore future plans for the department and discuss goals with the individual.

3. *What might be a self-fulfilling prophecy in this situation?*

The new nurse recruiter is expected to be unable to handle the paperwork of the job. If this is expressed in these terms or if the vice president accepts this "weakness" without attempting to explore it further, the person may live up to this expectation.

Chapter 10

1. *How can the vice president use (a) analyzing, (b) synthesizing, and (c) valuing to think about this situation?*

(a) To analyze the situation the VP can start simply by asking who? what? when? how? why? which? why not? This can lead to further questions such as, What will be the reaction of the 4 North, 4 South, and 5 North staff to their unit closing? What is the relationship of each of the three units and the head nurses to the nursing department and the organization? What is the cause of the problem? What other issues are involved, such as the reactions of the surgeons, reassignment of surgeons to other units, changes in case mix, and the impact on income for the hospital? Are there any overriding principles involved such as maintaining the loyalty of staff to their unit; beliefs about retention of staff/staff satisfaction; and feelings about closing beds on a temporary or permanent basis?

(b) To synthesize, the VP should think about the entire nursing department and the impact of unit closure on the whole department. She should consider concepts such as job satisfaction, unit leadership, retention of staff, and quality nursing care.

(c) Lastly, the VP should think about the value of her thinking and consider her feelings that have been brought to light in the first two steps. The value of her thinking about the skills and abilities of the involved head nurses is important. She should also consider the value of having a well-functioning team on 4 North.

2. *How should the vice president use the steps of the decision-making process to reach a decision about closing a unit?*

The VP should first ensure that the problem has been identified correctly. In this case, the leadership of 4 South should be fully considered. Why was nothing done to improve the situation before it became a crisis?

Secondly, an objective should be defined. In this case, the objective should include finding a solution in which there is adequate staffing of the surgical units and improved staff morale. However, it may be possible to achieve two other objectives: to fill three vacancies in the surgical ICU and to start a surgical ambulatory care unit.

Next, the VP would develop alternate courses of action including listing the pros and cons of closing each unit. She should also consider other feasible alternatives to staffing 5 North such as a staffing agency or floating staff on a more permanent basis such as a month at a time.

Once an alternative is chosen it is implemented and evaluated. In the case of this decision, however, it would be unlikely to reverse the decision and try another alternative in the foreseeable future.

3. *What would be one acceptable solution to this problem? Support your decision.*

In this case, the VP decided to close 4 North because it was the smallest unit. Instead of disbanding the 4 North cohesive team and the superior head nurse, she decided to move the entire team to 4 South and have the two teams integrated into one staff. The head nurse on 5 North was reassigned to open a small ambulatory surgical unit on the vacated 4 North. There was also enough staff available to transfer the three RNs to the ICU. The vacancies on 4 South then could take priority for recruitment efforts. In the meantime, more agency nurses would be available for that unit with 5 North stabilized.

Chapter 11

1. *For the CNE, is the initial request for office reassignment boss-, system-, or self-imposed time?*
This was self-imposed time. It is an example of subordinate-imposed time which is one of two types of self-imposed time; the other is discretionary time.

2. *Was the decision appropriately delegated?*
Yes.

3. *What category of activities for delegation does this decision fit?*
This fits the category of either trivial or chore activities.

4. *Was the task delegated to the appropriate person?*
Yes. The nurse recruiter had the most interest in room reassignment. Only a neutral third party might have been a better choice although this type of person may not exist.

5. *Could the task have been delegated to someone else?*
Yes. The administrative assistant to the CNE would also be an appropriate person.

6. *Did the nurse recruiter have appropriate guidance in making the decision?*
No. The CNE could have given more guidance as to whose offices could be moved. If the recruiter had known from the beginning that it was acceptable to move the CNE's secretary, a plan could have been developed in a much shorter time period.

Chapter 12

1. *Is this a temporary or permanent group? Is it a formal or informal group? What are the implications of this for the nurse executive?*
This is a permanent, formal group. As such, the nurse executive will need to permit the group to slowly proceed through the first two phases of group development—the formation stage through the power subphase to the problem-solving phase.

2. *Are there biases in the composition of the membership of the board?*
Most definitely. The board is heavily composed of nursing administrators. There is only one staff nurse and one nursing assistant representing the needs of the largest portion of nursing personnel. The board also has few people with clinical expertise.

3. *What was the purpose of the executive introducing members at the first meeting?*
The purpose was to clarify expectations and group purpose during the formation phase of group development.

4. *Were the concerns expressed by the two head nurses at the second meeting healthy?*
Yes. This was indicative of the need for groups to explore the commitment of one another to the purpose of the group.

5. *How could the board's work be better facilitated?*
Prior to meetings with the agenda, the members should be given a copy of the minutes of all committees. If these minutes are in a standard format, recommendations could be easily read and acted upon.

6. *Is the interaction between Nina and Mary an example of structure or process?*
At first the interaction might be seen as process. However, once it becomes routine it is structure.

7. *Which subgroups are evident in the case and how do they relate to the whole?*

Subgroups of people hold similar positions in the nursing department. The directors and the head nurses comprise the two largest of such groups. In the decision about the blood sugar monitoring, the head nurses formed a large coalition of votes.

8. *How was the decision to allow nursing assistants to electronically monitor blood sugars reached? Could a better approach have been taken?*
The decision was reached by vote. If the group had been allowed to discuss the issue further and even defer the decision for a month, the group might have been able to reach consensus. During the month, the quality assurance nurse could be asked to explore the difficulties with the accuracy of the machine. The nursing assistants could be asked to revise their job descriptions and to thoughtfully consider the issue of monetary compensation for the addition of one task. The new job description could be assessed by the Human Resource Department.

Appendix B

Additional Readings

Leadership Theory

Argyris, C. 1971. *Management and organizational development: The path from XA to YB*. New York: McGraw-Hill.

Bass, B.M. 1981. *Stogdill's handbook of leadership*. 2d ed. New York: MacMillan Publishing.

Blake, R.R., and J.S. Mouton. 1964. *The managerial grid*. Houston: Gulf Publishing.

Blake, R.R., J.S. Mouton, and M. Tapper. 1981. *Grid approaches for managerial leadership in nursing*. Houston: Gulf Publishing.

Davis, K. 1981. *Human behavior at work: Organizational behavior*. New York: McGraw-Hill.

Drucker, P.F. 1964. *Managing for results: Economic tasks, risk taking, and decisions*. New York: Harper and Row.

Drucker, P. 1985. *Innovation and entrepreneurship: Practices and principles*. New York: Harper and Row.

Fiedler, F., and M.M. Chemers. 1984. *Improving leadership effectiveness: The leader match concept*. 2d ed. New York: John Wiley and Sons.

Filley, A.C., and House, J.R. 1969. *Managerial process and organizational behavior*. Glenview, IL: Scott, Foresman.

Hershey, P. 1985. *The situational leader*. New York: Warner Books.

Hershey, P., and K. Blanchard. 1977. *Management of organizational behavior: Utilizing human resources*. 3rd ed. Engelwood Cliffs, NJ: Prentice-Hall.

Hollander, E.P. 1978. *Leadership dynamics: A practical guide to effective relationships*. New York: The Free Press.

House, R.J., and L.A. Wigdoe. 1967. Herzberg's dual factor theory of job satisfaction and motivation. *Personnel Psychology* 20:369-390.

Jenkins, C. and S. Sheman. 1979. *The collapse of work*. London: Eyre Methuen.

Kouzes, J.M., and B.Z. Posner. 1987. *The leadership challenge*. San Francisco: Jossey-Bass.

LaMonica, E.L. 1986. *Nursing leadership and management: An experiential approach*. Boston: Jones and Bartlett.

McClelland, D.C. 1985. *Human motivation*. Glenview, IL: Scott, Foresman.

Miller, L.M. 1978. *Behavior management: The new science of managing people at work*. New York: John Wiley and Sons.

Misshauk, M.J. 1979. *Management: theory and practice*. Boston: Little, Brown and Co.

Pascale, R.T., and A.G. Athos. 1981. *The art of Japanese management*. New York: Warner Books.

Smith, H.L., K. Mangelsdorf, N. Piland, and J.F. Garner. 1989. A retrospective on Japanese management in nursing. *Journal of Nursing Administration* 19(1):27-35.

Sullivan, J.J. 1983. A critique of theory Z. *Academy of Management Review* 8:132-142.

Tappan, R.M. 1983. *Nursing leadership: Concepts and practice*. Philadelphia: F.A. Davis Co.

Vroom, V.H., and P.W. Yetton. 1973. *Leadership and decision making*. Pittsburgh: University of Pittsburgh Press.

Young, L.C., and A.N. Hayne. 1988. *Nursing administration: From concepts to practice*. Philadelphia: W.B. Saunders Co.

Societal and Healthcare Transformation

Andreoli, K.G., and L.A. Musser. 1985. Trends that may affect nursing's future. *Nursing and Health Care* 6(1):47-51.

Califano, J.A. 1986. *America's health care revolution: Who lives? Who dies? Who pays?* New York: Random House.

Callahan, D. 1987. *Setting limits: Medical goals in an aging society*. New York: Simon and Schuster.

Cardoza, A., and S. Ulk. 1985. *Robotics*. Blue Ridge Summit, PA: TAB Books, Inc.

DeBella, S., L. Martin and S. Siddall. 1986. *Nurses' role in health care planning*. Norwalk, CT: Appleton-Century-Crofts.

Ferguson, M. 1980. *The aquarian conspiracy: Personal and social transformation in the 1980s*. Los Angeles: J.P. Trarcher, Inc.

Krasnoff, B. 1982. *Robots: reel to real*. New York: Arco Publishing.

Scott, W.G., and D.K. Hart. 1979. *Organizational America*. Boston: Houghton Mifflin.

Sheil, B. 1987. Thinking about artificial intelligence. *Harvard Business Review* 65(4):91-97.

Steele, S.M. 1979. *Value clarification in nursing*. New York: Appleton-Century-Crofts.

Transformational Leadership

Adams, J.D., ed. 1984. *Transforming work: A collection of organizational transformation readings*. Alexandria, VA: Miles River Press.

Adams, J.D., ed. 1986. *Transforming leadership: From vision to results*. Alexandria, VA: Miles River Press.

Brandt, R. 1979. On leadership: A conversation with James MacGregor Burns. *Educational Leadership* 36:384-387.

Brockett, C. 1976. Toward a clarification of the need hierarchy theory: Some extensions on Maslow's conceptualization. *Interpersonal Development* 6(2):77-90.

DePree, M. 1987. *Leadership is an art*. East Lansing, MI: Michigan State University Press.

Drews, E.M., and L. Lipson. 1971. *Values and humanity*. New York: St. Martin's Press.

Drucker, P. 1987. Management: The problem of success. *Academy of Management Executives* 1(2):13-19.

Horton, T.H. 1986. *What works for me: 16 CEOs talk about their careers and commitments*. New York: Random House.

Rescher, N. 1969. *Introduction to values theory*. Englewood Cliffs, NJ: Prentice-Hall.

Schoonover, S.C., and M.M. Dalziel. 1986. Developing leadership for change. *Management Review* 7(7):55-60.

Sredl, D. 1988. What's your LQ? *Nursing Management* 19(10):96Q, 96T, 96V.

Tichy, N.M., and M.A. Devanna. 1986. The transformational leader. *Training and Development Journal* 40(7):27-32.

Wahba, M.A., and L. Bridwell. 1973. Maslow's need hierarchy: A review of research. *Proceedings of the 81st annual convention of the American Psychological Association* 8:571-572.

Williams, J.C. 1986. Managerial leadership for the 21st century. *Baylor Business Review* 4(3):22-25.

Williamson, J.N., ed. 1986. *The leader-manager*. New York: John Wiley and Sons.

Zaleznik, A. 1977. Managers and leaders: Are they different? *Harvard Business Review*, 55(3):67-78.

Change

Conger, J.A., and R.N. Kanungo. 1988. The empowerment process: Integrating theory and practice. *Academy of Management Review* 13:471-482.

Haffer, A. 1986. Facilitating change: Choosing the appropriate strategy. *Journal of Nursing Administration* 16(4):18-22.

Lancaster, J. 1985. Creating a climate for excellence. *Journal of Nursing Administration* 15(1):16-19.

Lawrence, P.R. 1969. How to deal with resistance to change. *Harvard Business Review.* 7(1):17-27.

Lewin, K. 1951. *Field theory in social science.* New York: Harper and Row.

Schaller, L.E. 1972. *The change agent.* New York: Abingdon Press.

Welch, L.B. 1979. Planned change in nursing: The theory. *Nursing Clinics of North America* 14:307-321.

Wiener, Y. 1988. Forms of values systems: A focus on organizational effectiveness and cultural change and maintenance. *Academy of Management Review* 13:534-545.

Wilkins, A.L., and W.G. Dyer. 1988. Toward culturally sensitive theories of cultural change. *Academy of Management Review* 13:522-533.

Young, L.C., and A.N. Hayne. 1988. *Nursing administration: From concepts to practice.* Philadelphia: W.B. Saunders Co.

Vision

Bird, B. 1988. Implementing entrepreneurial ideas: The case for intention. *Academy of Management Review* 13:442-443.

Graham, P., S. Constantini, B. Balik, B. Bedore, M.C. Hooke, D. Papin, M. Quamme, and R. Rivard. 1987. Operationalizing a nursing philosophy. *Journal of Nursing Administration* 17(3): 14-18.

Kiefer, C.F., and P.M. Senge. 1984. Metanoic organizations. In *Transforming work: A collection of organizational transformation readings*, ed. J.D. Adams, 69-84. Alexandria, VA: Miles River Press.

Rockey, E.H. 1986. Envisioning new business: How entrepreneurs perceive the benefits of visualization. In *Frontiers of Entrepreneurship Research 1986.* eds. R. Ronstadt, J. Hornaday, R. Peterson, and K. Vesper, 344-360. Wellesley, MA: Babson College.

Schofeldt, R. 1982. *A brave new nursing world: Exercising options for the future.* Washington, DC: American Association of Colleges of Nursing.

Social Architecture

Billings, C.V. 1987. Employment setting barriers to professional actualization in nursing. *Nursing Management* 18(11): 69-71.

Cotton, J.L., D.A. Vollrath, K.L. Froggatt, M. Lengnick-Hall, and K.R. Jennings. 1988. Employee participation: Diverse forms and different outcomes. *Academy of Management Review* 13:8-22.

Counte, M.A., D.Y. Barhyte, and L.P. Christman. 1987. Participative management among staff nurses. *Hospital and Health Services Administration* 23(3): 97-108.

Kiel, J.M. 1984. *The creative mystique: How to manage it, nurture it and make it pay.* New York: John Wiley and Sons.

Killan, R.A. 1968. *Managing by design.* USA: American Management Association, Inc.

Locke, E.A., D.M. Schweiger, and G.D. Latame. 1986. Participation in decision making: When should it be used? *Organizational Dynamics* 15(4):65-79.

Mitnick, S.D., and B.D. Crumette. 1987. Hospital nurses as entrepreneurs. *Nursing Management* 18(11): 58-59, 63-64.

Porter-O'Grady, T. 1986. *Creative nursing administration: Participative management into the 21st century.* Rockville, MD: Aspen Publishers.

Quinn, J.B. 1985. Managing innovation: Controlled chaos. *Harvard Business Review* 63(3):73-84.

Saffold, G.S. 1988. Cultural traits, strengths, and organizational performance: Moving beyond "strong" culture. *Academy of Management Review* 13:546-558.

Shaskin, M. 1984. Participative management: An ethical imperative. *Organizational Dynamics* 13(2): 4-22.

Strasen, L. 1989. Redesigning patient care to empower nurses and increase productivity. *Nursing Economics* 7: 32-35.

Walton, R.E. 1985. From control to commitment in the workplace. *Harvard Business Review* 63(2): 77-84.

Wiener, Y. 1988. Forms of value systems: A focus on organizational effectiveness and cultural change and maintenance. *Academy of Management Review* 13:546-558.

Elements of the Social Architecture

Campbell, D.J., and C. Lee. 1988. Self appraisal in performance evaluation: Development versus evaluation. *Academy of Management Review* 13:302-314.

Drucker, P.E. 1985. How to make people decisions. *Harvard Business Review* 63(4): 22-26.

Huntsman, A.J. 1987. A model for employee development. *Nursing Management* 18(2): 51-54.

Jernigan, D.K. 1988. *Human resource management in nursing.* Norwalk, CT: Appleton and Lange.

Locke, E., G.P. Latham, and M. Erez. 1988. The determinants of goal commitment. *Advanced Management Review* 13:23-39.

Marriner-Tomey, A. 1988. *Guide to nursing management.* 3d ed. St. Louis: C.V. Mosby.

Prescott, P.A., and S.A. Bowen. 1987. Controlling nursing turnover. *Nursing Management* 18(6):60-66.

Nauright, L.D. 1987. Toward a comprehensive personnel system: Performance appraisal. *Nursing Management* 18(8):67-70, 75-77.

Nauright, L.D. 1987. Toward a comprehensive personnel system: Personnel selection. *Nursing Management* 18(6):33-34, 38, 40, 44, 46-48.

Nauright, L.D. 1987. Toward a comprehensive personnel system: Reward system. *Nursing Management* 18(9):58-60, 62-64.

Nauright, L.D. 1987. Toward a comprehensive personnel system: Staff development. *Nursing Management* 18(7):44-46, 48.

Sudela, K.D., and L.S. Landureth. 1987. Criterion referenced performance appraisal system: A blueprint. *Nursing Management* 18(3):54-58.

Sweeney, N.R. 1981. *The art of managing middle managers.* Reading, MA: Addison-Wesley.

Urtel, J., and S.E. Runtz. 1987. Eight steps to recruiting the right manager. *Nursing Management* 18(1):28-30, 32-33.

Trust

Bennis, W., and B. Nanus. 1985. *Leadership: The strategies for taking charge.* New York: John Wiley and Sons.

Bernstein, P. 1988. The trust culture. *Advanced Management Journal* 563(2):4-8.

Bradford, P., J. Gibb, and K. Benne. eds. 1964. *T-Group theory and laboratory method: An innovation in reeducation.* New York: John Wiley and Sons.

Cook, J. and T. Wall. 1980. New work attitude measure of trust, organizational commitment and personal need non-fulfillment. *Journal of Occupational Psychology* 53(3):39-52.

Hultzman, K.E. 1988. The psychology of performance management. *Training and Development Journal* 42(7): 34-39.

Likert, R., and J.G. Likert. 1976. *New ways of managing conflict.* New York: McGraw-Hill.

McClelland, V. 1988. Employees we trust. *Personnel Administration* 33:137-139.

Self-Esteem

Eden, D. 1988. Pygmalion, goal setting, and expectancy: Compatible ways to boost productivity. *Academy of Management Review* 13:639-652.

Hill, N.C., and J.B. Ritchie. 1977. The effect of self-esteem on leadership and achievement: A paradigm and review. *Group and Organization Studies* 2:491-503.

Niebuhr, R.E., and K.R. Davis. 1984. Self-esteem: relationship with leader behavior perceptions as moderated by the duration of the superior-subordinate dyad association. *Personality and Social Psychology Bulletin* 10(1):5-59.

Decision Making and Thinking

Abelson, R.R., and A. Levi. 1986. Decision making and decision theory. In *The handbook of social psychology.* 3d ed. G. Lindzey and E. Aronson, 231-309. New York: Random House.

Barros, A. 1986. The process of effective decision making. *Journal of Medical Technology* 3:525-528.

Bass, B. 1983. *Organizational decision making.* Homewood, IL: R.D. Irwin.

deBono, E. 1970. *Lateral thinking: Creativity step-by-step.* New York: Harper and Row.

Isenberg, D.J. 1984. How senior managers think. *Harvard Business Review* 62(6):81-90.

Janis, I., and L. Mann. 1977. *Decision making.* New York: The Free Press.

McGinnis, M.A. 1984. The key to strategic planning: Integrating analysis and intuition. *Sloan Management Review* 26(1):45-52.

Time Management

Applebaum, S.H., and W.F. Rohrs. 1981. *Time management for health professionals.* Rockville, MD: Aspen Publishers.

Bliss, E. 1976. *Getting things done: The ABCs of time management.* New York: Scribner's.

Buckley, K.W., and J. Steffy. 1986. *The invisible side of leadership.* In *Transforming leadership: From vision to results,* ed. J.D. Adams, 233-243. Alexandria, VA: Miles River Press.

Davidson, J. 1978. *Effective time management: A practical workbook.* New York: Human Science Press.

McFarland, G.K., H.S. Leonard, and M.M. Morris. 1984. *Nursing leadership and management: Contemporary strategies.* New York: John Wiley and Sons.

Reynolds, H. and M. Tramel. 1979. *Executive time management.* Englewood Cliffs, NJ: Prentice-Hall.

Ritscher, J.A. 1986. Spiritual leadership. In *Transforming leadership: From vision to results,* ed. J.D. Adams, 61-80. Alexandria, VA: Miles River Press.

Groups

Gibbard, G., J. Hartman, and R. Mann. eds. *Analysis of groups.* San Francisco: Jossey-Bass.

LaMonica, E.L. 1983. *Nursing leadership and management: An experiential approach.* Boston: Jones and Barlett.

McFarland, G.K., H.S. Leonard, and M.M. Morris. 1984. *Nursing leadership and management: Contemporary strategies.* New York: John Wiley and Sons.

Mullen, B., and G.R. Goethals, eds. 1987. *Theories of group behavior.* New York: Springer-Verlag.

Shaw, M. 1976. *Group dynamics: The psychology of small group behavior.* 2d ed. New York: McGraw-Hill.

Tappan, R.M. 1983. *Nursing leadership: Concepts and practice.* Philadelphia: F.A. Davis.

Index